Y0-BQW-257

DUCKWORTH'S THEOLOGY SERIES

Christian Thought to the Reformation.
By HERBERT B. WORKMAN, D.LITT.

The Christian Estimate of Man.
By SYDNEY CAVE, D.D.

Christianity and Some Living Religions of the East.
By SYDNEY CAVE, D.D.

Calvinism.
By A. DAKIN, B.D., D.TH.

Christianity: Its Nature and Truth.
By A. S. PEAKE, D.D.

Christianity According to St. John.
By W. F. HOWARD, D.D.

The Doctrine of the Atonement.
By J. K. MOZLEY, D.D.

The Doctrine of the Person o fChrist.
By SYDNEY CAVE, D.D.

The Doctrine of the Trinity.
By ROBERT S. FRANKS, M.A., D.LITT., LL.D.

Faith and its Psychology.
By W. R. INGE, D.D.

Form Criticism.
By E. BASIL REDLICH, B.D.

Groundwork of the Philosophy of Religion.
By ATKINSON LEE, M.A.

A History of Christian Thought since Kant.
By EDWARD CALDWELL MOORE, D.D.

The History of Israel.
By H. WHEELER ROBINSON, D.D.

An Introduction to the Study of Some Living Religions of the East.
By SYDNEY CAVE, D.D.

The Poetry of the Old Testament.
By THEODORE H. ROBINSON, D.D.

Prophecy and the Prophets in Ancient Israel.
By THEODORE H. ROBINSON, D.D.

Religious Ideas of the Old Testament.
By H. WHEELER ROBINSON, D.D.

A Short Comparative History of Religions.
By THEODORE H. ROBINSON, D.D.

The Text and Canon of the New Testament.
By ALEXANDER SOUTER, M.A., D.LITT.

The Text of the Greek Bible.
By SIR FREDERIC KENYON, D.LITT.

The Theology of the Epistles.
By H. A. A. KENNEDY, D.D.

The Theology of the Gospels.
By JAMES MOFFATT, D.D.

THE DOCTRINE OF THE ATONEMENT

THE DOCTRINE OF THE ATONEMENT

BY

J. K. MOZLEY, M.A., D.D.

LATE FELLOW AND DEAN OF PEMBROKE COLLEGE, CAMBRIDGE

GERALD DUCKWORTH & CO. LTD.

3 HENRIETTA STREET LONDON, W.C.2.

TO THE MEMORY

OF

MY MOTHER

PREFACE

THERE is no Christian doctrine which arouses fiercer resentment and opposition than the subject of the present study, just as there is none more passionately welcomed and confessed. The former feeling is not always a matter for surprise, nor the latter, under all circumstances, for approval. A misunderstanding of what the doctrine is and what it involves may explain and excuse something of the bitterness with which it has been assailed, while the same or a similar misunderstanding can induce states of religious consciousness and dogmatic assertions, neither altogether healthy in themselves, nor sweetened by true Christian charity in their expression towards others. Yet it is true, that even when misrepresentations are cleared away the Christian Doctrine of the Atonement marks a point at which differences, not least the differences between those who would all claim to have an appreciation of and some insight into spiritual realities and the truth of the Christian Gospel, become specially acute.

The present work is primarily historical and descriptive. The writer does not pretend to have begun his task without *prœjudicia*. But it has been his object to present the evidence, as regards both the foundations of the doctrine and the various expositions of the doctrine itself, with such fullness as has been possible and such accuracy as has been his to command, rather than to elaborate his own beliefs

A

and make his material serve as an apologetic for them. He is confident that in a book of this size the proportion represented on the one hand by the first six chapters, on the other by the seventh chapter, is the proportion alone consonant with an approach to a scientific handling of the subject.

The writer's obligation to others will be apparent from the text. In the first chapter, and in one or two other places, he has relied to what some may think an undue extent on the opinions of others. But it has seemed to him better to follow authorities, of whose general reliability he has been able to form some judgment, on certain questions or particular works with which his own theological education has left him insufficiently acquainted, than to indulge in arguments and interpretations which might be mere idiosyncrasies.

He is especially indebted to his father for suggestions in connection with the first three chapters.

CAMBRIDGE,
19th January 1915.

CONTENTS

THE DOCTRINE OF THE ATONEMENT

CHAPTER I

THE OLD TESTAMENT

IT would at one time have seemed natural enough for a writer, whose purpose was to expound the doctrine of atonement, to begin with an appeal to the Scriptures of the Old Testament. It is still—we trust—defensible, but it may need to be defended. Since Dr. Patrick Fairbairn produced his *Typology of Scripture*, and Dr. Alfred Cave his *Scriptural Doctrine of Sacrifice*, the method of handling the Old Testament has been so greatly affected as to have been almost revolutionised by two considerations : firstly, the wide acceptance of theories that have resulted from the higher criticism of the Bible ; secondly, the vastly increased knowledge of other religions, and the kinship that consequently emerges between rites and institutions, together with the conceptions lying behind them, which meet us in the religion of Israel, and customs whose origin escapes us, but which can be traced, in one form or another, literally from China to Peru. Many of those customs are concerned with that which is to be the subject-matter of this volume ; with the problem of the relationship of the fact of impurity, sin, and guilt, however primitively experienced, however inadequately conceived, to another fact, the existence of gods or God. 'Why start with the Old Testament,' the writer may naturally be asked, ' with the ideas and the ceremonies of one people,

when the whole world lies before you? What of all the
evidence collected in Dr. Frazer's book *The Scapegoat*?
Is not much of this as worthy of consideration as the ritual
of the Priestly Code? And what regulative value in
matters of dogma can the Old Testament, when read in
the light of modern criticism, be supposed to possess?'

An answer to these questions may be found, if we are
ready to admit that in religion, as well as in nature, there
is a survival of the fittest. And in religion, as in nature,
that which survives is indebted to that which has perished.
We can even say that the old lives on in the new. The
comparative study of religions is an interesting pursuit, but
it is often no more than a piece of archæological research.
But Christianity, despite the shocks it is always receiving,
is still something more than a department of archæology.
It lives with, at its heart, ideas, and beliefs akin to those
which Dr. Frazer has found among Kaffirs and Majhwars
and Mexicans,[1] which are indeed so world-wide that writers
of one school can make of this universality a reversed
Vincentian canon—' In no particular case can a belief be
true which has been held always, everywhere, and by all.'
Christianity is indeed the residuary legatee of all the old
symbolism of word and action which modern research is
revealing to us. If Christianity, as a religion of atonement,
is not true, then there is no true religion of atonement,
at the best there are only floating conceptions.

But how does this justify an examination of the Old
Testament? We do not now, most of us, regard the
Mosaic ceremonial as directly given by God to Moses;
the supposed parallelism between the Law and the Gospel
expressed in former days by the words ' type,' ' antitype,'
does not make the same appeal to us;[2] no longer do we

---

[1] Frazer, *The Scapegoat*, pp. 30, 36, etc.

[2] For the old view, cf. *e.g.* P. Fairbairn, *The Typology of Scripture*[4], i.
p. 68 : ' There are two things which, by general consent, are held to enter into
the constitution of a type. It is held, first, that in the character, action, or
institution which is denominated the *type*, there must be a resemblance in
form or spirit to what answers to it under the Gospel ; and secondly, that
it must not be *any* character, action, or institution occurring in Old Testament Scripture, but such only as had their ordination of God, and were

think of the prophets of Israel as predicting beforehand
in words unintelligible to themselves and their contemporaries the doings of the Messiah. To be told, as we are
told from time to time, that the Old Testament has gained,
not lost, through the methods and results of the higher
criticism, is not always as convincing to us as our teachers
think it should be. When we read that ' the New Testament constantly assumes a genetic connection between
Judaism and Christianity,'[1] we ask whether in this respect
our point of view can be the same as that of the New
Testament. We can easily see how the genetic connection
was formerly vindicated ; but how shall we vindicate it ?

We can vindicate the connection if we can answer in
the affirmative the two questions: Was Israel called ?
Was Jesus sent ? And between these two questions
comes yet a third : Was the Messianic Hope, as it was
envisaged by the great prophets of Israel and Judah, a
true hope ? The apologetic of the future will have to
concern itself with these questions.[2] But we have a right
to say that if Israel was chosen of God, not only for
privilege as the Israelites very readily believed, but also
for service which they much less readily believed ; if the
substance of the Messianic Hope, namely, ' the reunion of
Jahveh and Israel, when Israel had been purified from sin,
and the consequent universality of Israel's religion [3] was
justifiable ; if Jesus of Nazareth was in truth the Christ,
if He differed from the Jews ' not because He preached a
God other than Him whom they worshipped as their
national God, but because He knew that national God
better than they did';[4] if His mission was primarily but
not exhaustively to the lost sheep of the house of Israel ;
—if we can still make these affirmations, then we rightly
conclude that the two Testaments form a unity, though

designed by Him to foreshadow and prepare for the better things of the
Gospel.'
[1] Stevens, *The Christian Doctrine of Salvation*, p. 1.
[2] Reference may be made to Dr. H. F. Hamilton's fresh and important
work, *The People of God* (Oxford, 1912), which is largely devoted to a consideration of these questions.
[3] Hamilton, *op. cit.*, vol. i. p. xv.   [4] *Ibid.*, p. 213.

it be a unity different in some respects from that which our fathers supposed, and that Augustine's words are true to-day as when first uttered—' in vetere Testamento novum latet, et in novo vetus patet.' [1]

To say this is not to say that the religious ideas though not the religious worship, the moral but not the ceremonial law of the Old Testament, can be assumed as valid for ourselves. But we must beware lest in avoiding these often artificial antitheses we fall into the contrary error of Marcion and, to some extent, of Ritschl, and undervalue the importance of what we find in the Old Testament. When Wellhausen says, ' Jesus was not a Christian but a Jew,' [2] his words are not a mere platitude ; the truth contained in them is often overlooked. If we are to understand Jesus we cannot afford to neglect the Old Testament ; if we want a clue for the interpretation of His life and work, we are more likely to find it in the Old Testament than anywhere else. And perhaps the ' Rabbinism ' which critics find in St. Paul's use of the Old Testament has really got more affinity with the mind of Jesus than those who contrast the simple Gospel of Jesus and the theological subtleties of Paul allow.

So in beginning our study of the Atonement with the Old Testament we start with the premiss that the religious development of Israel is of such a character as to allow us, in connection with it, to think of a special revelation from God. To the Old Testament as a whole may be applied the words which Riehm uses of the Pentateuch— of the portion of the Old Testament which has been most drastically handled by Riehm's fellow critics : ' Every one who so reads the Pentateuch as to allow its contents to work upon his spirit, must receive the impression that a consciousness of God such as is here expressed cannot be derived from flesh and blood.' [3] And because we

---

[1] August., *Quaest. in Ex.*, lxxiii.
[2] Wellhausen, *Einleitung in die drei ersten Evangelien*, p. 113.
[3] Riehm, *Einleitung in das alte Testament*, § 28, quoted by Driver, *Introduction to the Literature of the Old Testament* [8], p. 9.

believe that this revelation came to rest and to the promise of further and wider activity in the person of Jesus of Nazareth and in all that proceeded from and depends upon Him, we hold that we are justified in conceiving of a genetic relationship between the Old and the New Testament. This will not imply that an Old Testament idea, whether expressed in teaching or in rite, will, in the New Testament, remain unchanged. ' In reading the Old Testament we must remember that it is a book of beginnings.' [1] And He who came to fulfil did not carry out His purpose by a mere republication of the old. It does imply a certain unity of religious conception and tendency. We should have a right to be surprised if we found something that we had recognised as of the very essence of Jewish piety, spread over all the books of the Old Testament, set on one side or utterly reversed in the New. In that case we should find it hard to explain what we meant, if we still spoke of a religious—I say nothing of a theological—unity as existing between the Old and New Testaments.

Now the problem of atonement is of fundamental importance in religion. For if religion involves the idea of relationship between man and God, whatever special connotation be attached to the term ' God,' then the problem of atonement is the problem of the way in which that relationship may still be regarded as existing, despite certain facts which appear to affect it adversely. There is a certain true relationship between man and God ; something happens which destroys or appears to destroy that relationship ; how can that relationship be restored ? That is the problem.

The idea of atonement presupposes the idea of relationship between man and God or gods. In religions and beliefs which, by undervaluing human personality and denying divine personality, have no place for such a relationship, there is also no place for atonement. Redemption may be held out to man as his highest good, but it will be

---

[1] A. B. Davidson, *The Theology of the Old Testament*, p. 531.

redemption from existence or, at most, from the material environment in the midst of which existence is set, rather than from moral evil. It is not so much that a right relationship must be restored to man, as that all relationships must be stripped from him.[1] But wherever God is regarded as personal, whatever care may be taken to differentiate His personality in this or that respect from the personality of man, there we have at once the conditions necessary for the raising of the problem of atonement. How is He related to man ? Can anything affect the relationship ? Does God care if this relationship is affected ? On what terms can the relationship be restored ? What part in the restoration is played by man, and what by God ? Answers of a widely different kind can be and are given. The question concerns religion at its very deepest.

The question is raised in the Old Testament. Strange indeed would it be if it were not, seeing that the whole of the Old Testament is written round the idea of the relationship existing between God and Israel. If no great stress is laid upon the personality of the individual man, if the nation, not each individual, is the unit which stands opposite to God, there is no depreciation of the personality of God. ' In the Old Testament conception of God,' says Professor Schultz, ' nothing stood out from the first so strongly and unmistakably as the *personality* of the God of Israel.' [2] And in a recent book the unity which, despite profound developments, characterises the religion of Israel from the twelfth to the fifth century is well described as ' that of a continuous faith that Yahweh is Israel's God, that His personality is as real and living as a man's, that the relation

---

[1] Cf. Bousset, *What is Religion* (E.T.), p. 209 : ' In Buddhism . . . the idea of moral deficiency and imperfection, of the agony of sin and the need for redemption from sin, is quite unknown. In Platonism, also, the highest faculty of the human being is not the will towards the good, but the clear reason which lasts for ever. What hinders and fetters mankind is not moral evil, but the material world.' Yet these are for Bousset the two typical religions of redemption, as contrasted with the religion of the law.
[2] Schultz, *Old Testament Theology* (E.T.), ii. p. 103.

between the corporate personality of Israel and the divine
Person is moral, and that no other deity counts at all.' [1]

But if in the Old Testament the relation between God
and Israel is moral, then the conception of God which fills
the Old Testament must also be moral, though the conception may be patient of differences in degree. And the
characteristic moral conception of God is expressed by
the term ' holiness.' ' All other ethical attributes are but
the further developments of this fundamental conception.' [2]
Doubtless the conception is partly conditioned by physical
considerations. God is exalted above finiteness and
limitation ; but He is also exalted above sin and evil.[3]
Moral as well as metaphysical perfection is implied. Nor
have we to deal with a conception of self-contained, passive
holiness. Rather is it essentially active. ' All that God
has disclosed of His ethical being—anger, vengeance, grace,
love, mercy—is only the championship of His moral purity
and perfection against everything which opposes Him
and His holiness, and has for its end the creation of a
kingdom of purity and goodness. From the time of the
Mosaic covenant, and through that which He then revealed,
He is known in Israel as the Holy One.' [4] When at
Sinai the people are forbidden to draw near to the mountain
upon which Jahveh has descended lest they should perish,[5]
this is not simply due, as Ritschl [6] argued, to the contrast
between the majesty of God and the weakness and creature-
liness of man. This, as Riehm [7] urged in answer, would
be to deprive the conception of holiness, as found in the
cultus, of all the ethical import which it undoubtedly

---

[1] H. Wheeler Robinson, *The Religious Ideas of the Old Testament*, p. 36.
[2] Dillmann, *Handbuch der alt-testamentlichen Theologie*, p. 252.
[3] See Exodus xv. 11 for the first occurrence of the conception ; Lev. xix. 2,
xx. 7, where physical ideas are excluded ; Num. xx. 13 includes, as Dillmann
points out, a physical and a moral conception.
[4] Dillmann, *op. cit.*, p. 257.   [5] Exodus xix. 20-25.
[6] Ritschl, *Rechtfertigung und Versöhnung*, ii. pp. 201 ff. Ritschl applied
this idea to the priestly ministrations of the law, but has failed to carry modern
scholarship with him.
[7] Riehm, *Alttestamentliche Theologie*, pp. 131-2. Cf. Schultz, *op. cit.*, i. 399,
for a mediating view—' Man is as a creature weak, and therefore also, on his
moral side, impure.

possesses in the prophetic writings, and to make of it an
entirely physical notion. Such a conclusion would be
altogether paradoxical. We can approach it only so far
as to allow that to the conception of holiness there belongs
an æsthetic or ceremonial side, to which the Levitical
law and the last chapters of Ezekiel bear witness, while
the prophets as a class attach exceedingly little importance
to it. Even so we must remember that ' there was no
distinction in the law between moral and what we have
been accustomed to call ceremonial. . . . The offences
which we call ceremonial were not symbolical, they were
real offences to Jehovah, against which His nature reacted.
. . . What might be called æsthetic or physical unholiness
was held offensive to the nature of God in the real sense,
in a sense as real as moral offences were offensive to Him ;
and the purifications were true removals of these real
causes of offence.' [1]

Allowing then for the fact of development, we may say
that throughout the Old Testament God is regarded as
both personal and moral. With Israel He is in covenant
—relationship by His own free act ; ' the most general
conception in what might be termed Israel's consciousness
of salvation was the idea of its being in covenant with
Jehovah.' [2] And this covenant relationship can be expressed yet more tenderly in terms of Fatherhood and
sonship.[3] The constantly emphasised difference between
Israel and other peoples is but the necessary result of what
God of His grace and mercy has done for Israel. Dillmann
defines the grace of God as the positive, revelationary side
of the divine holiness, visible both in the creation and
preservation of the world, and, more particularly, in
relation to Israel. Opposed to it is the negative, destructive quality of wrath, manifesting itself in vengeance,
and especially directed against those breaches of the
covenant of which the history of Israel was only too full.
But His wrath is as far removed as possible from blind

[1] Davidson, *op. cit.*, p. 159.   [2] *Ibid.*, p. 239.   [3] Hosea xi. 1.

hate ; to contrast the God of the Old Testament as
essentially wrathful with the God of the New Testament
as essentially loving and gracious is caricature.   Let it
be granted that in the Old Testament there is an antithesis
between the divine grace and the divine wrath which is
not wholly overcome, that God is regarded as changeable
in ways that we cannot make our own.[1]   Nevertheless
grace, not wrath, is uppermost in God : because God is
God and not man, because He is the Holy One, He will
not allow His anger free course,[2] nor will He keep it for
ever.[3]   And even though God seems to change, yet He
does not change as man changes.[4]   His wrath does not
contradict His grace, but is the inevitable reaction of His
holiness from whatever is opposed to that His essential
characteristic.   Of Jahveh, as of the God and Father of
our Lord Jesus Christ, it is true that 'because He is holy
and loving, He cannot be indifferent to sin,' [5] though,
for the Old Testament, we should emphasise the first
rather than the second adjective.[6]

We see then that the relationship in which Jahveh as
personal and moral stands to Israel can be affected by
whatever, from the side of Israel, is done contrary to the
fundamental fact of Jahveh's holiness, whether such acts
fall within what we should consider the sphere of ethics,
or whether they are æsthetically and ceremonially inhar-
monious with that supreme predicate.   Moreover, such
acts do not merely affect the relationship in such a way
that the consequences occur naturally and inevitably
without any direct action taken by Jahveh.   It is not
simply that Israel has deserted Jahveh, and that therefore
there is separation where there was contact.   In respect
of disobedient Israel the anger of Jahveh is a positive,
active attribute, bringing disaster upon the people.   Yet

[1] *E.g.* Jer. xvii. 7-10.   [2] Hosea xi. 9.
[3] Jer. iii. 12; Micah vii. 18; Ps. ciii. 9, etc.
[4] 1 Sam. xv. 29 ; Num. xxiii. 19; Ezek. xviii. 25.
[5] Murray in Hastings' *Dictionary of the Bible*, i. p. 198.
[6] The whole discussion of God's wrath and grace by Dillmann, pp. 258-
268, is worthy of close attention.

even in His wrath He thinks upon mercy ; but because
His wrath is not caprice or blind vengeance, the change
from wrath to grace cannot be unconditional. If the
disobedience of Israel remains, the wrath of Jahveh must
remain, even though that wrath seems to disappear in
the note of pleading with Israel, which sounds with such
noble pathos in the second Isaiah. How then is the
relationship to be restored ? We come to the problem
of atonement in the Old Testament, asking what solution,
if any, is to be found there.

So far it has not been necessary to make any sharp
distinction between different parts of the Old Testament.
Such differences as a more detailed consideration of the
points hitherto under discussion might reveal as existing
between 'The Religion of the Law' and 'The Religion
of the Prophets' would be only differences of degree.
God's covenant with Israel, God's grace, God's anger with
Israel in consequence of Israel's disobedience—all these
are facts in the legal and prophetic books alike, with the
conception of God as a personal, moral Being as the
foundation of the whole. But when we go on to ask how
can that which has been broken be restored, what will
serve to atone, we must prepare for answers of widely
divergent character, though even in this case we must
beware of a tendency to exaggerate the divergence. A clue
to the nature of the difference may be found in the words
in which Dr. Davidson sums up his study of the Old
Testament doctrine of redemption : 'There are two lines
on which atonement moves : that of the righteousness
of God in the extra-ritual Scriptures, and that of the
holiness of God in the ritual law. In the former He deals
with sin as the righteous Ruler and Judge of men. In
the latter He deals with it as a holy person with whom
men have fellowship, who draw near to Him, and among
whom He graciously abides ; ' yet a third, as he suggests,
may be found in Isaiah liii.[1]

[1] Davidson, *op. cit.*, pp. 354-5.

It will be well to begin by putting in the very forefront of our discussion that which lies at the base of both the legal and the prophetic conceptions of the method of reconciliation.[1] In the Law and in the Prophets alike Jahveh is depicted as the Mover in the work of reconciliation. Whatever means are necessary they are means appointed and approved by Him. It is always true that ' it is He who takes the initiative in the matter of man's redemption, and not man, who, desiring to return, seeks some acceptable medium by which this may be done.'[2] In virtue of this it is misleading to say that ' to understand the real Old Testament doctrine of atonement we have to look away from the Sacrifices and study the thoughts of the great prophets and psalmists. In their view there is no limit to God's willingness to be reconciled. If Israel draws near to Him in penitence, he may be sure that he will be welcomed with open arms.'[3] Exactly the same principle permeates the sacrificial system. However much they may have been abused, the sacrifices were never intended to be a substitute for, but rather the expression of, the penitent heart. As has often been noted,[4] it is just this fact that the ways and means of reconciliation are appointed by God, who of His own accord approaches the sinner, which sharply distinguishes the biblical from the heathen conception of sacrifice. ' Whatever the sacrifices may have been conceived to accomplish, and in

[1] As regards the two words ' atonement ' and ' reconciliation,' it may be said that whereas the idea of reconciliation is implied in the word ' atonement,' however the latter be interpreted, the reverse, if atonement is not interpreted as at-one-ment, is not necessarily the case. Thus Dr. Driver writes (Hastings' *Dictionary of the Bible*, iv. 128) : ' Since the Authorised Version of 1611 was made the word (atonement) has changed its meaning, and whereas it formerly expressed the idea of *reconciliation*, it now suggests chiefly the idea of *making amends* or *reparation*.' On the other hand, the title of Dr. G. C. Workman's book, *At Onement or Reconciliation with God*, may be noted as a brief commentary on the position he upholds that ' the term (atonement) denotes only action or result. It is the act of becoming reconciled to God, or the state of being reconciled to Him ' (p. 16).

[2] W. L. Alexander, *System of Biblical Theology*, ii. p. 11.

[3] Schultz, *op. cit.*, ii. p. 89.

[4] Cf. *e.g.* Maurice, *The Doctrine of Sacrifice deduced from the Scriptures*, p. 87.

whatever way they may have been regarded as operating, it is evident that they assume the antecedent graciousness of God, who, though prescribing conditions, offers a free forgiveness.'[1] So Riehm truly says of the Old Testament conception that ' there is nothing in the world in which, of its own nature, redemptive power resides.'[2] Dr. Davidson, who is not satisfied with Riehm's view that the blood atones simply because it is God's appointment or ordinance, and thinks it probable that ' deeper and mystical ideas gathered around the blood, and that men, if they did not see more in the offering of the life for atonement of sin than a mere ordinance of God, felt there was more in it, that there lay grounds under the ordinance which they might not see,' nevertheless has to admit that no rationale or explanation is given in the law which ' has contented itself with stating the fact that the offering of a life to God atones.'[3] The important passage, Lev. xvii. 11, ' for the soul of all flesh is in the blood, and I have given it to you upon the altar to make atonement for your souls ; for it is the blood that makes atonement by means of the soul that is therein,'[4] does not enable us to construct any definite theory ; the blood is, or contains, the life ; that we are told, but not why it should have the power to atone. Rather should we emphasise the words, ' I have given it to you upon the altar ' : it is an act of God's grace. And this means that in the Old Testament, as we shall find to be true of the New, Sacrifice ' is the fruit of Grace, and not its root.'[5] That the initiation is God's is seen to be equally true if we turn from the sacrificial system to that special conception of the means of recon- ciliation enshrined in Isaiah liii. There it is ' in accordance with the appointment of the God of Salvation, Who is gracious in holiness,' that ' this great multitude of sins,

1 Stevens, *op. cit.*, p. 16 ; cf. Schultz, *op. cit.*, ii. p. 100.
2 Riehm, *op. cit.*, p. 136.
3 Davidson, *op. cit.*, pp. 352-4.
4 Tr. Driver-White in *The Polychrome Bible*.
5 Forsyth in *Priesthood and Sacrifice*, p. 93.

and mass of guilt, and weight of punishment came upon the servant of Jehovah.' [1]

Throughout the Old Testament God is regarded as providing the means of reconciliation, and as ready and anxious to forgive if His people will but show themselves penitent. But how is this to be done ? What is necessary from the side of man ? We must pass from unity to diversity, from that which is common ground in the legal and the prophetical books, to that wherein their views, even if they are not to be considered as contradictory, can hardly be defended as complementary. First, let us examine the teaching of the Law, and then pass on to the less systematic conceptions of the extra-ritual books.

When we come to deal with the means appointed in the Law for the cancelling of the effects of sin, for the avoiding of the wrath of God and the re-establishment of true relations with Him on the part of an individual or of the whole people, we are faced at the very outset with the fact of sacrifice, and the problem of its real significance. Formerly, the question used to be posed in this way : ' Was sacrifice of divine or human origin ? ' Heated as the controversy often was, owing to the dogmatic issues supposed to be involved, its echoes are all that remain to-day ; [2] on the other hand, the argument as to the original meaning of sacrifice is living and unlikely to be settled in the near future. The old view, usually held along with the belief in the divine origin of sacrifice, was that sacrifice was essentially of a piacular and propitiatory character, and that in sacrifice an animal was slain in substitution for the life of a man justly forfeit. This view is simple and intelligible, but formidable objections can be raised against it. ' The expiatory theory not only

[1] Delitzsch, *Commentary on Isaiah* [4], ii. p. 296 (ed. 1890) (E.T.).
[2] For a discussion of the question from a point of view which ignores or rejects modern criticism of the Old Testament, see P. Fairbairn, *Typology of Scripture* [4], i. pp. 290 ff. ; W. L. Alexander, *op. cit.*, i. pp. 452 ff. ; A. Cave, *The Scriptural Doctrine of Sacrifice*, pp. 32 ff. Writers of this school had to explain how it is that the first sacrifices mentioned—those of Abel and Cain —are not said to have been in any way ordered by God

presupposes a primitive knowledge of God transcending the thoughts of childhood, but it credits man with a sense of sin, and with a valuation of death as the wages of sin, which belong to a later period of spiritual development.' [1] Robertson Smith goes so far as to connect the characteristic features of piacular sacrifice with ' a very primitive type of religion, in which the sense of sin, in any proper sense of the word, did not exist at all.' [2] From what is known of primitive sacrifice, we see that sacrifice, so far from being conditioned by the sense of sin, was often the expression of joy and the occasion of feasting, while non-bloody sacrifices, common features of the life of peoples living in agricultural conditions, bear out the statement that ' sacrifice is a far broader conception than propitiation.' [3]

Probably the ' gift theory ' of sacrifice is the one most commonly held to-day, since the conception of sacrifice as essentially a common meal, in which ' there was a sacramental communion between the Deity and its worshippers by means of blood,' [4] has become less popular, owing to its association, especially in the hands of Robertson Smith, with totemistic theories of the ' Divine-human affinity of animals, and of the assimilation of the Divine life through eating the totem,' [5] which have failed to establish themselves among anthropologists.[6] Possibly, as Loisy hints,[7] it is beyond our powers to say whether ' the notion of sacrifice as an offering preceded or followed the notion of sacrifice as a communion,' but if we confine ourselves to the evidence from the Old Testament which reflects the most primitive conditions, we shall certainly

[1] W. P. Paterson, *s.v.* ' Sacrifice ' in Hastings' *Dictionary of the Bible*, iv. p. 331.
[2] *Religion of the Semites*, new edition, 1907, p. 401.
[3] Gore in *Priesthood and Sacrifice*, p. 82.
[4] Marti, *Religion of the Old Testament*, p. 57 (E.T.).
[5] Paterson, *loc. cit.*
[6] For a brilliant criticism of Robertson Smith's exposition of this view see Lagrange, *Etudes sur les religions Sémitiques*, pp. 246 ff. He argues that the idea of offering alone (though not as tribute) will cover the cases of bloody and unbloody sacrifices.
[7] Loisy, *The Religion of Israel*, p. 78 (E.T.).

find more support for the former than for the latter
hypothesis. ' J and E,' says Dr. Welch, ' are at one in
the way in which they construe sacrifice. They regard
it as a gift, never as a propitiation.'[1] The term minḥa
oblation, used in the Priestly Code for a special kind of
sacrifice, the rules for which are given in Lev. ii., was
originally employed to denote sacrifices in general, bloody
as well as non-bloody.[2] The offerings were often food and
drink. In the anthropomorphic conception of the gods,
in virtue of which they are regarded as needing nourish-
ment, Piepenbring sees the origin of sacrifice, and, in the
Old Testament, stories such as those found in Gen. xviii.,
Judges vi. 17 ff., xiii. 15 ff., and references to the food of
Jahveh in Lev. iii. 11, xxi. 8, 17, Num. xxviii. 24, etc.,
point back to a time when sacrifices were looked on as
material gifts, and as such well pleasing to the divinity
to whom they were offered.[3] ' The characteristic of
sacrifice as a gift,' says Dillmann,[4] ' that which differentiates
it from other gifts, is that it is enjoyed by the divinity.'
If, then, we look for one positive explanation of primitive
sacrifice, the ' Gift theory ' is probably the most satisfactory and the simplest one. But we must beware of the
dangers of reading into acts, performed under conditions
of which we have but small knowledge, motives and
explanations which demand greater analytical capacities
than we can suppose to have existed in such remote ages.
There is truth in the remark, ' the more childlike and
ingenuous the conception of God formed by primitive
man, the more natural and easy was for him the introduc-

---

[1] Welch, *Religion of Israel under the Kingdom*, p. 18.
[2] Cf. Piepenbring, *Théologie de l'ancien Testament*, p. 56. In support of
his statement he refers to Gen. iv. 3-5, Num. xvi. 15, Judges vi. 18, 1 Sam.
ii. 17, and other passages.
[3] A well-balanced statement of the superiority of the ' Gift theory ' (including the gift as food) to the ' Communion theory ' will be found in Stade,
Biblische Theologie des Alten Testaments, i. pp. 156-9. He points out as
against Robertson Smith that the nomad life with its bloody sacrifices was
not the most primitive life, and that in many sacrifices there was no
meal.
[4] *Exodus und Leviticus*[2], p. 416.

tion of sacrifice.'[1] This so-called 'psychological' theory rests upon the supposition that to man, in the infancy of the race, the giving up of some portion of his possessions to his Divinity, ignorant though he might be of the precise ends that he was thereby serving, was a natural instinct which he followed out in practice without stopping to ask the kind of question which at once rises in a more developed mind.

But though we may accept as most probable the theory that a sacrifice was originally a gift, this does not prevent us from holding that from very early times sacrifices were more closely connected with human sin and error, that their object was not simply to please the deity but to regain the favour of the deity which had been alienated by some act or shortcoming. When we turn to the Old Testament we find considerable evidence pointing to this conclusion. Granted that the specific sin-offering and trespass-offering of Lev. iv. 1-vi. 7 is of late origin, this does not imply that there were no offerings for sin at a much earlier date. If 'the old history knows nothing of the Levitical sin-offering,' it is because 'the atoning function of sacrifice is not confined to a particular class of oblation, but belongs to all sacrifices.'[2] We find traces of this in the fact that even in P. the whole burnt-offering can have an expiatory significance.[3] Accordingly there is good reason to believe that the burnt-offering, the oldest of all the sacrifices, 'was at first offered also in those cases which afterwards required the expiatory sacrifices proper.'[4] It is in Ezekiel that we first get mention of special expiatory sacrifices,[5] and in post-exilic times the sacrificial system is completed with the careful elaboration of the idea of expiation. It is worthy of note that this elaboration went

---

[1] J. Pohle, *s.v.* 'Sacrifice' in *The Catholic Encyclopædia*, xiii. p. 320. Cf. somewhat similarly C. von Orelli in the *New Schaff Herzog*, x. p. 163, *s.v.* 'Sacrifice': 'The true solution of the theory of sacrifice must be found in the child-like dependence of man upon the gods.'
[2] Robertson Smith, *op. cit.*, p. 237.   [3] Cf. Lev. i. 4, xiv. 20, xvi. 24.
[4] Kuenen, *The Religion of Israel*, ii. p. 263 (E.T.).
[5] Ezek. xl. 39, xlii. 13, xliii. 19.

along with the deepening of Jewish religious ideas as a whole, which resulted from the bitter experiences of the two previous centuries. If the sin-offering now takes first place amongst the four main types of sacrifice,[1] ' this change points to a new tone and emphasis in the post-exilic religion. The rejoicing of the festal meal has been displaced by penitent humiliation before Yahweh, which reflected the later sorrows of the nation.' [2] To know what sacrifice came to be under the pressure of circumstances reacting upon man's heart and conscience is more important than to know what it originally was.

We see then that in the developed sacrificial system there is a special offering which is to follow upon and atone for sin, that is to procure for the guilty person the forgiveness of his sins, avert whatever consequences might otherwise have followed, and restore him to that state of relationship with Jahveh which was his before the sin. Not only for the individual but for the whole congregation is the sin-offering to be made whenever there is cause,[3] while once a year the whole people is to be cleansed from all its sins after special and solemn ceremonies.[4] We have now to ask what, if any, theory of atonement is implied in the ritual of the sin-offering.[5] A brief description of the ritual, first of the ordinary sin-offering and then of the Day of Atonement, must now be given.

Any one who had sinned in ignorance—for offences

---

[1] *I.e.* burnt-offerings, peace-offerings, sin-offerings, and trespass-offerings.
[2] H. W. Robinson, *op. cit.*, pp. 144-5. Cf. Dillmann, *Exodus und Leviticus*[3], p. 421 : 'The earnest desire for holiness, and the keen consciousness of sin and guilt which the Mosaic system more and more stimulated, made the provision of means for expiation and purification necessary.' An expiatory value certainly seems to belong to the burnt-offerings in Judges xx. 26, 2 Sam. xxiv. 18-25.
[3] Lev. iv. 13.   [4] Lev. xvi.
[5] The original distinction between the trespass-offering (āšām) and the sin-offering (haṭṭāth) seems to have been that the former was required ' only in expiation of the unlawful appropriation of the property of another, or of the tribute due to Yahwè. . . . In such cases restitution of the property with the addition of one-fifth its value must be made, and a ram offered as a "trespass-offering."' At a later period the āšām lost its distinctive character, so that a confusion of it with the sin-offering sometimes arises, *e.g.* in Lev. v. G. F. Moore in *Encyc. Bib.*, *s.v.* 'Sacrifice,' iv. p. 4203.

committed presumptuously 'with a high hand' there
was no atonement, but death followed [1]—whether priest,
ruler, or one of the common people, was to bring an animal
of value proportionate to the offence or to the sinner's
status, and after laying his hand upon its head kill it
before the Lord. The priest was then to sprinkle the
blood ceremonially upon the horns of the altar, and, after
that, to burn certain parts of the victim upon the altar.
The flesh belonged to the sacrificing priest, was regarded
as 'most holy,' and ordered to be eaten in the sanctuary.[2]
Of the Day of Atonement the fundamental idea was that
'the community as a whole was defiled by sin and was
therefore rendered unholy, and that it needed some special
and periodical purgation in order to restore it to its true
position as the people of God.'[3] First of all, the High
Priest offered a bullock as a sin-offering for himself and
his house, and sprinkled the blood upon the mercy-seat.
Then, having taken two goats and cast lots for them, he
offered one 'upon which the Lord's lot fell' for the people
and sprinkled the blood. Then when he had made an
end 'of reconciling the holy place, and the tabernacle
of the congregation, and the altar,' he brought the goat
upon which the other lot—for Azazel[4]—had fallen, laid
his hands upon it, confessed over it all the sins of the
people, 'putting them upon the head of the goat,' and sent
it away into the wilderness.

The old explanation of this ritual was that the animal
was substituted for the sinner, and endured in his place
the punishment due to sin. An able defence of this
position, joined with criticism of different theories, is
made by Dr. W. L. Alexander.[5] He asks the question,
How does sacrifice cast light on man's hope of pardon and
acceptance with God? To this—since he looks on death
as the penalty denounced against sin—he finds no answer

[1] Num. xv. 30.   [2] Lev. iv. and vi. 24 ff
[3] Ottley, *The Religion of Israel*, p. 148.
[4] An evil spirit, supposed to dwell in the wilderness.
[5] Alexander, *op. cit.*, ii. pp. 21-36.

except 'that God shall accept something in lieu of the sinner's death—something that shall answer the same ends (at least) as would be answered by his death.' So in this way 'the doctrine of substitution emerges as a natural principle, and takes its place in the *rationale* of a scheme of religion for the sinner.' This doctrine was established by divine revelation in the Mosaic ritual wherein sacrifice becomes 'a symbolical rite adumbrating by sensible objects and acts great spiritual truths concerning the ground and medium of the sinner's acceptance with God.' And, as against conceptions of the meaning of sacrifice associated with the names of Bähr, Tholuck, and Maurice, he quotes with approval a statement of Liddon's that such theories throw into the background 'the ideas which in these sacrifices are most prominent—those of a broken law, of consequent guilt, of liability to punishment, and of forgiveness through vicarious suffering.' Dr. Alexander's position, taken as a whole, is not commonly held to-day; but his argument that the idea of vicarious penalty is the true idea for the explanation of the sin-offering and of the Day of Atonement still meets with at least partial support. Dr. W. P. Paterson,[1] while he allows that 'the idea of penal substitution is not one which has been consistently transfused throughout the entire sacrificial system,' nevertheless suggests the possibility 'that the sacrificial forms of most recent growth, and the most likely, therefore, to reveal the ideas of the compilers, embody the idea of propitiation through penal substitution,' and indeed goes on to say that 'given the doctrine that sin entailed death, and that one being might suffer in room of another, it was a highly natural, if not an inevitable step, to go on to suppose that the rite of sacrifice combined the two ideas, and that the slain victim bore the penalty due to the sinner.' This does not necessarily carry with it the idea of the transfer of guilt from the man to the animal. Kuenen, who rejects any such interpretation,

---

[1] Hastings' *Dictionary of the Bible*, *s.v.* 'Sacrifice,' iv. 340.

since the blood of the animal remains clean, as, it may be
added, does the flesh, still thinks that it is simplest, and
therefore truest, to accept the view that 'according to
the Israelites' notion, Jahveh in his clemency permits
the soul of the animal sacrificed to take the place of that
of the sufferer.' [1]   But he thinks we should go too far if
we spoke of vicarious punishment in this connection.
It is indeed against this conception in particular that
modern scholarship has reacted.   Marti's [2] argument is
typical ; the laying on of hands is found as part of the
ritual of the burnt-offering and of the peace-offering
(Lev. i. 4, iii. 2), and therefore, in the sin-offering, cannot
be supposed to imply the transference of guilt.   The
blood sprinkling does not connote vicarious satisfaction ;
animals are killed in other sacrifices, and if in the animal's
death there is involved a doctrine of substitution, how
comes it that there is no sacrifice permitted in cases of
sins whose penalty is death ?   As to the ritual of the Day
of Atonement, here also the old opinion is not as firmly
established as might appear at first sight.   The culminat-
ing point is the sending away of the goat 'for Azazel,'
but we must remember that ' the flesh of this goat was
not burned ; atonement was not made by its blood, it
was not a sacrifice at all.' [3]

The difficulty, as Dr. Stevens sees, is to find any satisfactory alternative theory.   A clue is often supposed
to be given in the directions as to the sprinkling and
application of the blood.   'The blood,' says Bertholet,
' which, as the seat of the soul, is the essential means of
expiation, must be brought as visibly near to God as
possible.' [4]   The death of the victim is ' merely the means
by which the life (blood) of the victim is appropriated to

[1] Kuenen, op. cit., ii. p. 267 (E.T.).
[2] Marti, Geschichte der Israelitischen Religion [5], pp. 250 ff.   Cf. G. F. Moore
in Encyc. Bib., iv. p. 4226, who, after an exhaustive discussion, concludes
that a theory of poena vicaria is not derived from the Old Testament, but
imported into it.
[3] Stevens, op. cit., p. 11.
Bertholet, Biblische Theologie des Alten Testaments, p. 35.

God,' and as to the meaning of the sprinkling with blood
it is 'the appropriation to God of the animal's life, the
accomplishment of the penance demanded by Him through
the surrender of that sacred thing, the mysterious centre
of life.   This blood, given to God, forms, as it were, the
robe in which the priest arrays the sinner so that he may
appear before God.'[1]   Riehm, after rejecting as an
explanation of Lev. xvii. 11 doctrines of vicarious punishment and of the substitution of the pure soul of the animal
for the impure soul of the offerer, looks to the end purposed
by the atonement for the right answer : 'This is a protective
covering of the soul of him who needs atonement, a securing
of his life, if he comes into God's presence.'   An unbloody
sacrifice does not adequately correspond to this end, its
value is not comparable with the value of a man's soul ;
but blood is comparable to the soul ; in the blood of the
offering the sinner brings a $\psi v \chi \grave{\eta} v \ \grave{a} v \tau \grave{\iota} \ \psi v \chi \hat{\eta} s$, a life to
secure his life.[2]   As to the Day of Atonement, the expulsion
of the 'scapegoat' is 'a symbolical representation of the
fact that there is no longer any guilt in Israel ' ;[3] the idea
of the expiation of sin is made more solemn by the reference

[1] Schultz, *op. cit.*, i. pp. 392 ff. There is a valuable note on Lev. iv. 1 in
Driver-White (Lev., *Polychrome Bible*). Their view is much the same as
Schultz's. That a special protective power resided in the blood is the view
of C. von Orelli in the *New Schaff Herzog*, *s.v.* 'Sacrifice': 'It is evident
from Lev. xvii. 11 that the blood of the sacrificial victim was held to protect
the life of the sacrificer in virtue of the animal's life in the blood.' For the
modern Jewish view see the articles 'Sacrifice' and 'Atonement' in *The
Jewish Encyclopædia*. The writer of the latter—Dr. Köhler—says: 'The
life of the victim was offered . . . as a typical ransom of "life by life," the
blood sprinkled by the priest upon the altar serving as the means of a
renewal of man's covenant of life with God. The blood, which to the
ancients was the life-power or soul, forms the essential part of the Sacrificial Atonement' (vol. ii. p. 276).
[2] Riehm, *op. cit.*, pp. 137, 138. For a study of the religious significance
of blood, H. C. Trumbull's *The Blood-Covenant* should be consulted. He
argues that the blood-covenant effects a human-divine interunion, because
the blood is the life, for the obtaining of which death is necessary. Hence,
in the Mosaic sacrifices, blood always signifies life, not death. Cf. Nairne,
The Faith of the Old Testament, pp. 98, 99.
[3] Schultz, *op. cit.*, i. p. 404 (E.T.).   Cf. Kuenen, ii. p. 272: 'The
sending away of the other goat is a symbol of what the real sin-
offerings (*i.e.* the killing of the bullock and goat for Jahveh) have already
effected.'

to the whole people ; but the ritual of the occasion does not allow us to make any new generalisation.

Apart then from the question of the legitimacy of using the Levitical sacrifices for the construction of a Christian theory of atonement, it is clear that we can no longer assert with confidence that they involve a doctrine of substitution and vicarious punishment. On the other hand, the whole system is built up to show the necessity for the expiation of sin. Only the ideas of expiation and propitiation must not be confused. We may agree with Dr. Paterson that ' the *Expiation of guilt* is the leading purpose of the Levitical sacrifices,' [1] and with Dr. Stevens that it is ' opposed to all the presuppositions of Israel's religion' to conceive of Jahveh as ' propitiated by the sacrifices or by any other means, in the sense of being rendered merciful, or of being thereby made willing to forgive.' [2] The words in which Piepenbring sums up his discussion of pardon and expiation in the sacrificial system do justice to the evidence from which our conclusions must be drawn : ' expiatory sacrifice being, like every other sacrifice, a corban, a gift (Lev. iv. 23, 28, 32 ; v. 11), we must think of it as an offering made to God by a guilty person to make amends for a sin for which amends are possible, and to gain forgiveness for it. It is in reality a means of grace, a means given by Jehovah to those of His people who have sinned against Him in ignorance, that they may return to a state of grace, be reconciled with him, and continue to enjoy union with him.' [3] The sacrificial system assumes that sin makes a barrier between man and God ; and that before the covenant relationship with Jahveh, which the individual normally enjoys as a member of the covenant people, can be restored, the sin must be covered or wiped out. [4] For that Jahveh Himself

[1] In Hastings' *Dictionary of the Bible*, iv. p. 339.
[2] Stevens, *op. cit.*, p. 28.   [3] Piepenbring, *op. cit.*, pp. 279, 280.
[4] Herrmann's *Die Idee der Sühne im Alten Testament* is the fullest recent (1905) study of the word *kipper*, which in Hebrew corresponds to 'make expiation' and 'make atonement.' Driver's articles in Hastings' *Dictionary*

has made provision, and the final act of reparation is the presentation [1] and sprinkling of the blood, the most sacred of all earthly things, as the equivalent of life.

When we go on to consider the means looked on as effective for reconciling sinful man with God in those books of the Old Testament which stand in complete independence of the sacrificial system, we are at first ready to accept even extreme statements of the fundamental opposition between the legal and the prophetic religion of Israel. Thus Marti expresses the opposition in the most uncompromising way. 'The prophets were always the outspoken opponents of the sacrificial cultus practised by their contemporaries. In almost every one you can read the flat rejection of the cultus.[2] Dr. Welch, without committing himself so far as this, says of Amos that 'he shows a certain impatient disdain of the whole subject, which seems to suggest a negative attitude, not only to the ritual of his own day, but to any ritual of any day.' [3]

of the Bible, *s.v.* 'Propitiation,' and in the *Encyc. Rel. Eth.*, *s.v.* 'Expiation' and 'Atonement' (Hebrew), may be recommended to the English reader. The primary meaning of the word is either 'cover,' from the Arabic (so, with reserve, Driver in Hastings' *Dictionary of the Bible*, Piepenbring, Dillmann, Stade, Davidson, Marti, and the older writers generally), or 'wipe away,' from the Syriac (so Robertson Smith and Zimmern, to whom approximate Herrmann and, apparently, Driver in *Encyc. Rel. Eth.* The last-named thinks that the idea of 'ritual purgation' was attached to kipper from an early date). It is certainly easier to carry the idea of covering through the different classes of passages in which kipper occurs than the idea of wiping away. Three classes of passages may be distinguished—(i.) extra-ritual, a person 'covers the face of,' hence conciliates another person (but not Jahveh as direct object, cf. Davidson, p. 321), *e.g.* Gen. xxxii. 20, Ex. xxxii. 30 ; (ii.) extra-ritual. God is subject, the sinner (Deut. xxi. 8) or the sin (Jer. xviii. 23) the object, and kipper has the sense of pardon ; (iii.) ritual (Ezekiel and P.) priest is subject, the person or thing (not the sin) covered is the object, the sense being to make atonement for (Ez. xlv. 15, 17 ; Lev. iv. 20, viii. 15). In the LXX kipper is rendered by ἐξιλάσκεσθαι and its derivatives, but to propitiate God is never said. In *Encyc. Rel. Eth.* Driver gives it as his opinion that while the idea of propitiation was involved in kipper, 'the idea most distinctively conveyed by the word was probably that of "expiation."'

[1] Cf. Cave, *The Scriptural Doctrine of Sacrifice*, pp. 129, 253. While Dr. Cave represents, generally speaking, the old view, he sees clearly, as against Bähr, the importance in the sacrifice of the element of presentation as well as of that of atonement.

[2] Marti, *Religion of the Old Testament*, p. 148 (E.T.).

[3] Welch, *op. cit.*, p. 89.

Whatever be the exact truth of the matter, it is certain
that the prophets did not simply mean that sacrifices
were useless apart from righteousness ; such an interpretation fails to explain particular passages such as Amos v. 25
and Jer. vii. 22, and the atmosphere of—at least—aloofness
from the cultus which it is impossible not to feel.   To say
that ' they could not have regarded the sacrifices as essential
accompaniments of repentance or necessary media of forgiveness ' [1] is to do no violence to the evidence.

When Mr. Montefiore writes that ' the main doctrine
of Judaism on the subject of atonement is comprised in
the single word Repentance, and under repentance was
included and understood amendment,' [2] he leads us to the
heart of the prophets' teaching and of the piety of the
Psalms.   If even ' in the whole ceremony of sacrifice the
one really essential point is the confession of sin,' [3] confession is for the prophets the first of religious necessities.
In such psalms as the fortieth, the fiftieth, and the fifty-first
we note the superiority given to contrition, thankfulness,
and prayer as contrasted with external sacrifice.   That
man, confessing his sins, may look for forgiveness is referred
especially to Jahveh's regard for His own name,[4] but also
to His love for Jerusalem,[5] His remembrance of the faithful
ancestors of the people with whom He made His covenant,[6]
His respect for those who remain loyal to Him, even though
the mass of the nation fall away.[7]   But however the
motives which lead Jahveh to forgive be expressed, undoubtedly the only conditions which He requires of man
are of a moral not a ritual character.   Religion almost
becomes a moralism, were it not for the characteristic
Hebrew reference of ethics to the laws of God rather than
to the ideals of man.[8]   The prophets live in a region of

[1] Stevens, *op. cit.*, p. 18.   [2] Montefiore, *Hibbert Lectures*, 1892, p. 524.
[3] Schultz, *op. cit.*, ii. p. 100.
[4] Cf. Ex. xx. ; Num. xiv. 13 ; Deut. ix. 24 ; Is. xlviii. 9-11, etc.
[5] 1 Kings xi. 13, xiv. 21.
[6] Ex. xxxii. 13 ; Deut. ix. 27 ; 2 Kings xx. 6.
[7] 1 Sam. vii. 5 ; Ps. cvi. 23 ; Jer. v. 1.
[8] Cf. Ps. cxix. pass., and H. W. Robinson, *op. cit.*, p. 154.

categorical imperatives, binding alike upon nation and
individual. In the great religious reform of Josiah's
reign the moral zeal of the earlier prophets—Amos, Hosea,
and Isaiah—lays hold upon the southern kingdom only to
be baulked of full success by that spirit of compromise
between the prophetical and the priestly which runs
through Deuteronomy.[1] The prophetical insistence upon
true repentance and personal righteousness leads at times
to beliefs which seem to ascribe to good works some positive
share in the attainment of forgiveness, as when in Proverbs
xvi. 6 iniquity is said to be purged by mercy and truth,
and in Daniel iv. 27 the command is given to break free
from sins by righteousness and from guilt by mercy to
the poor.[2] Such incipient doctrines of merit are the danger
of an earnest moralism, but the intense religious feeling
and sense of dependence upon Jahveh which the prophets
and psalmists possessed and preached were an effective safeguard against an undue glorifying of human
achievement.

If the religion of the prophets had culminated in the
appeal for repentance for the past and right action for
the future, we should have to look upon them as separated
by an unbridgeable gulf from the ideals of the legal, priestly
cultus. Where repentance and good works are all that is
necessary, there may be a religion of reconciliation, but not
what is generally understood by a religion of atonement.[3]
But this was not the prophetic culmination. For the true
culmination there is already some preparation in earlier
passages. We hear of persons who make intercession to
God for others—Moses for the people, a prophet for
Jeroboam, Job for his friends.[4] The idea of mediation is,
to some extent, introduced, and not in dependence upon

---

[1] Cf. Glazebrook, *The End of the Law*, p. 119, 'in a larger measure the
obedience required by the Deuteronomic law meant sacrifice and ceremony;
and these elements, appealing more readily to the ordinary mind, soon
secured a practical precedence.'
[2] Cf. Dillmann, *Handbuch*, p. 472.   [3] See note 1, p. 11.
[4] Ex. xxxii. 11-14; 1 Kings xiii. 6; Job xlii. 8, 9

the law, for the mediators are not priests ; and yet 'such
passages are on the same ground as that occupied by the
teaching of the law, since the sinner cannot himself effect
atonement, but needs a mediator, who, as object of the
divine good pleasure, absorbs into himself the wrath of
God, and procures the divine grace for him who has made
himself unworthy of it.' [1] The culmination of such
passages and of the whole prophetic teaching is to be
found in that picture of the office and destiny of the
Servant of Jahveh, which reaches its zenith in the fifty-
third chapter of Isaiah.

The precise interpretation that we give to the Servant
of Jahveh is not immediately important. Whether the
Servant be Israel as a whole, who suffers for the nations,
or an ideal Israel, a faithful remnant who suffer for the
redemption of the people, or the mysterious ' Great
Personage' of Dr. Cheyne's *Mines of Isaiah Re-explored*,
the expiatory virtue of whose sufferings extended not to
Israel alone, but also to the remnant of the peoples of
N. Arabia ; whether or no we allow that there is in this
'golden passional' of the Old Testament an element of
symbolism which necessarily looks beyond the immediate
circumstances under which this unique portion of the
Old Testament was produced; [2]—whatever, in short, be
our conclusion as to the critical problems, historic and
linguistic, involved, at least we are face to face with ideas
of mediation, sacrifice, and expiation, which come with
the greater and more significant force because of their
totally unexpected appearance. Three points deserve
special attention. In the first place, the prophetic and
priestly lines of development meet in this great climax
of sacrificial death conceived as a personal moral action.
It is not enough to say that ' the office of the Servant is
prophetic not priestly. It is the suffering of actual

[1] Dillmann, *op. cit.*, p. 473.
[2] So Delitzsch, *Commentary on Isaiah* [4], ii. p. 281 (E.T.). He refers with
approval to Cheyne's Excursus on the Servant of Jehovah, and on The
Suffering Messiah in his *Prophecies of Isaiah* [3], ii. pp. 211-224.

experience which falls upon him. The vicariousness is ethical.' [1] It is ethical but it is also priestly ; the antithesis is here overcome. Riehm does not go too far when he says of the Servant, 'Israel is the priestly people, mediator between God and man, and in this priestly mediation is its kingly lordship over the peoples grounded.' [2] The reference to the trespass-offering in verse 10 is perfectly in accord with the general sense of the passage, and merely gives definitive expression to the office of the Servant, who has already been compared to the sacrificial lamb.[3] Secondly, there is the express teaching of the expiation of sins through vicarious suffering, and despite Marti's contention, it is paradoxical to regard this suffering as directed in its influence and effects towards the heathen alone and not towards God.[4] The idea of moral influence is involved, but it is not the dominating idea. What is done in Isaiah liii. is looked on as done between Jahveh and the Servant with the deliberate intention of an expiation for the sins of others. Whatever be the force of the substitutionary offering of the Servant, it is impossible to expel the idea of substitution from the passage.[5] Dr. Cheyne, in his last work on Isaiah referred to above, as

---

[1] Stevens, *op. cit.*, p. 33.

[2] Riehm, *op. cit.*, p. 343. Cf. Cave, *op. cit.*, p. 217, 'the sacrificial aspect is everywhere present,' and Piepenbring's interesting suggestion (p. 207) that the idea of the Suffering Servant arose when the exiled people could no longer offer sacrifices to Jahveh.

[3] Cf. Schultz, *op. cit.*, i. p. 319 (E.T.): 'The priest now appears in a far higher form, because his right no longer depends on his office, but on moral action.'

[4] Marti sarcastically writes (*Das Buch Jesaia* im Kurzen Hand-Commentar, p. 349): 'The heathen do not intend to be Christian theologians, they do not speak of the effect of the Servant's Suffering upon God, at least not of a power therein sufficient to induce God to change His mind, but of an influence upon their own outlook.'

[5] Dr. G. C. Wade, one of the most recent English commentators, fully recognises this. He argues (*Book of the Prophet Isaiah*, p. 344) on liii. 10, that amends for grievous sins could be made only by the sacrifice of life, but not necessarily that of the sinner (he refers to Micah vi. 7 and 2 Sam. xxi. 1-14), and that the text is in accordance with the principle. Quite rightly he continues: 'But Israel's death is not merely the substitution of one life for another; the innocence and submissiveness of the sufferer exert a moral influence upon those for whom he suffers, moving them to repentance and confession of their offences.'

clearly recognises the expiatory value of the sufferings
of the Servant as in his earlier commentary.[1] The sins
of the heathen or of the unfaithful Israelites are blotted
out, and they are brought into a new relation with Jahveh,
'justified' through the sufferings of the Righteous Servant.
But thirdly, if this be so, it seems hardly possible to rid
the chapter of that penal element which Mr. Montefiore,
in reference to this chapter, describes as 'a remnant of
a sacrificial theory which the teaching of the prophets
themselves had already been sufficient to explode.'[2]
Mr. H. W. Robinson, while admitting that we have here
the most important expression of the substitutionary idea,
yet refuses to allow that the value of the offering lies 'in
the penal transference to Israel of the guilt of the nations.
Israel actually suffers as the nations should have suffered ;
yet the purpose of that suffering is not to satisfy divine
justice, but to move the nations to penitence.'[3] But
the point of view of the nations, with which Deutero-
Isaiah obviously identifies himself, is that the Servant
is suffering what would have been the just reward of their
offences ; the contrast in verse 6 between the sins of the
nations and the suffering of the Servant compels us to
bring those sins and that suffering into the closest possible
connection.[4] We shall go wrong if we read formal theories

[1] Cf. his *Prophecies of Isaiah*[3], ii. p. 39, where he speaks of 'the idea of
Vicarious Atonement which some have laboured hard to expel from the
prophecy, but which still forces itself upon the unbiassed reader,' and p. 45,
where, on verse 4, he finds the chief meaning, not 'that the consequences of
the sins of the people fell upon him the innocent,' though this is present, but
'that he bore His undeserved sufferings as a sacrifice on behalf of His
people.' There are, says Dr. Cheyne, 'twelve distinct assertions in this one
chapter of the vicarious character of the sufferings of the Servant.' It will
be noted that the view that 'to bear the sins' simply means, as Dr. G. C.
Workman argues (*op. cit.*, p. 184), 'to bear the consequences of sins,' is
rejected in the above statement.

[2] Montefiore, *op. cit.*, p. 280.   [3] Robinson, *op. cit.*, p. 147.

[4] Dr. Davidson's careful statement seems to me to be unassailable. 'The
idea that the death of the creature was in the nature of penalty, by the
exaction of which the righteousness of Jehovah was satisfied, seems certainly
clearly expressed in Is. liii.; at least these two points appear to be stated
there, that the sins of the people, *i.e.* penalties for them, were laid on the
Servant and borne by him ; and secondly, that thus the people were relieved
from the penalty, and their sins being borne were forgiven.' Cf. Addis,

of atonement into the passage. The writer was not concerned with abstract θεολογούμενα. But we shall be equally wrong if we eviscerate the passage of what the writer's experience caused him to regard as fact. How the Servant can suffer for others, how he can endure the penal consequences of the sins of others—these are questions which Deutero-Isaiah does not raise. But we take the heart out of the words, and deprive the Servant of his noblest glory, if we look on his work as only an object-lesson, an incentive or even a piece of voluntary self-sacrifice : it is God who has brought him to stand where others should stand, to endure what others should endure ; and he stands and endures because it is God's will for him, without complaint. He is the victim, even before he is the priest.[1]

The prophetic and priestly lines, the problem of suffering,[2] and the value of sacrifice all come to rest in this great chapter. The offering which atones is an offering of reparation as well as of reconciliation. When the Maccabæan martyrs [3] are said to have become as it were a vicarious expiation for the sins of the nation, and divine providence to have saved Israel by reason of their atoning death (ἱλαστηρίου θανάτου), we have more precise terminology than in Isaiah liii., but no development of idea. We cannot wonder that the early Christian conception

Hebrew Religion, p. 217 : 'The heathen see that the Servant bore a punishment which they themselves deserved.'

[1] Delitzsch, *Commentary*[4], ii. p. 295 (E.T.) says : 'What falls on him is not punishment, and yet it is punishment ; it is punishment only in so far as he has identified himself vicariously ' (this is not quite the point) ' with sinners who are deserving of wrath. How could he have made expiation for sin, if he had merely subjected himself to its cosmical effects, and not face to face with God, to that wrath which is the correlative of sin ?' The last sentence has rather too modern a ring, but apart from that, and from the initiative being given to the Servant rather than to Jahveh, what is said here is implicit in the passage.

[2] In the book of Job, though it is taken up with the problem, there is no solution. As has been well said (H. W. Robinson, *op. cit.*, p. 175): 'If we ask what was the service which the suffering Job had rendered . . . the very point of the book is the mystery of this service ; the suffering must be borne under the pressure of an ever recurrent and finally unanswered "Why ?"'

[3] 4 Macc. xvii. 22, Bertholet, *Biblische Theologie*, p. 329, decisively rejects the idea of Hellenistic influence in this passage.

of the death of Christ was so greatly influenced by this description of the suffering Servant ; we may find that in this Christ Himself showed His followers the way.

Even in the picture of the Servant there is no complete synthesis of the priestly and the prophetic, the legal and the moral conceptions of the method of reconciliation. The religion of Israel was not a perfect religion, and in so great a matter as this we shall not be surprised to find unreconciled differences. The later prophets from Ezekiel onwards have no such burning words against the cultus as are found in Amos and in the early chapters of Isaiah, which sometimes appear to sound the note of 'abusus tollit usum.' But the moral element in sacrifice and mediation, even in punishment, rises before us uniquely, so far as concerns the Old Testament, in Isaiah liii. The moralism of the prophets might degenerate into a rationalism which ascribes everything to man and nothing to God ; the ritualistic piety of the Law into a magic which degrades both God and man. Only where the two elements fuse and interpenetrate, where the moral response is evoked through a sacrifice which God first supplies, and sacrifice can be made to do justice to those moral necessities which proceed from the nature of a holy God, can we be made possessors of the active ethic and the no less active piety which together go to build up the fabric of true personal religion.

of New Testament Studies.   However, in 1907, Dr. Sanday published his *Life of Christ in Recent Research*, and Schweitzer and the Eschatological Problem became household words.   The translation of Schweitzer's *Von Reimarus zu Wrede* in 1910 under the title of *The Quest of the Historical Jesus* ; the outspoken support given to the Strassburg *Privatdozent* by Professor Burkitt ; the no less outspoken criticism in the *Journal of Theological Studies* by the present Dean of St. Paul's, then one of Mr. Burkitt's professorial colleagues ; and something approaching to a full-dress debate on Schweitzer and his theory at the Cambridge Church Congress of 1910 ;—all contributed to make of the sketch which Dr. Sanday had given a complete picture, and certainly a very startling one.   Is Schweitzer the most recent blasphemer or the most recent apologist ?   There is no agreed answer.

But what has it got to do with the doctrine of atonement ? A very great deal.   So long as German Liberal-Protestant thought prevailed everywhere except in ' orthodox ' and ' ecclesiastical ' circles, Jesus was regarded as above all else a Teacher, who proclaimed the approach of a new ethico-religious community to which He gave the name of the Kingdom of God ; and He did not merely announce it ; He founded it.   To this Kingdom was attached a Gospel, the good news of God's Fatherhood, of His love for men, of His readiness to forgive sins, of the infinite value in the sight of God of every human soul, with, as the corollary, the obligation that the men in whose hearts the Kingdom had found a place should show themselves true children of their Father by treating one another as brethren bound together by the supreme law of the Kingdom, the law of love.   The most famous statement of this ethico-religious conception is that of Harnack in *Das Wesen des Christentums*.   Like many other theologians who had worked along similar lines, Harnack was greatly influenced by Ritschl's use of the idea of the Kingdom of God as the first principle of his theological system.   But whereas Ritschl could not fairly be accused of under-valuing the importance of the Person of Jesus, whatever might be thought of his positive doctrine of that Person, the Liberal School as a whole subordinated Jesus to the Gospel which He proclaimed.   Harnack's well-known words speak for others even more than they do for himself. 'The Gospel as Jesus proclaimed it had to do with the Father only, not with the Son.' [1]

Jesus was for the German Liberals a Teacher.   But if He was a Teacher, could He have thought of Himself as a Mediator, as one who had a special work to do in restoring right relations between God and man ?   Yet there were sayings of His in the earliest Gospel, St. Mark, which certainly seemed to imply that something of this kind was His belief ; [2]   in what light were they to be regarded ?   There were two possible solutions : the first, which is that of older 'mediating' writers such as Bey-schlag [3] and Wendt [4] and even of Oscar Holtzmann,[5] is to accept the sayings and rationalise them ; the second, which is that of Pfleiderer,[6] at the end of his career, Wellhausen,[7] and Wrede,[8] is to deny their authenticity. Such sayings are 'dogmatic' and therefore 'unhistorical' ; this, as Schweitzer [9] fairly points out, is the conclusion reached by writers of this second group.   But on one thing there was general agreement : Jesus was no dogmatist, and the Christian Church had greatly erred in trying to find support for her doctrines, about atonement as about other things, in the words of Jesus.   Paul, not Jesus, was the originator of such doctrines, and Pfleiderer and Loisy were not alone in suspecting Mark, or an Editor of Mark, of introducing Paulinism into the Gospels, and

---

[1] Harnack, *What is Christianity ?* p. 147 (E.T.).   [2] Mark x. 45, xiv. 24.
[3] Beyschlag, *New Testament Theology*, i. pp. 150-159 (E.T.).
[4] Wendt, *The Teaching of Jesus*, ii. pp. 218-246 (E.T.).
[5] O. Holtzmann, *Life of Jesus*, p. 464 (E.T.).
[6] Pfleiderer, *Primitive Christianity*, ii. pp. 482-493 (E.T.).
[7] Wellhausen, *Das Evangelium Marci*, pp. 65, 66.
[8] Wrede, *Das Messiasgeheimnis*, pp. 82 ff.
[9] Schweitzer, *Quest of the Historical Jesus*, p. 385 (E.T.).

attributing to Jesus the thoughts of Paul. The confident statement of Weinel,[1] ' not one word has Jesus to say of any doctrine of atonement,' may be taken as typical of much German Liberal theology, whether it is more or less ready to accept particular passages as embodying genuine words of Jesus.

Into the camp of German Liberalism burst like a bombshell Schweitzer's *Von Reimarus zu Wrede* in 1906. Its brilliant descriptive writing, its keenness of criticism and sense for the weak points in an adversary, and, not least, its construction of a picture of Jesus which is, at least, intelligible, and which, as latter-day construction goes, keeps fairly close to the text of the Gospels,[2] all pointed the shafts of the challenge which he issued to the upholders of the Liberal Portrait of Jesus. The Jesus of that portrait never existed : ' He is a figure designed by rationalism, endowed with life by liberalism, and clothed by modern theology in an historical garb.'[3] The picture substituted by Schweitzer, already painted in part by Johannes Weiss[4] some years earlier, is by this time familiar to English students of theology : the atmosphere which surrounds Jesus is permeated with eschatological conceptions, with the thought of the near approach of that Kingdom which the Baptist had announced ; the whole of the life and actions, as well as of the teaching of Jesus, is to be explained along eschatological lines, and the actions and teachings group themselves around three great secrets or mysteries. The first secret is that of the Messiah : Jesus knew Himself from the beginning of His ministry to be the Messiah ; the second is the secret of the Kingdom : this was close at hand, a supernatural event, the end of

---

[1] Weinel, *Biblische Theologie des Neuen Testaments*, p. 207.

[2] A point made by Dr. Sanday, *Life of Christ in Recent Research*, p. 88.

[3] Schweitzer, *Quest*, p. 396 (E. T.).

[4] J. Weiss, *Die Predigt Jesu vom Reiche Gottes*, 1892. In the second edition, 1900, Weiss is not quite as thorough going, but he is still confident (see the Preface) that Ritschl's idea of the Kingdom of God is very different from that of Jesus, and has its roots in Kant and the Theology of the Enlightenment.

the world-age ; and the third is the secret of the suffering ; this appears first as the general πειρασμός which must precede the Kingdom, with, as but one element in it, the suffering of Jesus Himself ; and then, in the revelation at Cæsarea Philippi, as the concentration of the eschatological woes upon Jesus, His suffering and death for others that the Kingdom may come, and that He may return from heaven, manifested as the Danielic Son of Man. Everything in the Gospel history is interpreted by Schweitzer along these lines, and the history ended as it did with the death of Jesus, 'because two of His disciples had broken His command of silence : Peter when he made known the secret of the Messiahship to the Twelve at Cæsarea Philippi ; Judas Iscariot by communicating it to the High Priest' ; [1] for the moment that the priests were able to inform the people that Jesus claimed to be not simply ' The Prophet ' as the people supposed when He entered into Jerusalem, but the Messiah,[2] all turned from Him as from a blasphemer.

At first sight it all appears revolutionary in the extreme : how on this hypothesis is Jesus superior to Bar Cochba, or any other deluded fanatic who makes assertions and promises which history will break to pieces ? Of what value can He and His teaching be to us ?

To deal fully with these questions would take us far beyond the limits of this chapter, even of this book. Yet the issues raised cannot be ignored, for they affect the whole dogmatic interpretation of the Gospels and the view that we shall take of recorded words of Jesus. Let us see, therefore, without going into detail, what conclusions we can come to as to Schweitzer's reconstruction.

Firstly, in his interpretation of the Kingdom of God he does a much-needed work in readjusting the balance. The Ritschlian conception of the Kingdom as a present

---

[1] Schweitzer, *Quest*, p. 394 (E.T.).
[2] Schweitzer, *Quest*, p. 392 (E.T.). ' The Entry into Jerusalem was Messianic for Jesus, but not Messianic for the people.' The people thought He was Elias.

moral power had prevailed unduly against that other conception of the Kingdom, which is unquestionably to be found in the Gospels, as a future supernatural phenomenon and gift.

Secondly, he explains, as the older Liberalism does not, the intimate connection of Jesus Himself with the Kingdom. He gives to the Messiahship of Jesus real importance, whereas critics had been too ready to make of it simply an honorary title, while laying all the emphasis on the teaching of Jesus. But a Teacher is only a Prophet, not the Messiah.

Thirdly, he does justice to the tragic note which is to be heard in the words of Jesus before Cæsarea Philippi. The 'Galilean Springtime' was never a springtime of unclouded skies. And when, after Cæsarea Philippi, the tragic note recurs again and again, he need neither deny its existence [1] nor reduce the solemnity and import of the strain. The predictions of the sufferings he declares to be 'dogmatic, and therefore historical; because they find their explanation in eschatological conceptions.' [2]

There are mysteries in the Gospel history upon which Schweitzer throws light. Only I think that with all his dread of a purely psychological treatment of the Person of Jesus and of the Gospel of Mark, he himself is at times the victim of the psychological method. The fault of the picture which he draws of the historical Jesus is its over-consistency. He makes no allowances; the consciousness of Jesus is wholly of one kind; no antitheses reveal themselves in His thought. Here Schweitzer and the thorough-going eschatologists outrun the evidence; it is only by a drastic and unnatural interpretation that some of the parables, such as the Unjust Judge, the Seed

---

[1] Even the parable of the Wicked Husbandman, which comes so naturally in the common synoptic tradition, cannot escape criticism, at least in its present form. Jülicher, *Gleichnisreden* [2], i. p. 406, and Pfleiderer, *Primitive Christianity*, ii. p. 57 (E.T.) see in it the product of early Christian theology.

[2] *Op. cit.*, p. 385.

Growing Secretly, and the Leaven can be made to give
evidence for the eschatological hypothesis ; the narratives
of the casting out of demons, and the accompanying
sayings, imply that the Kingdom is in some sense already
present ; [1] so does the contrast between the Baptist and
' the least in the Kingdom of Heaven ' with the corollary
that from the days of the Baptist the violent are beginning
to press by force into the Kingdom.   There are apparently
unreconciled conceptions, and if the history of the Quest
of the Historical Jesus has taught us anything, it should
be the improbability of the existence of any one magic
key to the secret of His personality, which includes the
three secrets to which Schweitzer has called attention but
transcends them all.   In his *Theologie des Neuen Testaments*, Feine has rightly tried to find in the Person of
Jesus a reconciliation of conceptions apparently so diverse :
' He is the king of the future kingdom ; but where He is
with these divine powers of His personality there the
powers of the kingdom are already active, there grows the
kingdom already in this world ' ; [2] and Professor Denney
points out how in His last public utterance Jesus identifies
Himself with the coming of the Kingdom of God, so that
the coming of the kingdom means His own exaltation and
return in glory.[3]   Working along these lines we can make
it clearer than Schweitzer has done that the Jesus of history
was not a deluded fanatic ; we can even begin to justify
Weinel's statement—' We know Him right well '—which
has shocked Professor Burkitt.   For Schweitzer has not
avoided (and here Dr. Inge's criticism holds good) making
a deep fissure between the Jesus of history and the Christ
of faith, and because of this he, like the Liberals he criticises,
is unable to do full justice to the Jesus of history.   But
if the Jesus of history was sent, then it is not absurd to

---

[1] See **Mark** i. 24, ii. 27 ; **Matt.** xii. 28 ; **Luke x.** 17.
[2] *Theologie des Neuen Testaments* [2], p. 77.
[3] Denney, *Jesus and the Gospels*, p. 370. This work is the most satisfactory recent criticism in English of Harnack's description—quoted above,
p. 33—of the Gospel as preached by Jesus.

see in Pentecost the fulfilment of the words which He
uttered concerning the advent in power of the Kingdom
before the death of all His hearers, whatever He meant
by them when He said them.[1]   The eschatological prayer,
'Thy Kingdom come,' began to be fulfilled at Pentecost,
and is still being fulfilled in the history of the Church.
For the Church stands in direct relationship to, and deriva-
tion from, the Jesus of history.   Particular critical problems
are here quite irrelevant ; on the Jesus of history depends
not only the fact of a Christian Church, but the character
of that Church's doctrine, ethic, and hope.   If the moral
teaching of the Gospels is an *Interimsethik*, are we any
better off ? do not we live in an *interim* ? [2]   'We do not
expect this world to break in pieces immediately, but we
know that in our pre-occupation with earthly things we
may hear the Voice of God, "Thou fool, this night shall
thy soul be demanded of thee." ' [3]   But the work of relating
the fact of the existence and character of the Church to
the Gospel picture of Jesus without denying the eschatological standpoint, without omitting other elements, and,
above all, without acquiescing contentedly in the shallow
antithesis of the Jesus of history and the Christ of faith,
has yet to be done.   What we have a right to urge is that
it ought no longer to be possible to draw the picture of
Jesus according to the old Liberal standpoint, and represent
the result as the most finished present product of scientific
draughtsmanship.[4]   In particular, with regard to the
death of Jesus, the older rationalism which shrunk from
recognising in the Gospels any 'dogmatic' significance
as attached to the Passion is undermined.   It is true that
Wrede can ask 'Why did Jesus go to Jerusalem ' ? and
can answer ' Not to die there, as the dogmatic view of the
Evangelists demands . . . but to work there with decisive

---

[1] I am much indebted to a letter of Professor Burkitt's at this point.
[2] Cf. a speech by E. G. Selwyn, *Church Congress* (1910) *Report*, p. 87.
[3] Feine, *op. cit.*, p. 87.
[4] The sketch of the life and teaching of Jesus in Weinel and Widgery,
Jesus in the Nineteenth Century and After, is curiously old-fashioned.

effect.' [1] But Wrede is only able to give this answer
because he has pursued a policy of ' thorough ' with regard
to everything in the Marcan tradition which implies that
Jesus thought of Himself as Messiah, and confidently
asserted the inevitability of his death. Wrede is prepared
to allow that now and then Jesus may have thought of
His death as a possibility ; but the idea was never a
dominant one. Pfleiderer can also bring himself to say
that Jesus, ' even at the Last Supper, gave expression
in quite unambiguous terms to His confident hope of the
immediate victory of His cause.' [2] But the Liberal
theologian who is not a radical exegete is hardly likely
to be thankful to Wrede and Pfleiderer, who, while they
refuse to attribute to Jesus ' dogmatic ' utterances, yet
equally refuse to deny that they are dogmatic, in which
conclusion they are supported by Loisy. Schweitzer very
clearly sees that, since the Marcan narrative as it stands
supports the dogmatic view according to which Jesus
went to Jerusalem to die, Wrede is forced to regard the
whole narrative of the last days at Jerusalem as unreliable,
' from beginning to end a creation of the dogmatic idea ' : [3]
in other words, from Wrede's point of view there can be
no confidence as to what really happened during the last
days of the life of Jesus, nor any satisfactory explanation
of His death. Pfleiderer indeed may speak of Mark xiv.
and xv. resting for the most part on authentic tradition,
but at how many crucial points this tradition becomes
unreliable any reader may learn for himself by a study
of Pfleiderer's pages (pp. 69-82). It is easy to see how
criticism such as that associated with the names of Wrede,
Pfleiderer, Loisy, and most recently the younger D'Alviella, [4]
forms material for the arguments and conclusions of the
Christus-Myth School. This school, with its insistence
that the Jesus of the Gospels is simply a mythical Saviour-

---

[1] Wrede, *Messiasgeheimnis*, p. 87.
[2] Pfleiderer, *op. cit.*, ii. 74.
[3] Schweitzer, *op. cit.*, p. 341.
[4] *L'Evolution du dogme catholique*, i.

God,[1] has proved a more formidable adversary of the
great liberal theologians of Germany than the many
absurdities to which it is committed would have led us
to suppose ; the fact is not without significance.[2]

What then do the Synoptic Gospels[3] record as to the
teaching and actions of Jesus which throw light on His
conception of the problem of atonement and reconciliation
and its solution ?   In the forefront of the Marcan narrative
stands the account of the Baptism of Jesus, followed by
that of the Temptation.   We ask what these events meant
to Him.   The answer often given[4] is that at the Baptism
Jesus became conscious of His Messianic office, and that
in the Temptation He was assailed by promptings to use
that office for His self-glorification.   Now the Voice which
came to Him at the Baptism designated Him the beloved
Son of God, the object of His good pleasure.   He is the
Son of the second psalm ; He is also the Servant of
Deutero-Isaiah's prophecies, who, in the first of the
passages which centre round Him, is described as the
Elect of God, in whom His soul delights (Isaiah xlii. 1).
But how different is the picture of the Triumphant Son
of the psalm from that of the Servant, finally the Suffering
Servant, of the prophecy.   Unless we are prepared with
Pfleiderer to argue that the oldest form of the words of
the Baptismal Voice was that of Codex D. in the Lucan
text, 'Thou art my Son ; this day have I begotten thee,'[5]

1 The title of W. B. Smith's book—*Ecce Deus*—describes the general attitude of this school, which, in regard to Jesus, is that of Professor Bury's
epigram on Lycurgus, 'He was not a man, He was only a god.'
2 The number of pamphlets called forth by the work of Drews in particular
recalls the great agitation of 1893 about the Apostles' Creed.
3 A writer, whatever may be his views on the Johannine question, must at
the present time refrain from using the Fourth Gospel to establish dogmatical
conceptions by the witness of Christ Himself.
4 *E.g.* O. Holtzmann, Wendt.
5 Pfleiderer thinks that the altered form of the received text was due to
'dogmatic reasons,' *op. cit.*, ii. p. 505.   Wendt, *Teaching of Jesus*, i. p. 100
(E.T.), accepts the usual text, and argues for the importance of the reference
to Old Testament passages, 'for that very reference was the reason why
Jesus could regard the words of that revelation as not only a recognition of
His personal religious relation to God, but as an express designation of His
Messianic character and vocation.'

we must allow that there were presented to the consciousness of Jesus two ideals not obviously harmonious. Is
it fanciful to suggest that the Temptation meant for Him
the facing of the question which the Community afterwards
had to face—can Sonship be reconciled with the role of
the Servant ? Can anything but success and triumph
await the Messiah ? [1] If this were true, then Keim's
famous picture of the Galilean Springtime of the Ministry,
with the young Teacher confident of success, of His power
to win the nation as a whole, would need considerable
alteration, for whatever the Temptation may mean, it
cannot possibly mean that Jesus repudiated the ideal of
the Servant of Jahveh or looked on it as without significance
for Himself. But in point of fact Keim must be thought
of as rather reading his picture in between the lines of the
Gospel narrative than as deducing it scientifically from the
text.[2]

---

[1] Cf. the discussion in Denney, *Death of Christ*, pp. 13 ff.

[2] If the question is raised, Why did Jesus go to John's Baptism? I do not
believe that any completely satisfactory answer can be given. On the one
hand it is asserted by Strauss, Bruno Bauer, and others that Jesus went,
like the rest, to the baptism of repentance with a view to the forgiveness of
sins which He felt that He personally needed. In this connexion O. Holtzmann quotes the fragment from the Gospel to the Hebrews in which Jesus
asks what sin He has committed that He should go to the baptism, and then
tentatively suggests that the very question may be a sin of ignorance.
Holtzmann treats this tradition with respect, but Denney rightly characterises it as altogether unlike Jesus. Moreover, if Jesus was baptized as one
who needed forgiveness, then what Wendt calls 'the miraculous impartation
of the knowledge of His Messiahship' becomes quite unintelligible. It will
not do to say that other men have been conscious of needing forgiveness, and
have also been conscious of special Divine vocation. The certainty of Messiahship—if Jesus believed and truly believed Himself to be the Messiah—
cannot be paralleled with anything else. On the other hand, the Matthaean
explanation (iii. 14, 15) naturally arouses some suspicion as to its genuineness. Modern 'positive' Biblical theologians, such as Feine and Schlatter,
insist on the fact that Jesus identified Himself with the community to which
the call to repent was addressed. Feine (*Theologie des Neuen Testaments*, pp.
46, 147) looks upon the voice from heaven as expressing God's good pleasure
at the determination of Jesus to take the sins of the people upon Himself
(cf. Denney, *op. cit.*, p. 21). This implies a sense of vocation and 'the most
intense inner communion with God' (Feine) before the baptism, which must
not be read into Mark. But the whole question cannot be answered simply
by the use of the so-called 'historical method,' for in the background lies the
further question, Who was Jesus? and so we come into the field of different
dogmatic presuppositions.

Keim started from a belief in the priority of the first Gospel. It certainly gave him more ground for his picture. But modern scholarship holds convincedly to the priority of Mark, and, as Schweitzer says, Mark knows nothing of a first period of success and a second period of failure. We have a passage in the second chapter (ii. 20) which, as it stands, is most naturally understood as a foreshadowing by Jesus of His own death, while in the next chapter we are definitely told that the Pharisees and Herodians are already beginning to plot against His life. As to the passage on fasting, there is nothing obscure about it or about the connexion of verses 19 and 20 with one another and with the preceding question, unless we are to demand that people shall speak according to the strict rules of the syllogism, under pain of having their words discredited.[1] The question is not as to the rationale of fasting, but as to the difference of behaviour of different sets of people. Jesus replies that the difference will one day cease, and, by a simple parable, indicates when that will be. And if it is a genuine word of Jesus, it is, as Wrede roundly declares, no mere foreboding but a prophecy of suffering,[2] for which we must find a place before the events and sayings connected with Cæsarea Philippi. It is no peaceful death to which Jesus looks forward.

The comparison with the Marcan and Lucan narratives prevents us from laying any stress on the prophecy of death which Jesus introduces in Matt. xii. 40, in connexion with the Sign of Jonah. But in any case the passage adds no further idea to those which we have already obtained ; and the evidence that we have entitles us to

[1] Loisy's elaborate note on the passage is a masterpiece of misplaced subtlety. He tells us that ' Christ explains nothing, neither the conduct of John's disciples, nor that of his own,' and argues that if Jesus compared His disciples to joyful attendants on a bridegroom, He must have compared John's disciples to attendants made sad by some accident, such as the death of a bridegroom. As it is, there is no application to John's disciples. But if John was already in prison the application is implicit in v. 20, and the introduction of the disciples of the Pharisees does away with any special importance in the conduct of John's disciples.

[2] *Messiasgeheimnis*, p. 19.

view with great suspicion ' Lives of Jesus ' which present
Him to us as one who during the first part of His ministry
lived in an atmosphere of blue skies and sunshine with no
sense of what was to come.   Wendt,[1] who thinks we may
fairly assume that Jesus at the beginning of His ministry
did not see clearly the necessity for the death He was to
experience, nevertheless admits that ' the general thought
of the necessity of His suffering did not emerge during
the course of His ministry, or at its close, as a new and
strange element in His consciousness.' And if the
passages [2] in which Jesus anticipates suffering for His
followers, and which come before the confession of Peter,
are kept in the order in which they now stand, that is an
additional reason for believing that He did not, even in
the first part of the Ministry, look forward to immediate
and overwhelming success for His cause ; but if His
followers were to suffer, was He to go free ?

Whatever doubt there may be as to the character of
the vision of the future which Jesus adopts in the early
Galilean ministry, there can be no doubt whatever as to
the period which follows upon Peter's confession. We
can—if we are convinced by his arguments—accept
Wrede's ' clean cut ' and eliminate the ' Messianic ' passages
and all that tells of suffering to come from the life of Jesus,
and see in them the apologetic efforts of the early Christian
community. Otherwise we must face the facts, refrain
from what Wellhausen calls the attempt of modern theology
to weaken the force of the evidence of Mark in order to
vindicate its historicity, and acknowledge the truth and
significance of the fact that when Jesus ' unfolds Messiahship it contains death.' [3] Three times, after Peter's
confession, during the journey southwards through Galilee

---

[1] *Teaching of Jesus*, ii. p. 219.
[2] Matt. v. 11, x. 17-23, 34-39. Whether Schweitzer be right or not in
interpreting the sufferings of Matt. x. as belonging to the eschatological,
Messianic woes, he is right when he says ' it appears as if it was appointed
for Him to share the persecution and the suffering' (p. 369).
[3] Denney, *op. cit.*, p. 32.

to Capernaum, and shortly before the Entry into Jericho
(Mark viii. 31, ix. 30, x. 32, with parallels in Matthew and
Luke), He tells His disciples that the result of their journey
to Jerusalem will be His death ; on the first occasion that
death is announced as not merely something which will
happen, but as something which must happen, ' a necessity
in accordance with a divine purpose' (δεῖ).[1] In some way
this necessity must be referred to the Will of God.   As
Feine says, it cannot express merely the idea of devotion
to duty, of a martyr's death for the truth, but ' can be
understood only as a necessity laid upon Him by God.'
H. J. Holtzmann, while dissenting from the views of those
who ' deduce the necessity of death simply from the
Messianic vocation,' and arguing that in the Gospels their
necessity simply arises from the historical circumstances
and is so regarded by Jesus, nevertheless insists that this
' contingent necessity ' was felt by Jesus to be binding upon
Him, because He recognised in it ' an essential piece of the
Divine Will,' necessary for the fulfilment of His mission.[2]

Scepticism [3] as to these successive declarations by Jesus

[1] Meyer on Matt. xvi. 21. Cf. Meyer-Weiss on Mark viii. 31 : ' Only after
the disciples have recognised Him as the promised Messiah can He begin to
teach them the fate that is appointed for the Son of Man, since this can
result only from that which must happen to the Messiah in accordance with
the decree of God foretold by the Prophets.'

[2] H. J. Holtzmann, *Lehrbuch der Neuen Testaments Theologie*, i. pp. 353-363.
The whole section is well worth studying. He points out that if we give up
the passages about suffering and death we should have to think of Jesus as
going to Jerusalem to overthrow the hierarchy (Wrede's ' effective working '),
and that we should have to re-interpret the Entry, the Temple-cleansing, the
Anointing at Bethany, the Words at the Last Supper, etc., so as to expunge
all idea of death. Schlatter, who in his *Theologie des Neuen Testaments* (i.
pp. 484-498) brings the necessity for death into the closest possible connexion
with the consciousness of Jesus that in His death He was fulfilling God's
will, and causing God's grace and righteousness to be glorified, so that He
sees the Cross as a duty which ' He grasps with resolute will,' yet holds
that Jesus became certain that He must die, when He perceived that Israel
had been called in vain ; and that goes back certainly to the woe uttered
over Capernaum (Matt. xi. 23), and indeed in Matthew to the Sermon on the
Mount.

[3] Cf. Pfleiderer, *op. cit.*, ii. pp. 34-36, 482-488. Jesus went to Jerusalem 'to
fight and conquer.' His death was, at most, a possibility to Him, as in the
case of Luther on the way to Worms : also Wrede's work. Sanday's description of Wrede's methods (*Life of Christ in Recent Research*, pp. 70-72)
constitutes an acute and entertaining criticism of them.

rests firstly upon the supposed incompatibility of such announcements of death with the existing situation, secondly upon the difficulty of explaining the consternation of the disciples at the death of Jesus, if He had told them 'plainly' (Mark viii. 32) that He was to die, and, moreover, to rise again.[1] The first objection only becomes weighty as a result of the wholesale re-writing of the Gospels, whereby for the 'Tendenz' of the ancient Evangelist is substituted the 'Tendenz' of the modern critic. The second objection is more serious, and Wrede and others have made great play with it. But the more we assent to the opinion of H. J. Holtzmann and Bousset that the Old Testament contains no doctrine of a suffering and dying Messiah,[2] the more intelligible does the unintelligence of the disciples (Mark ix. 32, Luke ix. 45, xviii. 34) become. They could not understand the 'must' die, and so they never really accepted the 'will.'[3] Moreover, the mention of the resurrection brought in a fresh difficulty, for what could the resurrection of the Messiah mean? (Mark ix. 10.) The rebuke which Peter received when, taking the words of Jesus literally, he remonstrated with the Master, convinced the disciples that here was some mystery which they could not understand. It is all very well to speak, as Pfleiderer does, of the 'unambiguous predictions of the Passion by Jesus,' but how could such a thing be unambiguous when it was spoken of the 'Son of Man'? If, as Pfleiderer believes, Jesus did not think of Himself as the Messiah, as the Son of Man of Daniel vii. 12, then it would be incredible that the disciples should

---

[1] There are other objections, such as the detailed character of the prophecies, especially Mark x. 33, 34; while some scholars (Loisy, J. Weiss) eliminate two of the passages as mere duplicates of the first. The first objection is not important, whatever be thought of it; and the idea that we are in the presence of 'triplicates' seems to me quite absurd, as a careful study of the Marcan passages will show.

[2] Holtzmann, op. cit., p. 357; Bousset, Jesus, pp. 196, 197 (E.T.). Is. liii. is, at any rate in its original sense, not Messianic.

[3] Accordingly I should not go so far as Professor Denney, who says they cannot but have understood His words about dying, and argues that what they did not grasp was its necessity and meaning.

not understand Him, if He said 'the end of My journey is to be crucified in Jerusalem' : but, as the words stand in the Gospels, the confusion of the disciples is not in the least incredible.[1]

In these three prophecies of His death, Jesus, while He speaks of the necessity for His death, has yet said nothing of the purpose which it is to serve. But shortly after the third saying the request of the sons of Zebedee gives occasion for an explanation of what it is that the Son of Man has come to do, and why it is He dies. Perhaps to this period we may refer the Lucan 'I have a baptism to be baptized with and how am I hemmed in until it be accomplished.' It is no time for questions and answers, but for reckoning with that which is daily approaching nearer. So as He has expounded to James and John the place of suffering, He expounds to the ten the place of service. Not in the exercise of authority but in the rendering of service is greatness to be sought by them, and the reason given is that the Son of Man, the Messiah, has come to do the work of a servant and to give His life a ransom for many. If Jesus said these last words, what did He mean by them ?

A. Ritschl, and a number of other writers, connect this passage closely with Mark viii. 35-37 and Psalm xlix. 8-10. According to these texts there is no possibility of an ἀντάλλαγμα τῆς ψυχῆς of something of value equivalent to a forfeited life. Neither for another nor for himself can a man provide what will be accepted in exchange. But this is exactly what Jesus claims to be able to do and says He has come to do. He brings His own life as

---

[1] It is interesting to note that O. Holtzmann, who accepts the passages in question as genuine, makes use of the prophecy of the resurrection to explain the beginning of the resurrection-stories : 'as soon as the disciples woke from their stupor at Jesus' death they could not fail to call His prediction to mind ; and when they did so, they would see in its fulfilment a guarantee of His speedy resurrection to glory' (*Life of Jesus*, p. 494). This is a credible hypothesis ; but how faith in the resurrection grew up, if Jesus had said nothing about it, and, in point of fact, did not rise again, it is exceedingly difficult to imagine : it would not be an atmosphere favourable to visions.

a λύτρον, that is, in the sense of the corresponding Hebrew word, a covering, and so a satisfaction or ransom [1] for many. He ends His life of service by an act of sacrifice, which has as its purpose and effect the liberation of the forfeited lives of many.[2] What is presented to us is not indeed a theory of atonement, but a perfectly definite statement that, apart from what Jesus does, lives would still be forfeit and that what He does is to die.

There are two ways of evading the force of this word as a word of Jesus ; the first is to admit its full force and then conclude that Jesus could not have said it ; the second is to allow its genuineness, and then to proceed, in Pfleiderer's unkind remark, to explain it away, to a greater or less extent. The first method is that of those drastic critics who conceive of the Gospels as dogmatic documents, but know that Jesus did not speak in dogmas. Thus Loisy [3] writes that ' the idea of the life given in ransom belongs to a different train of ideas from that of service, and the Son of Man who " comes " to ransom men by His death is the mythical Christ . . . not the preacher who went about proclaiming the near approach of the Kingdom.' Pfleiderer [4] finds the undoubted meaning in the surrender of the life of Jesus to death as an expiatory offering, ' to purchase the deliverance of many from eternal death.' But this is Paulinism based on Isaiah liii. and Pharisaic theology, and ' far removed from the thoughts of Jesus.' Wrede sees the Christian Community, convinced somehow or other [5] that the crucified Jesus was Messiah, putting into His mouth words which showed that He knew He was going to die, and why it had to be so. Wellhausen looks on the whole of the section

[1] See Driver in Hastings' *Dictionary of the Bible*, *s.v.* ' Propitiation,' iv. p. 128.
[2] Cf. Denney, *op. cit.*, p. 45. Dr. Denney seems to me to be justified in saying that this is the unambiguous meaning of the sentence.
[3] Loisy, *L'Evangile selon Marc*, p. 310.   [4] Pfleiderer, *op. cit.*, ii. 485-6.
[5] The extraordinary difficulty of explaining this conviction from Wrede's standpoint is well put by Bousset, *Jesus*, pp. 168 ff., quoted by Sanday, *op. cit.*, pp. 75, 76.

Mark viii. 27-x. 45 as thoroughly Christianised, apparently
objects to it being said of Jesus first (x. 39) that He is to
die before the disciples, then that He is to die for them
(x. 45), and finally characterises the passing from the thought
of service to that of the surrender of life as a ransom as
a μετάβασις εἰς ἄλλο γένος.[1] It is not quite this, for the
idea of service remains, but even if it were it would not
prove that Jesus did not say it.

On the other hand, Liberal theologians and exegetes,
who, while adopting a more conservative attitude towards
the genuineness of the recorded sayings of Jesus yet wish
to fix a great gulf between His words and the orthodox
or Churchly interpretation of them, go a different way.
The words are capable of a very different interpretation
—are not really patient of the orthodox interpretation at
all. Thus Beyschlag[2] argues that Jesus meant that by
His death men would be freed from the slavery of sin,
from such selfishness as the sons of Zebedee had just
shown ; so He would accomplish by dying ' what He
had only been permitted to prepare for by living ' :
apparently He is to be thought of as redeeming by a
supreme example of self-sacrifice. Wendt[3] emphasises
the idea of deliverance from the bondage of suffering and
death, connects the passage, very unnaturally as I must
think, with Matt. xi. 28-30, and writes that Jesus ' by the
voluntary God-consecrated sacrifice of His life to sufferings
and death delivers from their bondage to suffering and
death many, namely all those who will learn of Him,'
so that death is for them transformed ' from being a
dreaded foe to a means of salvation.' With regard to
this, Kähler's[4] common-sense remark that Jesus certainly

[1] Wellhausen, *Das Evangelium Marci*, p. 91.
[2] *New Testament Theology*[2], i. pp. 151-154 (E.T.).
[3] *Teaching of Jesus*, ii. 231 (E.T.). Cf. B. Weiss, *Biblical Theology of the New Testament*, i. 101 (E.T.). 'It is not directly stated from what it is that the ransom paid by Jesus in their stead redeems them ; according to viii. 36 f., however, it is undoubtedly the fate of death to which they are exposed on account of sin.'
[4] *Zur Lehre von der Versöhnung*, p. 167.

did not think of the many as being spared the physical
fact of death, while His promise to the sons of Zebedee
that they shall drink of His cup and share His baptism
shows that He promised them no easy death, has all the
merits of a necessary truism. Weinel [1] connects the
imagery with the belief of the Passover, with its commemo-
ration of the redemption from Egyptian slavery. Jesus
lays down His life to win for the people ' the new eternal
release, the true redemption.'   J. Weiss,[2] who, on the whole,
inclines to accept it as a true word of Jesus, will not go
further than to say that ' it is probable that He was convinced that His death would in some way benefit the
men with whom He had pleaded by word and deed.'   Of
English Liberal commentators, Dr. Menzies [3] is disposed
to refer the word to the belief of Jesus that His death
would bring about a general movement towards the
Kingdom, so that many would come in ' who might otherwise have been left outside it.'   Dr. G. B. Stevens [4]
translates λύτρον ἀντὶ πολλῶν, ' a ransom price for the
sake of obtaining the freedom of many,' ἀντί being used
as in Heb. xii. 2, with the force of ' to obtain,' rather than
with the force of ' instead of.'   He then argues that we
have no means of saying what it is from which Jesus
liberates men by His death, but, inasmuch as Jesus never
isolated His death, but correlated it with His life, He
must have thought of His death as consummating His
life's work, the foundation of the Kingdom of God.   ' He
died in the achievement of that result, and His death
was a potent means to its achievement.'   Accordingly
we must exclude from the text later ideas of ' atonement,
penalty, substitution, satisfaction.'

---

[1] *Biblische Theologie des Neuen Testaments*, p. 207.
[2] *Die Schriften des Neuen Testaments*, i. p. 175.
[3] *The Earliest Gospel*, p. 202.
[4] *The Christian Doctrine of Salvation*, pp. 45-48.   Cf. G. C. Workman,
At Onement, pp. 58-61, who paraphrases ' to give his life a service in behalf
of many,' and interprets the ransom as the making of ' a sacrifice of Himself
for the sake of rescuing man from sin through His self-denying service in
their behalf.'

It is hard to deny that the Liberal theologians modernise
over-much. The strongest point in their case is the
impossibility of answering from Mark x. 45 the question
—even Dr. Denney calls it the 'meaningless' question
in this context—'To whom was the ransom paid?' To
God, to the devil, to death, are all unsatisfactory answers.[1]
It is simplest to take the logion as expressing the conviction
of Jesus that He will lay down His life as a sacrifice for
sinners, and neither to denude it of this force nor to read
into it the possibly quite legitimate, but later, theories
of the Church.[2]

Labyrinths of textual and exegetical criticism await
the student who turns to the account of the Last Supper,
and to a consideration of what Jesus said, did, and meant.
Loisy[3] sees Pauline influence changing the original account
at each important point. His own view is that if we keep
to Mark xiv. 25 as a genuine utterance, and suppose that
something similar was said at the giving of the bread, a
saying reproduced in Luke xxii. 16, we are on the firmest
ground there is. The historic Jesus could not have called

[1] For a comprehensive statement, which may fairly be taken as representing the general sense, cf. Keim, *Jesus of Nazara*, v. p. 324 (E.T.), 'With the
idea of a "ransom for many," which the Passover suggested to him, he represented His death as an atoning sacrifice which was to be presented to God on
behalf of many, and would win from God remission of human guilt, remission
of the divine punishment of imprisonment and condemnation, therefore pro-
tection, forgiveness, grace for the many through the fall of one.'

[2] There is an excellent discussion in Moffatt, *The Theology of the Gospels*,
pp. 145-149. Dr. Moffatt sets the verse in the light of Is. liii., and interprets
according to the true significance of ὁ υἱὸς τοῦ ἀνθρώπου. To this the idea of
self-sacrifice, possible for any man, supremely so in the case of Jesus (O.
Holtzmann), is inadequate. I have not thought it necessary to go into the
question whether ἀντὶ πολλῶν should be taken simply with λύτρον, or with
ἦλθεν δοῦναι, or with δοῦναι alone. 'In the last case,' says H. J. Holtzmann
(*Lehrbuch*, i. p. 363), 'Jesus gives instead of many a λύτρον which they would
be compelled to give did they wish to be saved from destruction.' But there
is no idea in the passage of anything as due to be given by the many, though
this interpretation agrees with the 'orthodox' one in translating ἀντὶ as
'instead of' rather than 'for.' This, in itself, is linguistically preferable,
and according to Holtzmann, supported by the Syriac versions, but raises
the further question of what Aramaic word Jesus used. These minutiæ of
criticism do not affect the general sense of the sentence. There is a
very full discussion by Ritschl, *Rechtfertigung und Versöhnung*, ii. pp.
68-85.

[3] *L'Évangile selon Marc*, pp. 400-406.

bread His body or wine His blood shed for many. It is the Church's faith which attributes to Jesus the thought of an atoning death when He was thinking of something totally different. Johannes Weiss,[1] relying on Luke xxii. 17, 18, on the omission of all the words after σῶμά μου in Luke xxii. 19, 20, in D. and the Italian codices, and on the evidence of the *Didache* c. ix., argues that in what Jesus said and did at the Supper there was no reference to His death. The texts of Mark (Matthew) and Paul with their references to a (new) covenant and blood shed for many ' do but show the tradition which existed in the Gentile-Christian communities about the year 60.' Wellhausen, who characterises as a bad joke the idea that Jesus at the Supper had not His death in view, but was looking forward hopefully to a speedy victory of His cause, adds a further difficulty by the highly questionable statement that ' Jesus at this moment obviously does not proclaim Himself as either present or future Messiah.' [2]

Is the idea that at the Supper Jesus used no symbolism in reference to His death tenable ? There is really nothing to be said for it except the ' Western ' text of Luke. Granted that there is a real difficulty in Luke's text, whether we have to explain the presence of two cups or of one cup distributed before the bread, is this strong enough to overthrow all the other New Testament evidence that we possess, the significance of the Passover associations—whether the meal was the Passover or not—and ' the character expressly stamped upon the meal in the evangelists as a meal in which Jesus . . . was preoccupied

---

[1] In *Die Schriften des Neuen Testaments*, on Mark xiv. 22, and Luke xxii. 15, cf. Pfleiderer, *op. cit.*, ii. 488-493, ' it was natural for the Apostle (Paul), to whom the crucified Christ had become the keystone of his faith, to give to the Lord's Supper a mystical reference to His atoning death, and to seek support for this new mystical conception in a corresponding re-interpretation and extension of the traditional words by which Jesus had originally made the common meal a symbol of the inner fellowship, the covenant of brotherhood, among His followers.' In other words, Paul fakes the evidence in the most barefaced way to suit his own ideas. Was not one of the older apostles honest or courageous enough to protest?

[2] *Evangelium Marci*, p. 122.

with the idea of His parting ? ' [1] Unless we are convinced
of the ' Paulinism ' of Mark we may emphasise, as Feine [2]
does, the fact that while Mark and Paul give different
reports of the words said at the giving of the cup, they
agree that Jesus spoke of the making of a covenant by
the mediation of His blood. If εἰς ἄφεσιν ἁμαρτιῶν in
Matthew is a gloss by the Evangelist, it is in perfect harmony with the context ; would not Jesus, when He spoke
so solemnly of a covenant in His blood, turn His thoughts
back to those passages in the Old Testament where a
covenant is spoken of as made or to be made between God
and His people ? In Exodus xxiv. 8 we read of the
blood of the covenant which ratified the Book of the
Covenant ; but this was not all. In Jer. xxxi. 31 ff.
the definite promise of a new covenant is given, and its
final blessing (v. 34) is that God ' will forgive their iniquity
and remember their sin no more.' The Matthaean addition
makes the connexion clear, and the instinct which prompted
the insertion was a true one. [3]

If then we are not prepared to evacuate the symbolism
of the Supper of all reference to the death of Jesus, which,
as Kähler [4] has pointed out, is in itself so unnatural that
it is only possible if we charge Paul with a ' thorough-
going obscuration ' of the Gospel of Jesus, we must ask
what is the implication of the actions and words of Jesus ?
Dr. Stevens looks on the words as adapted to carry our
thoughts not in the direction of ideas of propitiation by

[1] Denney, *op. cit.*, p. 47 ; the whole discussion by Prof. Denney is full of
power—and of common sense.

[2] *Theologie des Neuen Testaments*[2], p. 159, cf. p. 160, ' in the synoptic account,
as with Paul, we have in the forefront the tradition that Jesus regarded His
approaching death as a sacrificial death for His own, and that for Him His
death was the effecting of a—new—covenant, and we see no reason for
doubting this tradition.' Feine thinks Mark's account as to the words said
at the administration of the cup more exact, but that Paul rightly includes
the command of Jesus that the rite should be repeated.

[3] Cf. O. Holtzmann, *op. cit.*, pp. 462, 463. Jeremiah's words indicate, as
the result of the new covenant, two blessings—forgiveness of sins and the
complete fulfilment of God's will. ' Both these results Jesus looks forward
to as the effects of His death.'

[4] *Op. cit.*, p. 168.

sacrifice, 'but rather towards the conception of a new relation of fellowship with God and obedience to Him constituted by Jesus' death.'[1] Wendt allows that Jesus looked on His death as a sacrifice, well-pleasing to God, whereby the Kingdom of God, with all that that meant of fellowship between God and man, would be 'brought to an established condition.' 'He regarded His death as virtual obedience to God, in which the conduct required by God of the members of His Kingdom was represented as fulfilled, and accordingly He also viewed His death as a pledge that God would on His side keep faithfully to this gracious relation, and would perform His promises of blessing to the members of the Kingdom.' But, according to Wendt, the conception of His death as having special significance for the forgiveness of sins was a thought of the Church, and, though a justifiable one, must not be assigned to Jesus Himself.[2]

The objection felt by many scholars[3] to the frank admission that Jesus at the Supper spoke of forgiveness as mediated through the outpouring of His blood rests upon the belief that any such utterance would be irreconcilable with all that Jesus had said in the course of His ministry as to God's willingness to forgive sins, and with the fact that Jesus had forgiven sins Himself.[4] Keim, who holds that Jesus did attribute atoning efficacy to His death and interpret the new covenant through the medium of sacrificial ideas, looks on this sacrificial purpose as 'a

---

[1] Stevens, *op. cit.*, pp. 50, 51.

[2] *Teaching of Jesus*, ii. 235 ff. (E.T.). For a somewhat similar attempt to 'ethicise' the sacrificial language of Jesus cf. E. P. Gould, *St. Mark* (Int. Crit. Com.), in loc. 'Jesus' use of the language of sacrifice in connection with His death does not indicate that He means to give to that death the current idea of sacrifice, but that He means to illustrate the idea of sacrifice by His own death.' Support for this might be found in the statement by Dr. Sanday (*op. cit.*, p. 127), 'I believe that our Lord rarely took up a Jewish idea without putting into it more than He found there': nevertheless there is, along these lines, the danger of making our own ideas the measure of the words of Jesus.

[3] *E.g.* Beyschlag, *New Testament Theology*[2], i. 159 ; Wendt, *Teaching of Jesus*, ii. 242.

[4] *E.g.* Mark ii. 5 ; Luke vii. 48, xv. 11 ff. ; Matt. vi. 14.

relapse into obsolete opinions' when 'measured by the profoundest ideas of the Old Testament and of the teaching of Jesus Himself,' though he sees in it the condescension of Jesus to the weakness of men.[1] This difficulty raises the whole Christological problem. If we do not ascribe to the Person of Jesus a unique value with all that that implies, then we are faced with an insoluble antinomy. On the other hand, if the consciousness of Jesus that He is Messiah and Son (Matt. xi. 25-27) is regarded as the legitimate basis for a Christology, and as the one key to the difficulties to be found in the Gospels, then, just as Feine urges that the two conceptions of the Kingdom as present and as future find their unity in the Person of Jesus, and the burden of His moral commands cease to be a burden when looked at in the light of His Person, so with regard to forgiveness. That and the fellowship with God that results from it are, throughout the ministry, mediated through Jesus. The four parables of forgiveness in Matt. xviii. 23-35 and Luke xv. 'cannot be separated from the Person of Jesus ; in other words, they were spoken out of Jesus' Messianic consciousness ' ; for ' the love of God which seeks sinners and receives the returning Penitent first became truth and reality in the Person and Work of Jesus.' [2] So we say that ' where Jesus was, there already was the Kingdom and there the Kingdom's powers.' [3] A similar emphasis on the idea of mediation through Jesus as running through the Gospels is laid by A. Schlatter in his *Theologie des Neuen Testaments*. He rejects the ' rationalistic ' explanation of the parable of The Prodigal Son as proclaiming the blessedness of repentance alone.

---

[1] *Jesus of Nazara*, v. 328-331 (E.T.).

[2] Feine, *op. cit.*, p. 62; cf. Denney, *op. cit.*, p. 57, ' The love of God is no doubt unconditionally free to Jesus, but it is not an abstraction. It does not exist *in vacuo* ; so far as the forgiveness of sins is concerned—and it is with the love of God in this relation that we have to do—it exists in and is represented by His own presence in the world.' Prof. Denney insists that the presence of Jesus in the world implies mediation, and ' propitiation is merely a mode of mediation.'

[3] Feine, *op. cit.*, p. 169.

The parable is drawn from Jesus' own attitude to sinners; it is no abstraction separated from His own ministry. Indeed Schlatter goes so far as to say that as the future attitude of the elder brother is not described, 'this picture has its conclusion in the prophecy of Jesus' death as inevitably as has the parable of the husbandmen.'[1] Schlatter's warning against false abstractions is valuable, even though we fail to follow him in his final interpretation of the parable. What is specially valuable in this theologian is the unity which he makes of the saving powers of Jesus' life and those of His death, without sacrificing the full significance of the latter.[2] 'Jesus died in order to be able to do with an eternal completion what He always did—call, forgive, free while making visible the glory of God's grace.'[3] . . . 'Jesus ends His work, as He began it. He began it with the call to repentance, which promised men the forgiveness of sins. He ends it with the act of the Cross whereby they receive forgiveness. There is only this difference: Jesus' right and power to forgive men so that they have God's forgiveness, is now completely grounded and unveiled. God gives Him this power because He accepts from God the Cross.'[4] The death of Jesus brings into effect the new covenant and the new community[5] based on the fact of the forgiveness of sins.

We cannot help dogmatic considerations influencing us here and there in our interpretations, and 'critics' as well as 'traditionalists' need to beware of dogmatic

---

[1] *Op. cit.*, p. 87.

[2] He writes (p. 511), 'Why God should demand a ransom Jesus has not asked. . . . Strange as it may seem to us that Jesus should not set Himself up against God's right, the fact is so.'

[3] P. 512. [4] Pp. 541-2.

[5] Schlatter constantly brings into close connexion the redemptive work of Jesus and the building-up of the Community. Cf. also Ritschl, *Rechtfertigung und Versöhnung*[2], ii. 51-61, 'the expectation of the forgiveness of sins in the Old Testament rests upon the positive foundation of the idea of the divine covenant with Israel' (p. 58). Ritschl finds the same to be true of the New Testament; cf. Feine, *op. cit.*, p. 170, 'the Christian Church is a necessary product of the sayings of the atoning power of His death for many.'

bias. The question whether Jesus could have spoken as He is said to have done at the Supper and in the Ransompassage is largely bound up with whether we think Jesus was such as the Liberal theologians have pictured Him, or incomparably greater, the πλεῖον of Matt. xii. 41. The greatest of all Liberals, Harnack, does indeed, both in his *History of Dogma* [1] and in his *What is Christianity?* [2] allow that Jesus gave expression to a conviction of the necessity and saving significance of His death for the remission of sins, and tries to find a place for the truth of that conviction ; but even in matters of doctrine there are more 'traditional' elements in Harnack's thought than in that of many of his colleagues. Whether the dogmatico-religious views of the death of Jesus which Kähler and Schlatter [3] have expressed are legitimate can only be answered when we feel able to answer the question Who was Jesus ?

It is peculiarly difficult to understand the scene in Gethsemane by the use of the historical method alone, unless with J. Weiss and Loisy we attribute the picture to Mark or a later editor, working on the basis of Petrine recollections. If with Weiss we explain Mark xiv. 34 as meaning ' My sorrow is so great that I sink under its burden ; it is as though death were drawing near to Me,' [4] we must still feel the difficulty involved in such overwhelming grief. Schweitzer [5] and the eschatologists cannot help us here, unless they are prepared to admit to the full the truth of Jesus' thought of His atoning death, or to say that, for the time, the dogmatic edifice to which Jesus

---

[1] Vol. i. 66 (E.T.).   [2] Pp. 159 ff.

[3] I should like to associate myself with one to whom I owe much—Dr. P. T. Forsyth—in deploring (see the Preface to his *Person and Place of Jesus Christ*) the fact that the German scholars and theologians, whose works are translated into English, are almos t wholly of one school of thought. Of course we want as much of Harnack as possible, but of the others, need all be 'liberals' ? Not only has the modern ' positive' school a good deal to say for itself, but some of its representatives, especially Kähler and Schlatter, are men of outstanding ability.

[4] *Die Schriften des Neuen Testaments*, i. 209.

[5] He leaves Gethsemane out altogether.

clung broke down for Him, and that He was supported by no faith in the meaning of His Person and Work. How are we to think of the Agony in the Garden ? That the resolution of Jesus broke down in the face of death is incompatible with what we know of Him ; that He felt acutely the guilt of the people in putting Him to death may be true, but is inadequate as an explanation. But if His death had for Him a special character, if Mark xiv. 21 ' the Son of Man goeth even as it is written of Him,' and xiv. 49, ' this is done that the Scriptures might be fulfilled,' together with Luke xxii. 37 ' this which is written must be fulfilled in Me, And He was reckoned with transgressors : for that which concerneth Me hath fulfilment ' bear true witness to what was passing in His mind, revealing mirrored there the picture of the Suffering Servant, with all that that could show of suffering and guilt and penalty heaped upon the innocent, then some light does fall upon that scene.[1] I can see no satisfactory alternatives to this conclusion in the light of the Marcan narrative, unless we suppose that even at the Supper Jesus expected to triumph, while in the Garden it flashed across His mind that He was destined to fail : then His prayer would point to the strongest reaction from the idea of victory coupled with the desire to acquiesce in whatever might be the Father's will, however strange it seemed. But such a solution is singularly unconvincing.

And what of the great cry from the Cross ? Schweitzer and the eschatological school have their answer ready. Jesus at last was undeceived ; at last He knew that the eschatological hope was vain, though it is not quite clear why, if He had come to Jerusalem to die, His faith should fail Him on the Cross. Liberal theologians [2] suppose that

---

[1] Cf. Garvie, *Studies in the Inner Life of Jesus*, pp. 374-388. Dr. Garvie, after rejecting other views, writes, ' What Jesus dreaded and prayed to be delivered from was the interruption of His filial communion with God, the obscuration of the gracious and glorious vision of God's Fatherhood ' (p. 383). He argues for the psychological probability that Jesus anticipated in Gethsemane the experience to which the ' Cry of Desolation ' from the Cross points.   [2] *E.g.* Stevens, *op. cit.*, p. 51.

in this cry there is wrung from Jesus the question 'Why has Thou abandoned Me to suffering?'[1] On the other hand, interpretations have been given which imply that Jesus endured the torments of the lost,[2] that herein, above all else, consisted the agony of His atoning death. We cannot speak with confidence, but that to Jesus, for the moment, there seemed to be a barrier, such as had never existed before, not even in Gethsemane, is the most natural sense of the word. But why this barrier arose and what it meant cannot be decided simply on the evidence which lies before us.[3] It may be a dogmatico-religious piece of exegesis when Kähler tells us that we do not know what separation from God means, because we do not know what it is to love God, whereas Jesus knew all that love of God meant, so that the terror of that hour was that He had to be 'far from the God, whom He never doubted, to whom even then He clung with all the fibres of His life.' Yet if what we call the finality of the Christian Religion is not merely the finality of a principle, but of a Person—Jesus— can we divorce dogma from history where we have already united eternity and time?

[1] J. Weiss thinks it likely that Mark xv. 34 was taken over from Matt. xxvii. 46, and that the original text of Mark had reference only to the loud cry with which Jesus expired (xv. 37). Matthew put the first words of Ps. xxii. into the mouth of Jesus 'simply as a fulfilled prophecy from the Messianic psalm.' Loisy also sees here the activity of the primitive community, which would interpret the words, not as utterances of despair, but, as in the psalm, as utterances of the innocent sufferer.

[2] Cf. Denney on Calvin, *Death of Christ*, p. 63.

[3] See Garvie, *op. cit.*, pp. 405-425 ; Denney, *op. cit.*, pp. 63-65 ; Kähler, *Zur Lehre von der Versöhnung*, pp. 180, 181.

CHAPTER III

THE NEW TESTAMENT INTERPRETATION

IT was from the conviction, finally established by the Resurrection, and deepened by the experiences of Pentecost, that Jesus of Nazareth was the Messiah that the Primitive Community gained assurance of the blessings of forgiveness of sins, power for a new life of unbounded moral possibilities, and future blessedness. But the pure joy which this new-born religious knowledge brought with it had as its necessary corollary, constant and painful controversy with those whose bitterness against the new teaching matched the eagerness of the disciples of Jesus to persuade them of His Messiahship. And the inner experience together with the external polemic produced and developed what St. Paul was afterwards to call ὁ λόγος τοῦ σταυροῦ the word of the cross—in which was involved both κήρυγμα and διδαχή, both proclamation of a fact of religious value, and its interpretation.

It is a mistake to suppose that apologetic needs alone impelled the Community to connect the death of Christ with the forgiveness of sins. Doubtless the taunts which the Jews must have levelled at the ascription of the great title 'Messiah' to one who had been crucified, led the disciples to ponder over the fact that God had allowed the Messiah to suffer so ignominious a death and to desiderate an explanation. But, even if we lay no stress upon those words of Jesus as to the necessity and the effects of His death, words which, unless we accept the position of critics like Loisy and Wrede, did remain fresh in the memory of the Community, we have a right to urge that the exigencies of formal apologetic cannot, except they meet and mingle with an intense corresponding inner conviction, create something so living and so dynamic as the New Testament ' word of the cross.' [1] The Passion of Jesus exercised its own constraint over heart and conscience, feeling and intelligence ; but this must be forgotten before it can be alleged with any confidence that Jesus was identified with the Suffering Servant— and that almost from the first [2]—simply because the Cross was a stumbling-block to the Jews, and some way had to be found whereby that stumbling-block might be transformed into something else. [3]

Nevertheless, we must frankly admit that though, as Weizsäcker says, ' the primitive church taught, and proved from Scripture, that the death of Jesus exerted a saving influence in the forgiveness of sin,' [4] there is nothing in those chapters of Acts which reflect most clearly the life and thought of the disciples in the earliest age of the Church's history, nor in the Epistle of James, if that document is to be reckoned as an early product of Palestinian Christianity, which rises to the level of a theory concerning the saving value of that death. It is natural that insistence should be laid upon this by those who fix a great gulf between the Gospel of Jesus and the dogmatic of Paul, and represent the latter as diverting the current of Christian thought into channels of his own making, and overwhelming by the might of his superior personality

---

[1] Cf. Denney, *The Death of Christ*, p. 79. ' A doctrine of the death of Jesus which was merely the solution of an abstract difficulty—the answer to a conundrum—could never have become what the doctrine of the death of Jesus is in the New Testament—the centre of gravity in the Christian world.'

[2] Acts iii. 13, iv. 27.

[3] Cf. Lidgett, *The Spiritual Principle of the Atonement*, p. 72. ' It would have been impossible to interpret the tragedy of the cross in the light of Isaiah liii., had not the character, spirit, and mission of our Lord first suggested with irresistible force the fulfilment of the ideal of the Servant of Jehovah. Given both the fulfilment and the resurrection, and the doctrine of the Atonement would inevitably be suggested.'

[4] *Apostolic Age*, i. p. 131 (E.T.).

and genius the Galilean disciples and their simpler message.[1]
But the evidence which can be obtained from Acts, and
from a comparison of that book with St. Paul's Epistles,
does not, when handled without critical and theological
praejudicia, lead to such a conclusion. The argument
from silence is notoriously dangerous, and in the present
instance the silence, whether it be of the leaders of the
Community or of the author of Acts, cannot be taken as
implying either that before the conversion of St. Paul
nothing worthy of the name of an explanation or theory
of the death of Christ had been given, or that he transformed
the simple teaching of the original apostles, who were
content to identify Jesus with the Suffering Servant,
into an elaborate and systematic analysis of God's dealings
with man, alien to the unsophisticated minds of the
recipients of the Galilean Gospel.

In the first place we must remember that to give an
account of Christian doctrine is not the object of the
author of Acts. Not to tell what the followers of Jesus
believed, but to show how by their labours knowledge
of the Gospel was spread throughout the empire and
reached the capital is his motive. Important as are the
speeches, in which more light is thrown upon the beliefs
of the Church, they are subsidiary to the narrative. And
if the speeches recorded in the first half of the book are
relied on as proving that Peter and the others held nothing
equivalent to a definite theory, explanatory of the death
of the Messiah, precisely the same argument could be held
with regard to the speeches delivered by Paul and preserved in the second half of the book. Only one verse,
Acts xx. 28, recalls to us the characteristic Pauline insistence upon the value and meaning of the Cross ; yet we
know that years before his speech to the Ephesian Elders
at Miletus, to the Jews at Jerusalem, to Felix and to
Festus, he had come to value and to interpret the death
of Jesus as the very heart of the Gospel, as, in Dr. Denney's

[1] Cf. Wrede, *Paul*, pp. 155-169 (E.T.).

E

admirable words, 'the hiding-place of God's power, the
inspiration of all Christian praise.'[1] Inferences drawn
from these speeches alone as to St. Paul's presentation
of the Gospel would stray far from the truth; this should
be remembered when the earlier speeches of St. Peter
are used as though we could extract from them a compendium of primitive belief.[2]

Secondly, if apologetic needs played a part in the
positive importance—whatever precisely that might be
—attributed by the primitive Church to the death of
Jesus, there were also apologetic interests which might
often involve the obscuring of certain aspects of the Cross.
That Jesus as the Messiah had suffered for the sins of others
was the enthusiastic, not the formal, verdict of those who
had known Him in the days of His flesh and in His resurrection triumph, but it was not a belief that would make
a natural appeal to hostile crowds, who would see in such
a doctrine merely an additional outrage upon their own
convictions.[3] And as Dr. Dale points out, it was first
of all necessary to insist upon the crucifixion as a crime
committed with the consent of the people, and to be
repented of by them.[4]

Then, thirdly, the beginnings of what we must call a
doctrine of the death of Christ are to be found in Acts,
and in the earliest chapters. When St. Peter speaks of
Jesus as 'delivered up by the determinate counsel and
foreknowledge of God,[5] and the Community confess that
all that Herod and Pilate, Gentiles and Jews had done
was the result of God's fore-ordering purpose,[6] it is clear

---

[1] *Op. cit.*, p. 79.
[2] In this connexion may be mentioned the suggestion of Titius, *Die
Neutestamentliche Lehre von der Seligkeit*, part iv. p. 166, that St. Luke in
the Acts as well as in his Gospel connects forgiveness so intimately with
repentance and with baptism for remission of sins that he fails to apprehend
the closeness of the connexion between forgiveness and the death of Christ.
[3] Feine, *Theologie des Neuen Testaments*, p. 151, refers to the researches of
Dalman, Schürer, Baldensperger, and Bousset in support of his opinion that
the idea of a Suffering Messiah was quite foreign to Jewish thought in New
Testament times.
[4] Dale, *The Atonement*. p. 113.   Cf. Acts ii. 23.
[5] Acts ii. 23.   [6] Acts iv. 27, 28.

that faith already sees in the Cross something much greater and deeper than contingent wickedness. It is significant also that in Acts v. 30 and x. 39 reference is made to Deuteronomy xxi. 23, the passage quoted by St. Paul in one of his classic references [1] to the meaning of Calvary. Possibly Feine goes too far [2] in using these passages to show that the primitive Community already looked on the death of Jesus as an expiatory sacrifice, though he appears to be clearly right in refusing to attribute their presence in Acts to the passage in Galatians; but they may induce us to question the confident statement of Beyschlag that ' there is nowhere mixed up with these discussions of the death upon the cross a suggestion of its having been necessary to salvation; of its having been required as an atonement for the sins of the people, as a satisfaction to God.' [3]   Nor can we safely follow Beyschlag when in the course of the same argument he lays great stress on the absence, in the conversation between Philip and the Eunuch, of any reference to the atoning character of the Servant's Sufferings in relation to the people's guilt. In the passage quoted from Isaiah the direct allusion, as Beyschlag remarks, is only to the innocence and patience of the Sufferer and His final exaltation, but that Philip who, as St. Luke says, took his cue from this passage in preaching Jesus, dwelt on no other points than these is really beyond the power of Beyschlag or of anybody else to prove.   And the fact that whenever in the early chapters of Acts Jesus is spoken of as the Servant it is in close connexion with the thought of His sufferings points the other way; for, according to late Jewish theory suffering possessed atoning value and compensated for guilt.[4]

The evidence from Acts does not by any means conclusively prove that the primitive Community neither possessed nor desired any dogmatic theory as to the

---

[1] Gal. iii. 13.   [2] Op. cit., p. 203.
[3] New Testament Theology, i. p. 312 (E.T.).
[4] H. J. Holtzmann, Lehrbuch der Neuen Testaments Theologie[2], i. 79.

death of Christ ; rather are there stepping-stones by which
we may pass, as did St. Paul, to a wider outlook. The
Epistle of James raises too many difficult problems as to
its own origin and purpose for any dependence to be laid
upon it in coming to a decision as to the beliefs of the early
Church. Dr. Dale [1] argues with much skill that the
existence of the heresy so sternly opposed at the end of
the second chapter, and the manner of the author's opposition, are quite compatible with a belief on the part of the
early Church that there was a direct relation between
Christ's death and the remission of sins, but incompatible
with any belief that ' the sole purpose of the life and death
of Christ was to effect a change in the moral and spiritual
character of men.' But the reference of the ' faith '
which the writer rebukes to a pretentious and barren faith
in the death of Christ as the treasury whence inevitably
flowed the free gifts of salvation, or, indeed, to faith in
Christ at all, is exceedingly uncertain.

But apart from Acts and the Epistle of James there
is nothing whatever in the New Testament which can be
pressed into the service of the contention that St. Paul
elaborated to the point of invention, and over the heads
of the older apostles, a dogma of the death of Christ, while
there are two powerful considerations which go to support
Jülicher's statement ' that in Paul's teaching as to satisfaction and redemption he has the primitive Community on
his side.' [2] First, and most definitely, St. Paul, in 1 Cor.
xv. 3, tells his converts that he had received, without any
doubt from the original apostles, the doctrine which he
in his turn was preaching, ' that Christ died for our sins
according to the Scriptures.' It is difficult to describe
by any other term than bathos Beyschlag's opinion that
when St. Paul spoke of ' receiving ' he was thinking solely
of the fact of the death, which he then passed on to the
Corinthians with a religious interpretation of his own.[3]

---

[1] Op. cit., pp. 176-190.   [2] Jülicher, Paulus und Jesus, p. 34.
[3] Op. cit., i. p. 313. Wrede, Paul, p. 168 (E.T.), with equal lack of

Secondly, there is the argument from probability, strengthened by the known facts of St. Paul's controversy with the Judaisers and of the strained relations which, as the Galatian letter goes to show, existed for some time between him and the ' pillar-apostles.' How can St. Paul assume as common ground, as a belief held alike by himself and by the Judaisers, that Christ's death has true saving significance ? He never accuses his opponents of denying that significance; he does accuse them of insisting upon practices which, if looked on as necessary to salvation, take away the unique value of the Cross. That is why his argument is so powerful ; but it would not have been powerful at all if the Judaisers could have appealed to St. Peter and others against the novelty of his doctrine of the Cross. Gal. i. 11, 12, in which verses St. Paul speaks of his gospel as independent of human authority, may seem to stress unduly St. Paul's independence, but it is obviously safer to rely on the calm words of 1 Cor. xv. 3 than on the impassioned and perhaps slightly exaggerated outburst of the opening of the Epistle to the Galatians ; and the difference is one of form and of a point of view rather than of substance. But on the main question there is little room for doubt ; had St. Paul preached with all the fervour at his command a doctrine of the death of Christ which differed profoundly from the beliefs of the primitive Community, it is incredible that he should have made his view prevail without a struggle of which we must have heard more than the echoes—and we do not hear even them.[1]

When we turn from the primitive Community to the doctrine of St. Paul, we find ourselves in the presence of

felicity tries to carry the war into his opponents' camp when he writes, ' it requires a very literal interpretation of Paul's words to make out that what was delivered to him includes "*died for our sins.*"'

[1] Cf. Mignot quoted in Rivière, *Le Dogme de la Rédemption*, p. 65. Wernle, *Beginnings of Christianity*, i. 240 (E.T.), goes so far as to say that before St. Paul the death of Jesus was regarded as a punishment, ' but not for His own sins, but for the guilt of the Jewish people.' This is quite possible, but, as the statement runs, it goes beyond our sources.

conceptions of such variety and richness attached to the
death of Christ that we are in constant danger either of
paying too much attention to dialectical minutiæ or of
overlooking some point which may appear trivial to us,
but which, for the Apostle, was of the highest consideration.
In addition to this, the attempts that have been made by
theologians of one school to find in St. Paul not the foundations alone but the very fabric of later dogmatic, and the
efforts of scholars of quite other prepossessions to rid his
words of implications uncongenial in certain respects to
the beliefs and assumptions of modern times, have raised
serious obstacles to an impartial exegesis and true understanding of his thought. Yet for all the profundity of
his conceptions and the occasional obscurity of his language
and argument, there is a certain simplicity about St. Paul
which differentiates him from St. John, so that the Epistle
to the Romans lies open to the understanding of the reader
or the commentator more readily than the fourth Gospel.

The secret of this is that St. Paul's thought never moves
very far away from its centre. That centre is the Cross.
And the Cross was for him the centre not of theological
reflexion alone, but of faith and feeling and devotion to
God in a supernatural love,[1] evoked by what God in the
Cross had done for him, so that he could take it to himself,[2]
and for the world in giving His Son to redeem it.

Three elements combined to enable St. Paul to work out
his doctrine of the Cross. First, there was his own
experience of Jesus as the Deliverer.[3] From the time
when he was struck down on the road to Damascus he had
a sense, unknown before, of freedom and of power for
work and for endurance. Too much may sometimes be
made of the part played by the Apostle's experience in

---

[1] Romans v. 5.
[2] Cf. Wernle, *op. cit.*, i. 238. 'The sense of pardon and blessedness which
Paul derived from the Cross was a real personal experience. Henceforth it
is for him the fixed centre round which all history turns, the source of all
comfort, of all peace with God.'
[3] Cf. 1 Thess. i. 10.

the formation of his theology : such exaggeration is natural
in an age which stakes as much upon the word ' experience '
as does ours.   Schweitzer's criticisms of H. J. Holtzmann,
for whom ' the whole of Paulinism is a " systematisation
of the Christ-vision " and a " generalisation " of that
which the Apostle had experienced in his own soul, and
consequently ascribed to all who walk in the same way
as an experience which they must necessarily undergo,' [1]
are not unjustifiable.   Yet Holtzmann's position, which,
in respect of the extreme importance to be attached to
St. Paul's own experience, is that of Kaftan [2] also, makes
more intelligible the relationship of religion and theology
in St. Paul than does Wrede's view that in his teaching
redemption is something purely objective and faith
' simply an obedient acceptance of and assent to the
preaching of redemption.' [3]   Wrede does indeed insist
that ' the religion of the apostle is theological through and
through : his theology is his religion,' but this would
certainly not be the case with Christians who tried to make
St. Paul's view of redemption, as depicted by Wrede,
their own.   But whether we speak of St. Paul's religion
or of his theology we must admit that each alike returns
again and again for new inspiration to that moment
which then, and for ever after, reflected upon the Cross
the bright light which streamed from the risen Christ.
His doctrine of redemption is from the very outset preserved from barrenness and formalism, because the crucified
Jesus is the risen Lord.   And the power of the risen Lord
which he knows and upon which he draws is always the
power of one who had died.   The Apocalyptic vision of

---

[1] Schweitzer, *Paul and his Interpreters*, p. 113 (E.T.).   Cf. *ib.*, 'it is not
enough for him to regard the system as had been usual among scholars since
Baur, as a personal creation of the Apostle ; he goes the whole way with
Holsten in maintaining that the personal creation was nothing else than the
interpretation of a unique personal experience.'

[2] *Jesus und Paulus*, pp. 34-5, ' where Paul speaks of redemption he speaks
of something which he and Christians have experienced.   It is not a doctrine,
which he develops, for which he demands faith.'

[3] Wrede, *op. cit.*, p. 113 (E.T.).

the triumph of the Lamb that had been slain,[1] was for St. Paul the reality of realities.

Secondly, St. Paul did not turn his back upon the theology of his fathers. Schweitzer, as is his custom, makes no reservations in his determination to show that the Apostle took nothing from Jewish Hellenism and exercised no influence upon the creators of Greek-Christian theology,[2] while, in addition, there is no real parallelism between the Mystery-religions and Paulinism. Whatever modifications may be needed in Schweitzer's presentation of the case, he has thrown a burden of proof on facile assertors of 'Paul's Hellenism' which, in the absence of substantial supports, is likely to prove somewhat heavy. On the positive side we shall be safe in insisting upon the reality (of the appearance there can be no doubt) of the influence of the Old Testament upon the Apostle, especially when taken in connexion with the ideas of later Judaism.

Thirdly, St. Paul worked upon the basis of the faith and rudimentary theology of the primitive Community, to which reference has already been made.

The system which we associate with his name and speak of as Paulinism is so closely knit together that only by accommodating ourselves to the methods of later theologians can we divide it up into the doctrine of God, Christology, redemption as objective fact—atonement, redemption as subjective experience—justification, the Church, the Sacraments, and so on. Everything in St. Paul leads up to, turns upon, and results from one great thought—God redeems us in the Cross of Christ. The Cross is God's word to man, final revelation. Those who with Dr. Forsyth insist that revelation can truly be found only in redemption, can base themselves upon the whole tenor of St. Paul's thought.

For St. Paul the necessity of redemption is the inevitable outcome of the actual position in which man, be he Jew or Gentile, finds himself. Conscience and law have alike failed to enable man to be righteous before God. But this lack of righteousness is not something which God can finally pass over, though He may do so for a time.[1] Were He to do so, His own righteousness, that comprehensive moral attribute upon which the prophets had so passionately insisted, would be dragged down by the unrighteousness of men. God, therefore, stands over against sinful humanity as one who ' visiteth with wrath.' [2] Neither the thought of the Apostle taken as a whole, nor particular passages such as Rom. v. 10 and xi. 28, and 2 Cor. v. 18-21, restrict the enmity of which he speaks to that felt by man against God, though Beyschlag [3] contends vigorously for this interpretation. The wrath of God is an indispensable element in St. Paul's system ; apart from it religion would suffer ethically. But this implies punishment, for in punishment is to be seen the natural expression of righteous wrath. To identify the divine righteousness in such a passage as Rom. iii. 24-26 with punitive justice, as Pfleiderer does,[4] is to narrow unduly the conception, but St. Paul has no doubt at all that punishment can in itself be a righteous act, quite apart from its effect upon those subject to it.

The actual circumstances then make redemption necessary for man, if he is not to fall under the righteous wrath of God. But man himself is powerless ; any redemption, whatever it may ultimately do for and in

---

[1] Cf. Acts xvii. 30 ; Rom. iii. 25.   [2] Rom. iii. 5.

[3] *Op. cit.*, ii. 160-163. Despite Ritschl's attempt (*Rechtfertigung und Versöhnung*, ii. pp. 227 ff.) to get rid of the idea of God's hostility to man from St. Paul's thought, modern scholarship has steadily taken the other line. Of comparatively recent works, cf. Holtzmann, *Lehrbuch*, ii. 106, Pfleiderer, *Primitive Christianity*, i. p. 327 (E.T.), Stevens, *Christian Doctrine of Salvation*, p. 59. Titius, *Neue Testamentliche Lehre von der Seligkeit*, part ii. p. 196, defines the enmity between God and man as 'an objective relationship existing on both sides, though not in perfect correspondence.' One who approaches the texts without prejudice can hardly, he thinks, come to any other opinion.

[4] *Paulinism*, i. 94 (E.T.). But see his *Primitive Christianity*, i. 328 (E.T.). 'The righteousness of which the manifestation is here in view is, it is true, not simply retributive justice, since indeed, instead of punishment, atonement takes place.'

him, must come to him from without. And this can and
does happen because wrath, though a truly moral attribute
of God, is not the highest of attributes. Above wrath
stands love, and God in virtue of His love so deals with
the situation that neither shall His holiness and righteousness be impaired, nor man be destroyed. From His love
flows His gracious purpose to save. Love which appears
to man as grace, unmerited favour, is not to be opposed
to righteousness, and it is certainly misleading when
Holtzmann interprets Rom. iii. 24-26 as showing that
' God's grace must be relieved of opposition to his righteousness before it can express itself in action.' [1] On the other
hand, a false unity is reached in the position taken up by
Ritschl that God's righteousness means for St. Paul
God's gracious purpose of salvation. That is to identify
righteousness with love, and to leave out of account those
other elements in his conception of righteousness which
have been noted.[2]

In accordance with His love, God's purpose for man is
not punishment but salvation. Why then should not the
Pauline view of redemption culminate in a free forgiveness,
in which God welcomes back the repentant sinner without
the introduction of ideas which seem to imply that something of the nature of a transaction or bargain is necessary
before reconciliation between God and man can take place.
There is no formal answer in St. Paul's writings to this
question so eagerly asked to-day. But three answers
suggest themselves. In the first place sin is not a number
of isolated acts, but an organic whole co-extensive with

---

[1] *Op. cit.*, ii. 118.

[2] Dr. Garvie, *Studies of Paul and his Gospel*, pp. 157-160, makes righteousness include both wrath and grace ; ' as righteous God does not merely condemn and punish sinners ; it is His righteousness, His moral perfection,
which prompts Him to seek their salvation, so that they too may become
righteous even as He Himself is.' This is an attractive attempt at a
synthesis of different but alike moral qualities and Dr. Garvie's interpretation of δίκαιον καὶ δικαιοῦντα in Rom. iii. 26, which he almost makes
to mean righteous and *therefore* declaring righteous, is probably correct
(cf. Sanday-Headlam *in loc.*). Yet could St. Paul have said ' God com-
mendeth His *righteousness* toward us, in that while we were yet sinners,
Christ died for the ungodly ' ?

humanity and perpetuating itself as guilt ; consciousness
of guilt is consciousness of acts committed, with the weight
of the personality behind them, in opposition to the moral
character of the universe, that moral character which,
far more profoundly than any principles of physical
cohesion, binds all things together into a unity. Now
forgiveness is essentially an event and experience peculiar
to each individual as an individual sinner. We cannot
speak of corporate forgiveness. But guilt is corporate ;
it implies a dislocation of the moral order for which
humanity as a whole is responsible, and realises its corporate
responsibility. Forgiveness, therefore, can deal with the
situation caused by sin in connexion with the individual,
but not on the greater scale of the race. Secondly, forgiveness just as it does not solve the problem of past
guilt also does not give full assurance of future power ;
the guilt of humanity as a whole is not rolled away, and no
new principle is introduced which can work towards the
moral transformation of humanity, the final realisation
of the divine purpose in humanity. Thirdly, the life and
death of Jesus Christ demand adequate explanation ;
His history must be integrated into the purposes of God
towards man, and this is not secured if reconciliation
depends upon forgiveness alone. ' Paul sees the blessing
of the death on the Cross in that it reveals to him that
love of God as Father, which Jesus has portrayed in the
parable of the lost son.' [1] These are true and striking
words, but we naturally ask how St. Paul sees in the death
of Christ the love of God. As Holtzmann points out, we
cannot, in interpreting St. Paul, limit the redeeming power
of the Cross simply to a supreme revelation of God's love
towards His enemies.[2] On the contrary, we must allow
that for St. Paul love touches its highest possibility when
it is revealed in the work of expiation. God loved us ;
Christ died for us ; the blessings of justification and recon-

[1] Vischer, *Der Apostel Paulus*, p. 135.
[2] *Op. cit.*, ii. 110.

ciliation are ours ; [1] that is the movement of his thought. Difficulties are often raised as to St. Paul's use of the word ἱλαστήριον, meaning propitiation or propitiatory,[2] in Rom. iii. 26, and it is objected that it is not clear who is propitiated, that God cannot be thought of as propitiating Himself, that in any case propitiation cannot be other than inconsistent with the idea of love.[3] But we must keep such objections away from our exegesis of St. Paul or we shall unquestionably modernise him, and perhaps not improve upon his meaning.

Are we then shut up to saying that St. Paul teaches a penal substitution of Christ, the pre-existent Son of God, for sinful men, whereby expiation is made for guilt, God is propitiated, and is reconciled to man, while man on his side must be reconciled to God by faith in the divinely appointed Substitute ? Each of the statements here made is true in itself as a reflexion of some portion of St. Paul's ideas ; yet the impression we obtain by putting them together in this way is not a satisfactory reproduction of the Apostle's thought, in which there are *nuances* that do not deliver up their secrets to so precise and rigid a treatment. For St. Paul there is a penal element in the Cross. 'Christ on the Cross has endured what mankind had to expect.' [4] He goes to the very limits of possible language in saying that Christ was made sin and a curse for us, but even such expressions do not involve the idea that Christ was vicariously punished. Though, as Herrmann says of the verdict of Christian experience,[5] St. Paul thinks of Christ as suffering what we should have suffered, His sufferings had not the same quality or

---

[1] Rom. v. 8-10.

[2] Cf. Sanday-Headlam *in loc.* They take the word as adjective accusative masculine, and argue against the introduction of the conception of the 'mercy-seat,' which is favoured by Ritschl and others, who rely on the LXX of the Pentateuch. Another rendering is 'propitiatory sacrifice,' θῦμα being understood, but this also is more difficult.

[3] Stevens, *op. cit.*, p. 124, makes much of these difficulties as against those who would take St. Paul's idea of expiation as 'a hard dogmatic theorem.'

[4] Feine, *op. cit.*, p. 306.   [5] *Communion with God* (E.T.), p. 135.

character as ours would have had.[1] ' God reckons Christ's sufferings to mankind as punishment endured by it ' ; [2] but that is not to equate suffering and punishment. In other words, St. Paul's doctrine is not one of atonement and expiation through punishment, but rather of expiation instead of punishment, in which respect he anticipates Anselm. Beyschlag, therefore, is perfectly right in pointing out that in St. Paul's view ' Jesus does not die the eternal death which we as sinners have deserved,' [3] but wrong in supposing that this consideration, and others which he urges, evacuate the Apostle's system of ideas of expiation, satisfaction, and penalty. As to substitution, the conception is embedded in St. Paul's writings, and cannot be got rid of by appeals to points in the phraseology such as the use of ὑπέρ not ἀντί in 2 Cor. v. 21 and other places to describe the effect of Christ's death.[4] Those who do not like the idea of substitution in itself are reluctant to admit its presence in St. Paul, and often end in obscuring his meaning without giving any clear idea of their own. Sabatier, for example, first allows that ' Paul's theology positively contains the idea of substitution and exchange.' He then proceeds to give an incorrect interpretation of Rom. iii. 25, making faith, as well as Christ's death, ' the essential means whereby atonement is effected,' and coupling with it, apparently as an actual factor in atonement, the experiences recorded in Rom. vi. 1-10 : so he reaches the conclusion that ' strictly speaking it is not Christ who expiates the sins of humanity ; humanity expiates in Him its own

---

[1] Pfleiderer puts it very well (*Paulinism*, i. 96), 'This is only so far "vicarious punishment," that one life, which had incurred the penalty of death, is set free through the vicarious suffering of death by another, without this other one, who suffers death vicariously for him who is worthy of death, suffering this penalty *on his part also as a punishment* ; the penal character of the expiatory suffering ceases through the vicarious quittance of the penalty.'

[2] Jülicher, *op. cit.*, p. 26. 　　　　　　[3] *Op. cit.*, ii. 137.

[4] Baur, *Paul*, ii. 154 (E.T.), insists that ὑπέρ contains the idea of substitution as well as that of something done in the interest of men ; the ideas are ' constantly passing over into each other, and present in each other.'

sins,' by a moral dying and rising again.[1]   This is
to miss the point entirely and to overlook the fact
that the identification of sinners with Christ, and their
participation in His death and resurrection, is the result
of His original and unique death. When St. Paul in
2 Cor. v. 14 writes ' one died for all, therefore all died,' he
is not, at that point, concerned with Christian experience,
but, as Dr. Denney says, ' with the idea that Christ's death
was equivalent to the death of all.'[2]   But while we must
do full justice to the element of substitution, we can also,
without indulging in ' rationalising misinterpretations,'
sharply criticised by Pfleiderer and other scholars not
prejudiced in favour of orthodoxy, render it less unaccept-
able to those who start with a bias against it if we lay
stress on the three following considerations as vitally
inherent in St. Paul's thought. In the first place, Christ
did what He did for us out of His own love ; He did not
simply accept a condition imposed upon Him by the love
of the Father.[3]   Secondly, what is of value in Christ's
death is not the physical suffering which is left unempha-
sised, nor even the dying as a physical fact, though it has
also an ethical significance as the penalty of sin, but the
spirit of active obedience which made the death possible.
Christ's Lordship over us, says Schlatter, ' rests upon His
death and has its foundation in His obedience towards
God.'[4]   Therefore we can speak of what He did and not
only of what He endured. It is not as though He acted
during His life and endured in His death ; but the death

---

[1] *The Atonement*, pp. 43-48 (E.T.).   [2] *Op. cit.*, p. 142.
[3] Cf. Romans v. 5-8 ; Eph. ii. 13-16. As to the latter passage Holtzmann,
ii. 283, holds that the ascription of reconciling activity to Christ as subject
is against the Pauline authorship ; he contrasts Col. i. 20, 21. But 2 Cor.
viii. 9, Gal. ii. 20, Phil. ii. 2-7, imply initiative taken by the Son of God,
from His love, for man's salvation. Cf. Feine, *op. cit.*, p. 311 ; Weinel, *Bibl.
Theologie des Neuen Testaments*, p. 255.
[4] *Theologie des Neuen Testaments*, ii. 262 ; Rivière, *op. cit.*, pp. 45-47, does
full justice to the importance of Christ's free act of love, His voluntary and
active obedience in connexion with ideas of expiation and substitution ;
while the article entitled *The Moral Meaning of the Blood of Jesus*, reprinted
in Forsyth's *Cruciality of the Cross*, is a powerful exposition of the same line
of thought.

in which He stood in men's place was a reconciling action
on their behalf, a greater action than any He had done
before.[1] So we may speak of 'the finished work' of
Jesus, without detracting from the natural meaning of
the last word of the phrase. If, as is truly said, the idea
that he could repeat the work done by Jesus 'would be
from the standpoint of Paul the most complete folly,' [2]
this is incompatible with any exposition of the saving work
of Jesus in His death which ascribes to Him a merely
passive role. Thirdly, St. Paul does not regard Christ
as a daysman between God and man ; He is the Son of
God made man. His work is of avail for the race, He can
be a substitute for the race, because He is of the race ;
though He is Adam's polar opposite He represents the race
as truly as Adam did, though with far different results.
It is this which explains what is sometimes called the
mystical element in St. Paul's theology, that element
which appears in Rom. vi., Gal. ii. 20, and, in its grandest
form, in the Epistles to the Colossians and the Ephesians.
It should be clearly understood that the doctrine of
substitution leads on to this. Holtzmann [3] rightly finds
the basis of Romans vi.-viii. in Romans iii.-v. When in
one of the articles in *Foundations* [4] it is said that St. Paul's
doctrine is not so much that Christ died for men as that

---

[1] The old distinction between 'obedientia activa' and 'obedientia passiva'
is formal and unsatisfactory. Holtzmann, while favouring the thesis that
even in St. Paul saving power attaches to the death only in connexion with,
and as a culmination of, the previous life, allows that emphasis falls upon the
death as 'the last, all-decisive proof of all the voluntary service upon which
the Son of God had entered when He took the form of a servant' (ii. 120).

[2] Schlatter, *op. cit.*, ii. 363.

[3] *Op. cit.*, ii. 124. Cf. Pfleiderer, *Primitive Christianity*, i. 331, 'This
mystical view . . . appears in Romans vi.-viii., not indeed in place of his
earlier forensic view, but as an essential supplement to it, and in such fashion
that the latter is seen beneath it as abiding foundation.' Stevens, *op. cit.*,
pp. 71, 72, thinks that the apostle has not united the two lines of thought
'in such a way as to show in what consisted their unity or connection for his
own mind,' and leaves the impression that we must treat them as either
identical in idea or as involving a real duality, the 'ethico-mystical' element
being the product of St. Paul's own experience, the 'objective-juridical' the
survival of his Pharisaic training. But is not the idea of substitution
involved in St. Paul's experience ? Cf. Garvie, *op. cit.*, p. 182.

[4] P. 177.

men died in Christ, confusion is caused by a failure to do justice to the vital, and not merely the logical, order of the Apostle's thought. But the fact that the doctrine of substitution can and does lead on to this further conception is proof enough that St. Paul does not move in the atmosphere of the market-place or of the law court, but in that of real religious needs and their satisfaction. Only, religious needs meant more for St. Paul than those who expound him sometimes allow us to perceive. With all his insistence upon the reality of the gift of the Spirit who dwells in the hearts of God's children, he would hardly recognise his own doctrine in the statement that he finds ' both the only possibility and the real fact of Atonement in the presence in man's heart of the Spirit of Christ and of God.' [1] Kähler puts the matter incomparably more truly when he represents St. Paul's conception of the Christian position in the spirit as ' simply the result of participation in the expiatory redemption, and therefore unthinkable apart from its permanent basis in that which frees from guilt and from the wrath to come, from accusation and the judgment of condemnation.' [2]

It is sometimes argued that St. Paul's conception of atonement is conditioned by his belief in the rights of the Law, which demand satisfaction, a belief calculated to make his doctrine less accessible to modern religious feeling,[3] and, in accordance with this, stress is laid upon those passages which introduce the idea of ransom and refer to the curse pronounced in Deuteronomy xxi. 23 against death by ' hanging upon a tree.' [4] But a serious difficulty at once confronts such an interpretation. If

---

[1] Beeching, *Bible Doctrine of Atonement*, p. 77.

[2] *Zur Lehre von der Versöhnung*, p. 271.

[3] Cf. Pfleiderer, *Paulinism*, i. 102-5 (E.T.); Holtzmann, *op. cit.*, ii. 115, 116. J. S. Lidgett, *Spiritual Principle of the Atonement*, p. 47, writes on Gal. iii. 13, ' His being made a curse is His entering into the whole of those evil consequences which are the mark of the displeasure of the law.'

[4] 1 Cor. vi. 20, vii. 23, ' Ye were bought with a price ' ; Gal. iii. 13, Gal. iv. 5, ' that he might redeem (ἐξαγοράσῃ) them that were under the law.' Cf. the word ἀπολύτρωσις in Romans iii. 24, Eph. i. 7, Col. i. 14, and τὸ χειρόγραφον ὃ ὑπεναντίον ἡμῖν ἦν in Col. ii. 14.

in 1 Cor. vi. 20 and vii. 23 something more precise is
intended than what Dr. Denney calls ' the idea that the
work of man's salvation was a costly work, and that the
cost, however we are to construe it, is represented by the
death of Christ,' [1] if we not only allow but insist on the
meaning ' bought from the Law for God by the death of
Christ,' [2] we are almost forced to the conclusion, which
Bousset expressly draws, that for St. Paul the Law is
' an evil or hostile power,' like the sin to which tribute is
paid, according to Jülicher's [3] exegesis of Rom. vi. 10, and
analogous to the supernatural powers which brought
Jesus to the Cross (1 Cor. ii. 8) but met in it their final
defeat (Col. ii. 15).   In that case the thought of the Law
as the will of God, the respect paid to the Law by the
Apostle, even when he is most insistent upon its limitations,[4] would have vanished, and Anselm's antithesis
of justice and mercy in God be anticipated by a far
deeper antithesis, causing justice to sink to the level
of Shylock's standard, and become an evil greed for the
literal fulfilment of a bond.   But it is quite unnecessary
to take the passages in this way and to suppose that for
St. Paul the idea of ransom involved an arithmetical
problem, a commercial transaction between God and the
Law personified.   Deliverance from earthly and spiritual
bondage is the only thought that we have a right to press.[5]
As for Galatians iii. 13 we must interpret it neither of a
curse of the Law, conceived of independently of God, nor
as implying an essential significance in the particular
kind of death which Christ died.   Deuteronomy xxi. 23
is for St. Paul a passage which he can use as a proof-text,
but to suppose that in itself it is regulative of his theory,
so that apart from it he could not have applied the idea
of a ' curse ' to the death of Christ, is in accordance neither

[1] *Op. cit.*, p. 133.
[2] So Holtzmann, *op. cit.*, ii. 115 ; Bousset on 1 Cor. vi. 20, in *Die Schriften des Neuen Testaments*.
[3] *Die Schriften des Neuen Testaments*, ii. 241.
[4] Romans iii. 31, vii. 12.   [5] Cf. Beyschlag, *op. cit.*, ii. 155.

with the method in which the New Testament writers use the Old Testament, nor with the richness and variety of the moral and religious meaning attributed to that death.[1] Nor because St. Paul omits after the word 'cursed' the ὑπὸ τοῦ θεοῦ of the LXX does it follow that he gave to the Law a separate standing and power apart from God. He may have thought the additional words misleading; he may simply have abbreviated. In any case he does not say that Christ was personally accursed, but that He was made a curse, an expression parallel to 'made sin' (2 Cor. v. 21), of which we can safely say that whatever it does mean it does not mean 'was made a sinner.' And when we remember the denunciations and threats against sin to be found in the Law, and that the curse of the Deuteronomic passage is the concomitant of a penalty of sin, we see how little there is really to be said for Bousset's view that what demands the death of Christ is the Law, thought of as a foreign force 'only loosely related to God.'[2] Another mistaken attempt to limit the sense of the passage in Galatians by the original force of Deuteronomy is to be seen in Kaftan's[3] contention that we go beyond St. Paul if we apply his words concerning redemption from the curse to Gentiles as well as Jews. But the punishment denounced against sin, especially the punishment of death to which allusion is made, goes, in the Apostle's view, back

---

[1] Cf. Denney, *op. cit.*, p. 161, 'The Old Testament here gave Paul an expression—an *argumentum*, if we will; it did not give him his gospel.'

[2] On Gal. iii. 13, in *Die Schriften des Neuen Testaments*; B. Weiss, *Biblical Theology of the New Testament*, i. 424 (E.T.), writes, 'If Christ has become a curse according to the will of God, in order to redeem us from this curse, then the passage says, only in a form which is conditioned by the context, exactly the same as 2 Cor. v. 21, that God has treated the sinless One as a Sinner, in order that He need not treat sinners as such.' This is also the interpretation of Beyschlag, Bousset, and Rivière. On the other hand, Wrede (*Paul*, p. 98) connects the idea of Christ made sin closely with the Pauline view of 'the flesh of sin,' in which the Son of God was made man. Somewhat different from this is Dr. Lidgett's 'becomes one with our sin'; with which we may compare Du Bose, *Soteriology of the New Testament*, p. 321, 'The fact that Our Lord was subject to the natural death of men who are fallen was a passive endurance on His part of a consequence of our sin. It was a part of that sin and that curse for sin which "He was made for us" by the simple fact of entering into our nature as it was.'

[3] *Dogmatik*[6], p. 487.

far beyond the enactments of the Jewish Law to God's ordinance when Adam sinned.[1] As for the 'bond written in ordinances' which St. Paul in Col. ii. 14 speaks of Christ as having blotted out, that, as Weiss[2] points out, refers not to the law as demanding punishment from the transgressor, but as declaring us guilty by transgression.

Christ, out of His love, which is as the love of God His Father, offers to God a sacrifice which proceeds from and does not give birth to God's gracious purpose of salvation. This sacrifice may, however, be spoken of as propitiatory,[3] since through the expiation of sin which results from the sinless taking upon Himself sin's penalty, God's attitude to sin is made perfectly plain, and that wrath which stands for His holy reaction against all that is unholy can be laid aside without injury thereby being done to God's moral character and government. Hence the direct result of Christ's death is reconciliation. Despite Weinel's statement that according to St. Paul not God but man is reconciled and that 'the wrath of God is never brought into connection with reconciliation,'[4] it is as impossible to remove from the texture of St. Paul's thought the idea of God being reconciled as to restrict the hostility which exists before reconciliation to man's opposition to God. If St. Paul thinks of God as giving up His wrath against men, then, for him, God is reconciled to man, though in view of the fact that the initiative is with God throughout

---

[1] Romans v. 12.   [2] B. Weiss, *op. cit.*, ii. 81.

[3] Cf. Sanday-Headlam, *Romans*[4], p. 91, ' When we ask, Who is propitiated ! the answer can only be "God." Nor is it possible to separate this propitiation from the death of the Son.' St. Paul does not appear to have made great use of Old Testament ideas of sacrifice. Ritschl indeed, in the second volume of his great work, lays stress on the importance of the sacrificial system for St. Paul's doctrine, but we can hardly go beyond the balanced statement of Dr. Stevens (*op. cit.*, p. 63), 'While Paul has made a less frequent and explicit use of sacrificial ideas than we should have expected, it is clear that the system supplied one of the forms of thought by which he interpreted Christ's death.'

[4] *Bibl. Theologie des Neuen Testaments*, p. 254 ; cf. Kaftan, *Dogmatik*, p. 489, who argues that the idea of the reconciliation of God with men is that of the 'ecclesiastical dogmatic,' and has no foundation in the Pauline doctrine of καταλλαγή.

he may avoid the phrase.[1]   In the passage where at first
sight it might appear as though there could be no question
of God being reconciled (2 Cor. v. 18-20), a more careful
study shows the reverse to be the case.   Reconciliation
is defined as non-imputation of trespasses ; this is God's
gift in Christ to the world ; but this is something which,
at first, affects only the relationship of God to the world.
It is on the basis of this that the appeal to be reconciled
to God can be made to men.[2]   This reconciliation of
man to God forms, as Dr. Garvie says,[3] ' the link between
justification and sanctification,' though its connexion
with the former is the closer, the two conceptions almost
passing into one another,[4] inasmuch as each necessarily
connotes the other, while each is the immediate effect of
Christ's death when apprehended by faith.   Sanctification
or the new moral life is one stage further removed, though
B. Weiss pushes the distinction much too far in his representation of the new moral life as something demanded
by, but not a saving effect of, the death of Christ.[5]   The
idea of a demand to which the grateful should respond
is forcibly presented in 2 Cor. v. 15 ; we are, as Dr. Denney
affirms, in the sphere ' of love transcendently shown and
of gratitude profoundly felt.' [6]   But besides that there
are passages such as 1 Thess. v. 10, Gal. i. 4, Rom. xiv. 9,
in which a more direct working of Christ's death in free-
ing from sin itself is suggested.   Beyschlag's phrase, ' an

---

[1] Holtzmann, *op. cit.*, ii. 106, argues strongly on this side, and bids us
beware of bringing in rationalistic conceptions of God's unchangeableness.

[2] Du Bose, *Soteriology of the New Testament*, p. 60, writes, ' *Our being
reconciled* to God no doubt means that we are to accept in faith the fact of
an objective reconciliation in Christ.   But it does not mean that *only* ; it
means that we are to receive through faith the fact of a subjective reconciliation also, so as not only *to have* been made one, but *to be one* with God in
Christ.'   This is very true, but there are times when the objective side is too
easily forgotten.

[3] *Op. cit.*, p. 169.

[4] Cf. Titius, *op. cit.*, part ii. p. 196, ' The close relationship of the two
ideas is seen in this, that in Rom. v. 9-11 the idea of justification is reached
through that of reconciliation, in 2 Cor. v. 18-21 the idea of reconciliation
through that of justification.'

[5] *Op. cit.*, i. 431-434.   *Op. cit.*, p. 143.

infectious power of the death of Christ,' [1] gives true expression to this element in St. Paul's appreciation of what the death of Christ does for us.[2] And at this point the importance of the Resurrection as ' a link of connection between the saving deeds and the ethical aspects of salvation ' [3] is to be noted. Despite Sabatier's phrase, ' the redemptive value of the resurrection of Christ,' [4] the resurrection is not, in St. Paul's Epistles, regarded as along with the death on the Cross, having atoning efficacy, or as itself justifying. What it does is to create the possibility of a saving faith, and to stimulate aspiration to rise with Christ in a life of new moral power, of which the condition is vital union with the living Christ.[5]

Before we pass from St. Paul a word must be said as to the supposed changes which come over the theology of redemption first in the Epistle to the Colossians, and, still more, to the Ephesians; secondly, in the Pastoral Epistles, changes which play some part in the rejection by certain critics of the Pauline authorship of these works. As to Ephesians and Colossians, unless we are prepared to say that St. Paul must always have regarded the work of atonement from one point of view, there is no real ground for the opinion that St. Paul could not have written them. We have already seen [6] that the ascription of reconciling activity to Christ in Eph. ii. 14 is not un-

---

[1] *Op. cit.*, ii. 139.

[2] So Feine (*op. cit.*, p. 312) can speak of an important side of the Apostle's treatment of the death of Christ being that of its effect upon man : 'This is not simply separated from the objective way of regarding it.'

[3] Stevens, *op. cit.*, p. 67.   [4] *Op. cit.*, p. 48.

[5] That Christ was raised 'for our justification' (Rom. iv. 25) means, as Pfleiderer points out (*Paulinism*, i. 119), that the resurrection is 'the intermediate cause of subjective justification,' since faith in Christ's death as an expiation can only come into existence on the ground of the resurrection. Cf. Holtzmann, ii. 121, 122, and B. Weiss, i. 434-437. Beyschlag, on the other hand, argues for a more direct relationship of the resurrection to the work of redemption : 'According to Paul,' he writes, 'a man is justified only ἐν χριστῷ (2 Cor. v. 21 ; Eph. i. 7) ; that is, in living connection with Him ; and this connection manifestly can only exist with a living Christ, not with one who is dead and parted from us.' But the condition ἐν χριστῷ is for St. Paul the condition of one who is already justified.

[6] P. 174.

Pauline, while the cosmic effect of Christ's work, indicated in Eph. i. 10 and Col. i. 20, the extension of reconciliation to the heavenly existences, and the bringing of both Jew and Gentile to God in one body (Eph. ii. 15), give very little ground for Weinel's statement that 'Paul's doctrine of reconciliation is forgotten.'[1] And if we take to heart what Wartan says of such passages as Rom. vi. 1-11, Gal. ii. 20, vi. 14, and 2 Cor. v. 14, that through them runs the thought 'when Christ died the old world died.'[2] We need not be surprised if St. Paul came so to apply this as to leave nothing in the universe unaffected by Christ's death, its triumph, and its grace. As to the Pastorals there is more room for doubt. Despite the words $\dot{a}\nu\tau\dot{\iota}\lambda\upsilon\tau\rho o\nu$ $\dot{\upsilon}\pi\grave{\epsilon}\rho$ $\pi\acute{a}\nu\tau\omega\nu$ of 1 Tim. ii. 6, more characteristic of the general trend of these epistles is Titus ii. 14, with its conception of moral renewal as the immediate purpose of Christ's gift of Himself. The saying that Christ 'has brought light and immortality to light through the Gospel' (2 Tim. i. 10) inclines towards a Johannine point of view, even if we cannot go so far as Titius in seeing here 'the Pauline thought in the course of transition into the Greek way of thinking.'[3] There is not adequate ground in this for rejecting the Pauline authorship : an attitude of conservatism and protest against loose moral standards and strange theological ideas is taken up by the author, and we cannot say that such an attitude is inconsistent with what we know of St. Paul ; while if there is some lack of freshness and creative power running through these letters, this would not surprise us were they written at

---

[1] *Biblische Theologie des Neuen Testaments*, p. 523. Cf. Pfleiderer, *Paulinism*, ii. 112-114. He argues that $\check{a}\phi\epsilon\sigma\iota\varsigma$ $\dot{a}\mu\alpha\rho\tau\iota\hat{\omega}\nu$ in Col. i. 14 implies a human state of freedom from guilt, not a divine act of pardon, and is an un-Pauline notion. But Col. ii. 14 asserts just that divine act, while Eph. i. 7 conjoins the ideas of forgiveness and the blood of Christ, where 'objective atonement' is as manifestly supposed as in the reference to the blood of Christ in Rom. iii. 25. Eph. i. 7 also refutes Pfleiderer's statement (ii. 175) that in this epistle Christ is not the expiatory sacrifice, but the sacrificing priest. The latter idea is certainly that of v. 2, but St. Paul may as easily have united the two conceptions as did the writer to the Hebrews.

[2] *Dogmatik*, p. 476.   [3] *Op. cit.*, part iv. p. 168.

the end of a life of almost unparalleled activity and endurance.

The traces of Pauline influence in the first Epistle of St. Peter are, if not exaggerated,[1] not incompatible with the Apostolic authorship, especially when St. Paul's own relationship to the primitive teaching is not forgotten. In these pages the tradition is followed though ' with a note of interrogation, in brackets and in the margin,' as Dr. Sanday used to say about the miracles. Four passages come under review for our purposes. In i. 2 Christians are spoken of as elect through foreknowledge of the Father and sanctification of the Spirit ' unto obedience and sprinkling of the blood of Jesus Christ.' In i. 18 their past redemption from a vain manner of life is ascribed to the precious blood of Christ, who is compared to a spotless Lamb. Christ in i. 24 is said in His own self to have borne our sins in His own body upon the tree, that we being dead to sin might live unto righteousness, and in ii. 18 to have suffered once for our sins—the just for the unjust—that He might bring us to God.

That St. Peter attaches expiatory value to the death of Christ, and regards Him, after the manner of St. Paul, as standing in our place, and doing and enduring in our interest something which had to be done and endured, is the obvious sense of these passages when taken in union with one another; and attempts, such as Beyschlag's,[2] to expunge or reduce this sense are not convincing. Yet there is a more immediate connexion between Christ's sufferings and the new moral life of Christians than we observed in St. Paul. Rescue from the power of sin, as well as freedom from its guilt, is both the purpose and the effect of Christ's death. B. Weiss labours to restrict St. Peter's meaning to a liberation from guilt; but though he rightly protests against a ' dragging in ' of the idea

---

[1] Dr. Bigg thinks such exaggeration common; cf. his Commentary, pp. 15-21.

[2] *Op. cit.*, i. 394-398.

of moral effect in the words προσαγάγῃ τῷ θεῷ in iii. 18,[1]
he leaves the impression of being excessively dominated
by the formal distinctions of orthodox Lutheran theology.[2]
Still, that what Christ did is from one point of view a
'finished work,' which is just what it could not be if the
reference of its effect were solely to moral renewal, is clear
from the aorist ἐλυτρώθητε in i. 18, from the forcible
collocation ἡμῶν αὐτός before ἀνήνεγκεν in ii. 24, and from
the use of ἅπαξ when the suffering of Christ is spoken of
(iii. 18).

The most important passage, ii. 21-25, is influenced
throughout by Isaiah liii., and, as is the case with the
prophecy itself, by the sacrificial ritual of the Old
Testament, to which also the Lamb without blemish of
i. 19 points. Pfleiderer, in his *Paulinism*, appeals to this
passage in favour of the notion that it is the removal
of the power of sin, rather than its guilt, with which
St. Peter is generally concerned. 'The sense,' he says,
referring to v. 24, 'is evidently that by his death upon
the Cross He took away our sins, removed them, so that
they no longer defiled our life.'[3] This view is modified
in his later work,[4] though there too he gives it as his
opinion that in this writing the moral influence rather
than the propitiatory effect of Christ's death is prominent.
But the words ἀνήνεγκεν ἐπὶ τὸ ξύλον neither represent the
cross as an altar up to which sin is carried, and there slain,
nor speak of the simple removal of sins without implying
that they are borne by Christ. The former is excluded by
the Old Testament ritual, since the victim was not brought
to the altar, while the idea of associating sin with the altar

---

[1] Dale (*Atonement*, p. 137) holds that the language 'suggests the conferring of a new dignity and privilege rather than the creating of a new
disposition.' He compares the use of προσαγωγή in Eph. ii. 18 and
Romans v. 2.

[2] *Op. cit.*, i. 232-234.   [3] ii. 153.

[4] *Primitive Christianity*, iv. 247 (E.T.); ii. 24 'expresses the thought that
Christ took our guilt upon Himself and made atonement for it upon the
cross, as on an altar, by His sacrifice of expiation, but in doing so has also
laid on us the obligation to renounce sin.'

is in itself inadmissible.[1] And the view that the removal
of sin and the annihilation of its power over man is the
sense of ἁμαρτίας ἀνήνεγκεν is refuted, first by the original
meaning of Isaiah liii. 12, which is 'took up and bore,'[2]
secondly by the addition of the words ἐν τῷ σώματι αὐτοῦ,
which imply a far closer relationship between Christ's
sufferings and men's sins than is allowed by the idea of
simple removal. The passage is, in fact, analogous to
2 Cor. v. 21 and Gal. iii. 13,[3] and expresses the same idea.
Sin is removed because Christ takes it upon Himself, or,
from another standpoint, because He takes the sinner's
place.[4] 'It is the penal substitution which we have found
in St. Paul, though it lacks the juridical form given to it
by him.'[5] And however much we may rightly stress the
value assigned in this epistle to Christ's example, and the
moral efficacy attributed to His death, we must still see
behind these that feeling of liberation from guilt and of
debt to Him 'who suffered what we should have suffered,'
which, as Herrmann says, is the necessary confession of
Christian experience.

The Epistle to the Hebrews is more wholly concerned
with the work of Christ than is any other book of the New
Testament. The thought develops by a contrast of the
two covenants : the old Mosaic covenant with its priests,
who are themselves sinners, and its sacrifices, which are
shown by their continual repetition to be not only imperfect
but really powerless to deal with sin ; and the new covenant,

---

[1] Cf. Denney, *op. cit.*, p. 96, 'That which is slain at the altar is always regarded as a gift acceptable to God.'

[2] See Cheyne's note on Isaiah liii. 4, in *Prophecies of Isaiah*[3].

[3] As in Galatians, so in this epistle, the introduction of the word 'tree'
probably goes back to Deut. xxi. 23.

[4] Denney speaks of 'the singular and even poignant impression of reality'
left on the mind by the words ἐν τῷ σώματι and ἐπὶ τὸ ξύλον. On the other
hand, Gunkel in his commentary in J. Weiss' *Die Schriften des Neuen
Testaments*, ii. 554, thinks that the passage reveals 'a man of the second
generation' who approaches the Cross from the side of sacred prophecy, and
that the words 'in his body' spring from the belief that Christ as a heavenly
being could suffer only by assuming an earthly body. Gunkel does put a
'perhaps' before introducing this latter conception !

[5] Rivière, *op. cit.*, p. 62.

foreshadowed by the person of Melchizedek and predicted
in the words of Jeremiah, which has one sinless High
Priest, and one perfect offering in which the Priest is also
the sacrifice. If the readers of the epistle can only realise
this, they will cease to look longingly back to the old Jewish
cultus, since all that it attempted to do is secured in Christ,
who abolishes the old only because He fulfils it and establishes for ever, in a perfect way, those blessings at which
it aimed. It is misleading to say that ' the whole point
of the exposition turns on the *contrast* between Christ's
sacrifice and the Levitical offerings.' [1] Though it is true
that the author ' ethicises the whole subject of sacrifice,'
there is no suggestion that the Levitical cultus did not
seek for true ethical blessings, but only that it was powerless to gain them for the people.

For this writer then, as for St. Paul, the death of Christ
is a ' decisive act of salvation,' [2] organically connected
with the Old Testament, which is interpreted along the
lines of cultus rather than of law. It has a universal
character ' in respect to the distinction between present
and past,' [3] and is presented as a finished work in relation
to sin.[4] That it makes real expiation for sin, and so brings
real forgiveness, is the most natural teaching of many
passages,[5] and follows from the impotency of the sacrifices
of former times. In accordance with St. Paul the idea of
substitution has a place,[6] and though the use of it is
incidental rather than central, yet ' even more than in
Paul is the work of salvation a work done " outside of us "
on our behalf.' [7] In ii. 9 the death of Christ is, quite in

---

[1] Stevens, *op. cit.*, p. 126.   [2] Feine, *op. cit.*, p. 654.
[3] Titius, *op. cit.*, part iv. p. 175.   [4] Heb. ix. 26-28.
[5] ii. 17, vii. 27, ix. 12, x. 18, and others.
[6] Feine (p. 653) sees in ii. 7 the idea not of substitution, but of the
covering of sin before the eyes of God ; but he admits that the former idea is
present in ix. 28, where εἰς τὸ πολλῶν ἀνενεγκεῖν ἁμαρτίας goes back to
Isaiah liii. 12. Weiss (ii. 210) sees in the writer's view of Christ as priest as
well as sacrifice the way in which he combines, in a manner peculiar
to himself, the idea of sacrifice with that of assumption of punishment.
[7] Stevens, *op. cit.*, p. 79.

accordance with St. Paul's conception, regarded as pro-
ceeding from God's grace.

Yet the differences which separate this writer from
St. Paul are often made more of than the agreements
between them, and the conclusion drawn that his doctrine
of atonement is not really St. Paul's. Thus stress is laid
on the absence of the characteristic Pauline thought of
God's wrath and righteousness, and positively on the
connexion, even more direct in this epistle than in that
of St. Peter, between the death of Christ and the new
moral life. Beyschlag, commenting upon the words
καθαρίζειν, ἁγιάζειν, and τελειοῖν, which are used to describe
the power of the sacrifice and blood of Jesus, finds the root
ideas to be those of cleansing from sin and moral perfecting.
Accordingly, ' his main interest is in the moral effect of
the Saviour's death,' while the ' pardoning effect of the
death of Christ is . . . only the conscious reflex of a
cleansing, sanctifying effect, which the death of Christ
exercises on the heart.' [1] There is also a difference from
St. Paul in the writer's notion of faith. For St. Paul
the content of faith is the historical Christ, especially
in His death and resurrection ; but in this epistle the
object of faith is rather the world of transcendental reality,
and faith itself a looking upward and forward, not a looking
back.[2] In one passage, where, undoubtedly, Christ is
presented as doing for men in His death something which,
in its results alone, has a moral bearing upon man (ii. 14),
it is the overthrow of the devil, who had ' the power of
death,' and enslaved men through their fear of it, which
is expressed. With this may certainly be compared the

---

[1] Beyschlag, *op. cit.*, ii. 320-328. Cf. Holtzmann, ii. 344, who, while
allowing that the typical Pauline conception is to be found in the epistle,
e.g. in ix. 28, gives greater prominence to the idea that atonement appears
not as an act between God and Christ apart from men, ' but as a gift with a
power effective for real sanctification.' But see Denney, pp. 220-224. He
makes ἁγιάζειν correspond to the Pauline δικαιοῦν, and gives τελειοῦν a
religious rather than a moral bearing. Christ brings men into the ideal
religious relation to God.

[2] Cf. Stevens, *op. cit.*, p. 91.

Pauline thought of Christ's triumph over supernatural forces, and yet it is difficult to think that St. Paul would have related death, and all that death means for men, to the power of the devil without the introduction of the thought of sin and the law.[1]

But it is especially in his doctrine of the High Priesthood of Christ that the author is supposed to go beyond St. Paul, and, indeed, to throw quite a new light upon the doctrine of atonement. Not on the cross but in heaven is the act of atonement completed, when Christ appears in the holy place through His blood ;[2] since, on a line with the Levitical sacrifices, the climax of the act of sacrifice is the sprinkling of the blood. And if to this conception is added the further one that Christ in heaven ever presents His sacrifice before the Father, atonement appears rather as a never-ending process than as an act done once for all. The words, 'He ever liveth to make intercession' (vii. 25), are taken as implying a perpetual ministration, and not merely an appeal to a past finished act. 'He is now and always a ministering priest in the true tabernacle, the immediate presence of God.'[3] And just because heaven represents the higher and real world, there is reality, which can be called either continuous or timeless, about Christ's work in heaven, which cannot be predicated of anything He has done in the lower world.

Metaphysics, exegesis, and religious interest have combined to represent in this way the teaching of the Epistle to the Hebrews. The influence of the first in its idealistic form is opposed to any final importance being assigned to an act done in time. The exegesis made influential by the writings of Dr. Westcott and Dr. Milligan has urged that in the New Testament—especially in the Epistle to the Hebrews and the first Epistle of St. John—as well as in the Levitical sacrifices, blood always represents the

---

[1] Cf. Pfleiderer, *Primitive Christianity*, iii. 293 (E.T.), who looks on the thought of this verse as 'a substitute for the objective side of the Pauline doctrine of redemption.'

[2] ix. 12.

[3] Stevens, *op. cit.*, p. 87.

life which can be made available for use only when
liberated by death. And religious interest has sought for
some work worthy of the ascended Christ, and has found
it in the perpetual offering or presentation of His sacrifice.
These are questions which demand a far fuller treatment
than can be afforded here.[1] But this may be said : the
problem is one of relationship, of the connexion which
in this epistle is thought of as existing between Christ's
offering of Himself upon the Cross and His heavenly work
or ministry. What we have no right to do is to form an
idea of that ministry in reliance upon certain passages
of the epistle, and then to make that idea regulative for
other passages which, *prima facie*, do not seem to point
in the same direction. Dr. Stevens, who has no lack of
sympathy with the modern interpretation, can yet speak
of ' the one great priestly act of Christ done once for all—
the yielding up of His life on the cross,' [2] and so agree with
Dr. Denney that in this epistle there is ' the conception
of a *finished work* of Christ, a work finished in His death.' [3]
That this is the natural interpretation of more than one
passage [4] can hardly be disputed. But if this be so the
writer occupies the Pauline position, though in support
of that position he reasons from the cultus not from the
law, and though from it he passes to other ground, where
St. Paul has not preceded him.

The atmosphere of this epistle and of the Epistles of
St. Paul is admittedly different. The warnings which the
writer delivers are decisive against any lack of moral
force or fervour on his part ; nevertheless, there is a
certain delight in the intellectual and even the æsthetic [5]

---

[1] Dr. Tait's book, *The Heavenly Session of our Lord*, is a recent contribution to the subject. It is strong on the side of exegesis ; here and there
rather one-sided.

[2] *Op. cit.*, p. 87.   [3] *Op. cit.*, p. 225.

[4] *E.g.* vii. 27, ix. 14, x. 10, 12, 14.

[5] Cf. Denney, *op. cit.*, p. 214, ' The interpretation of Christ's death by moral
æsthetics rather than by moral law.' Schlatter, *Theologie des Neuen Testaments*, ii. 446, has a well-balanced statement of the differences between
St. Paul and this writer.

perfection of Christianity, which reflects the subtle questionings and refined taste of Alexandria, and is not an echo of St. Paul. We do not wonder that so original a mind has its own way of appreciating the Gospel, and of emphasising its finality. But the novelty of his apprehension does not constitute a break in the substance of that common teaching which St. Paul says he received, and which he moulded but did not transform.

Of the Johannine writings the Apocalypse may first be considered. Of the importance which, in this work, is attributed to Christ's death as a fact there can be no question. Twenty-nine times is Christ spoken of as the Lamb, a title which is constituted by the thought of suffering and death, going back as it does to the suffering Servant of Isaiah liii., perhaps also to the Lamb of the Passover.[1] Prominent is the idea of the innocence and of the patient and exemplary sufferings of the Lamb of God, but that is not all. Though the Apocalypse has no definitive theory of the death of Christ, Holtzmann is hardly justified in saying that 'it knows nothing of a substitutionary endurance of suffering.'[2] The notion of Christ's death as a ransom is to be found in several passages.[3] As to the remarkable text, xiii. 8, we must distinguish between eternal atonement viewed as an eternal truth,[4] and eternal atonement as implying something which has been part of God's eternal purpose. That the latter is the implication of the text is a view which, despite the opposition of many modern commentators who would

[1] So Holtzmann, i. 548, and Feine, p. 637.

[2] *Op. cit.*, i. 549. At the same time Holtzmann admits that the writer inclines towards the Pauline doctrine.

[3] i. 5, v. 9, xiv. 3. Of ἐν τῷ αἵματι Dr. Denney writes (p. 243), 'It seems to me far the most probable interpretation to make ἐν represent the Hebrew בּ of price.' Beyschlag (ii. 385) will admit only the thought of moral deliverance or cleansing.

[4] Cf. Dr. Inge in *Contentio Veritatis*, p. 298. Both Dr. Inge and Dr. Denney, who criticise him, seem to confuse the two. Atonement is no afterthought, since God knows that it will be required. No questions as to the relation of the historical to the eternal, of temporal fact and supra-temporal reality, need be raised.

take the words 'from the foundation of the world' not
with 'the Lamb slain' but with 'written in the book
of life,' seems to do most justice to the order. The fact
that in xxi. 27 the words 'written in the book of the
Lamb' reappear is obviously not decisive, since the
words 'from the foundation of the world' are omitted in
this passage, and we cannot rightly argue that this phrase
is to be construed with 'written' in the former passage.[1]
As in St. Peter's epistle, so in the Apocalypse, the new
moral life is closely connected with the work of Christ;[2]
but that 'the Apocalypse agrees in a remarkable way with
Paul's fundamental conception'[3] is a judgment which
does not exaggerate the impression produced by that
vision of the Lamb, and that triumphant praise of His
work which forms the centre of the Apocalyptic pictures.

The Gospel and first Epistle of St. John reveal the
writer as one who, like the author of the letter to the
Hebrews, has his own point of view and his own method
of emphasis. He probably came under the influence of
St. Paul, but he is very far from simply reproducing St.
Paul; and both in what he omits and in what he puts
forward he shows that he is not dependent upon any
other man's presentation of the Gospel. Characteristic
of him is his thought of revelation, and even if, as is the
case, he makes no sharp contrast between revelation and
redemption, but rather brings them together, he yet
thinks of the life and of the words of Christ in a way to
which there is no parallel in St. Paul. This fact is grasped,
though exaggerated by Holtzmann when he says of St.
John's Gospel that 'the redeeming work of the incarnate
Son of God can . . . consist only in His own self-revela-
tion.'[4] In this respect the Gospel shows a wider separation

---

[1] Stevens, *op. cit.*, p. 130, relies on this parallelism. On the other hand,
Feine (p. 637) accepts the other interpretation, and refers to 1 Peter i. 18.

[2] *E.g.* vii. 14.

[3] Titius, *op. cit.*, part iv. p. 165. He is referring to vii. 14, but his words
may be extended to the book as a whole.

[4] *Op. cit.*, ii. 520. Cf. Feine, p. 608, 'In John the whole earthly life of
Jesus, not first and principally His death, brings salvation.'

from St. Paul than does the epistle. In it the Pauline ideas of substitution, and of the abrogation of guilt through Christ's acceptance of the penalty of sin, are not prominent. The death of Christ 'is not a vicarious expiation of the guilt of sin and the curse of the law—these conceptions were remote from John's whole trend of thought.' [1] It represents rather the highest proof of love, and—a thought which has already appeared in the Epistle to the Hebrews —the destruction of the devil's power. Thus His death is not only an act of sacrifice but an act of judgment. Certainly it is not for St. John a riddle, something difficult to adjust with his other conceptions, but Christ 'in His death reveals His Sonship, and with that His lordship and His favour towards the community.' [2] But the Gospel does not attach to Christ's death the blessing of forgiveness as a proof of His favour, and as that which God gives for His sake ; [3] there is not the same sense as there is in St. Paul of everything which can be thought of as a blessing of salvation being stored up in the Cross. 'He does not obscure the Cross . . . nevertheless, the life is mightier than the death.' [4]

It is a true representation of St. John's doctrine which emerges from such quotations as the above, but, for all that, it is not the whole truth. Though St. John has his own point of view, he both knows and accepts that valuation of the death of Christ which belongs to the Pauline epistles. St. John may not make it as verbally clear as does St. Mark and St. Paul that Christ came to die ; but his Gospel [5] represents that death as necessary, while his epistle [6] expressly refers to it as a propitiation for our sins. Thus for St. John the revelation of Christ not only includes the revelation of His death, but without that death the revelation of Christ's person, life, and teaching would be unable to attain its end. Whether we translate $\alpha i\rho\omega\nu$ in i. 29

---

[1] Pfleiderer, *Primitive Christianity*, iv. 212 (E.T.).
[2] Schlatter, *op. cit.*, ii. 121.
[3] Cf. Weinel, *Bibl. Theologie des Neuen Testaments*, p. 392.
[4] Schlatter, *op. cit.*, ii. 178.   [5] iii. 14, xi. 50, xii. 24.   [6] ii. 2, iv. 10.

'beareth' or 'taketh away,' and do or do not regard the saying as a word of the Baptist, the real importance of the passage—that Christ as the Slain Lamb removes the sins of others—remains unaffected. And when the word ἱλασμός is used in the epistle (ii. 2, iv. 10), though the reference is to Christ Himself, it is only natural to suppose that the propitiation is regarded as flowing from Christ in His death.[1] Therefore we must not restrict the power of Christ's sacrifice to moral cleansing and the breaking of sin's power, but allow too the thought of the removal of guilt.[2]

St. John's teaching completes the circle of New Testament ideas concerning the Atonement. That doctrine is found most fully presented in the Epistles of St. Paul. But St. Paul does not stand alone, representing only one type of teaching. There is good reason for believing that what he taught was already, though in less definite form, the Gospel of the primitive community; and from his teaching St. Peter, the writer to the Hebrews, and even St. John, do not so greatly diverge that we can speak of different or opposed theologies. Through the New Testament runs one mighty thought: Christ died for our sins; He bore what we should have borne; He did for us what we could not have done for ourselves; He did for God that which was God's good pleasure. Apart from this there is no New Testament doctrine of salvation.

---

[1] Cf. Denney, *op. cit.*, p. 273. Westcott's note on ἱλασμός in his edition of the epistles really leaves unanswered the one fundamental question—in what does the propitiation consist? Sin is said to be neutralised by it, and the believer joined to Christ to enjoy its efficacy, since barriers to fellowship with God have been removed. But that it is more than an exhibition of love which breaks down the sinner's recalcitrancy is not in the least clear.

[2] Cf. Dale, *op. cit.*, pp. 158, 159, who appeals to the 'for His name's sake' ii. 12, and rightly stresses the word παράκλητον in ii. 1. Pfleiderer, *Primitive Christianity*, iv. 216, says of ii. 2 and iv. 10: 'The thought which is lacking in the Gospel of the expiation of sin (ἱλάσκεσθαι), or the cancelling of guilt through a vicarious work of Christ, is again taken up from the Pauline theology.' He refers the epistle to a different author.

CHAPTER IV

THE ATONEMENT IN GREEK THEOLOGY

WHEN we pass outside the canon of Scripture to those early Christian writers who, with whatever weaknesses in other directions, bear convincing witness to the power of a creative revelation, in which lies the secret of the affirmations of a new faith, of the aspirations of a new hope, of the energies of a new love, we must, if we are not to go constantly astray in interpreting their words, remember that, while they form a link between the New Testament foundation and the formulated doctrine of later times, the relation which they bear to the one and the other is by no means so clear as to be capable of precise definition. The same or similar words may point to the same or similar ideas ; but not necessarily so, since a word which has been at one time the expression of one idea, may, to a less or greater extent, alter its meaning under the influence of another idea. Hence it follows that the preservation of a word does not, as a matter of course, involve the preservation of the idea which the word was originally intended to convey.

In such respects no doctrine demands more careful treatment than that of the Atonement. For English students, indeed, a warning is conveyed in the very word.[1] Before the ideas of the New Testament were moulded into the forms of mediæval and reformation theology, we meet with writers making use of words in such ways as often to render it uncertain how far the apparently underlying idea was present to their minds or

---

[1] Cf. p. 11, note 1.

not. So we are confronted with a double possibility of error. On the one hand, we may take a passage written in the second century, and jump to the conclusion that its meaning is what it undoubtedly would have been had it come from a twelfth or sixteenth century author. So the learned American Calvinist, Dr. W. G. T. Shedd, asks of a passage in the Epistle to Diognetus, ' Is not the whole doctrine of vicarious satisfaction contained in these words?'[1] But the answer is not so obviously ' Yes ' to an open-minded commentator, as he clearly thinks it ought to be. On the other hand, it is possible for scholars who start from different presuppositions, and have no interest in adjusting the expressions used by ancient writers to the systems of Anselm or Calvin or Grotius, to push a legitimate caution much too far, and so refuse to allow any parity of ideas, however nearly akin the language of writers separated by centuries may be. We may, for instance, find Dr. Foley's remark that ' the period of the Post-Apostolic Fathers . . . cannot be said to have contained any distinct germs of the later dogmatic teaching '[2] in need of considerable modification. And in respect of the use of Scripture by the Church Fathers, over and above the precise meaning of the particular text in question, ' it is hard to say what arose from their own understanding of Christ's redemptive act, and what was said simply in reliance on the words of Scripture.'[3]

Of the Apostolic Fathers Clement of Rome speaks in four places of the blood of Christ in connexion with redemption. In the most important of these passages he says, ' Let us gaze steadfastly upon the blood of Christ, and know that it is precious to His Father, since it was shed for our salvation, and won grace of repentance for all the world.'[4] Elsewhere he speaks of those who believe and hope in God, having redemption (λύτρωσις) through the blood of the

---

[1] *History of Christian Doctrine*, ii. 219.
[2] Anselm's *Theory of the Atonement*, p. 45.
[3] Thomasius, *Dogmengeschichte*[2], i. 400, note 2.   [4] vii. 4.

Lord;[1] and again of our Lord Jesus Christ because of the
love which He had towards us, giving by the Will of God
'His blood for us, and His flesh for our flesh, and His soul
for our souls.'[2] Clearly, for Clement, the love of Christ
and the Will of God co-operate in effecting man's salvation,
the blood of Jesus freely outpoured being regarded as
the means. But it is impossible to say how far these
expressions imply independent reflection. Dr. Moberly
interprets χάριν μετανοίας as implying that Christ's blood
is 'the real possibility of human penitence. Human
penitence—not vicarious penitence only in man's stead,
but reality of penitence in man himself : this is its beauty,
its joy, its preciousness, in the presence of God.'[3] But
one cannot feel certain that any such thought was in
Clement's mind.[4] Just as Clement speaks of Christ's
blood, so does Ignatius of Christ's passion or death. Christ
died for our sake ' that by believing on His death you may
escape death.'[5] The Philadelphian Church 'rejoices in
the passion of our Lord,' and is saluted ' in the blood of
Jesus Christ, which is eternal joy.'[6] Even angels shall
be judged if they do not believe in the blood of Christ.
To those who teach the docetic heresy must be preferred
the Gospel ' in which the passion has been manifested
to us, and the resurrection accomplished.'[8] Ignatius'
devotion to Christ's Cross is as notable as his love for His
Person. ' My spirit is devoted (περίψημα) to the Cross,'
he cries :[9] he would be an imitator of the passion of his
God :[10] he knows of the life of Christ in men only if they
choose to die in (εἰς) His passion :[11] the blood of Jesus

---

[1] xii. 7.   [2] xlix. 6.
[3] *Atonement and Personality*, p. 326.
[4] Harnack, *History of Dogma*, i. 202 (E.T.), looks on χάριν μετανοίας
as simply the way in which Clement, slightly altering the traditional word-
ing, connects forgiveness with the death of Christ : 'It is meaningless to
deduce the χάριν μετανοίας (that is, if taken literally) from the blood of
Christ.'
[5] *Trall.*, ii. 2.   [6] *Philadelph.*, Intr.   [7] *Smyr.*, vi. 1.
[8] *Smyr.*, vii. 2. Cf. *Smyr.*, v. 3 : 'Till they repent concerning the passion
which is our resurrection.'
[9] *Eph.* xviii. 1.   [10] *Rom.* vi. 3.   [11] *Magn.* v. 2.

Christ can even be spoken of as love.[1] Ignatius like Clement presents us with no theory, but it is interesting to note that though he lays such stress on the Incarnation he cannot be classed with ' the best of the Fathers,' whose ' definite conviction,' according to Dr. Foley, it was ' that in essence the Incarnation was itself the Atonement.' [2] The saving words ' in essence ' will not save Ignatius for this view. The Didache and Hermas never connect redemption with the death of Christ. For the Didache Jesus is the revealer of knowledge, faith, and immortality,[3] while Hermas speaks of the Son of God as first cleansing the people's sins by undergoing much toil, and then showing them the way of life and giving them the law.[4] On the other hand, the author of the Epistle of Barnabas, and the writer to Diognetus, emphasize the death on the Cross. The former connects the forgiveness of sins with the sprinkling of the Lord's blood ; [5] the Son of God suffered that His wounding might make us alive,[6] and of that suffering many types are to be found in the Old Testament.[7] ' Barnabas ' has no one clear view of the purpose of the death of Christ. His antipathy to the Jews makes him see in it the one thing needful to complete the sum of the sins of those who had persecuted the prophets, but along with this he joins the redemption from darkness of hearts paid over to death and delivered up to the iniquity of error.[8] The writer to Diognetus in the passage already referred to [9] speaks of God as Himself taking our sins, which the reward of punishment and death awaited, and giving His Son as a ransom for us, ' the Holy for the wicked, the Innocent for the guilty.' ' For what else could cover our sins except His righteousness ? In whom was it possible for us sinners to be justified (δικαιωθῆναι) save in the Son of God alone ? O sweet exchange and unexpected benefits ! that the wickedness of many

---

[1] *Trall.* viii. 1 ; cf. *Rom.* vii. 3.   [2] *Op. cit.*, pp. 16, 17.   [3] x. 2.
[4] *Sim.* v. 6, 2-3.   [5] v. 1.   [6] vii. 2.
[7] *E.g.* the scapegoat, and Abraham's three hundred and eighteen servants.
[8] xiv. 5.   [9] P. 195 ; *Epistle*, ix. 2-6.

should be hidden in One who was righteous, and the
righteousness of one justify many wicked.' It is a remarkable passage, combining, as it does, ideas of man's sin
deserving punishment, of God taking our sins in His love
and giving His innocent Son as a ransom for us, and of the
consequent covering of sin by righteousness, represented
as an exchange.[1] M. Rivière correlates with this reference
to justification as the work of the Son of God alone the
statement of ' Barnabas ' that the Son of God could not
suffer except for our sakes;[2] and calls attention to these
as ' the two fundamental principles upon which little by
little the whole theology of redemption will be built up.'[3]

There is little to detain us in the Greek Apologists of
the second century. Christ for them is pre-eminently
the Teacher of divine truth, and the Saviour from the
power of demons. Only Justin tries to do more justice
to the facts of His life, and, especially, to the death on the
Cross. ' By His blood He cleanses those that believe on
Him ';[4] His Passion is the mystery of salvation, through
which men are saved by God.[5] Of the curse pronounced
against hanging on a tree in Deuteronomy xxi. 23 he seems
to make a double application, once connecting it with the
curse pronounced against wrongdoing, and seeing in the
Passion Christ, by the Will of the Father, taking the curses
of all men upon Himself and suffering for humanity, and
later applying it simply to the curses pronounced by the
Jews against Christ and Christians.[6] Through the Cross
and the water of Baptism we are redeemed from our sins.[7]

---

[1] Lidgett (*The Spiritual Principle of the Atonement*, p. 424) remarks that
this epistle ' might stand with equal propriety at the head of the so-called
moral doctrines of the Atonement, and of those which look upon it as a
satisfaction for sin.' Rivière (*Le Dogme de la Rédemption*, pp. 111, 112)
finds the idea of substitution clearly stated, but without formal reference to
Christ's death. Foley (*op. cit.*, p. 23) rules out the idea of substitution (but
the thought of punishment and of the innocent for the guilty tells against
him), and insists that the ' exchange' is one ' of situation in the sinner himself.' Cf. Moberly, p. 331.

[2] vii. 2.   [3] *Op. cit.*, p. 111.   [4] *Ap.*, i. 32.   [5] *Dial.*, 74.

[6] *Dial.*, 95, 96. καταρας αναδεξασθαι, in c. 95, probably means, as Dr.
Lidgett (p. 426) suggests, evils which have resulted from sin.

[7] *Dial.*, 86.

Ritschl seems to leave this element in his thought out of account when he restricts Justin's conception of Christ's redemptive activity to that of a Teacher of faith and obedience, and, at His second coming, a Judge who grants the boon of immortality to the virtuous.[1] Nevertheless, Justin's soteriology is little developed, despite his use of Old Testament prophecy in its interest, and the idea of expiation is not prominent.

In the various Gnostic schools we find as the underlying religious idea man's need of redemption. But the religious passes into the metaphysical, even into the physical, since redemption is from the limitations of matter rather than from moral evil,[2] and is effected by illumination and true knowledge. In the systems of Basilides and Valentinus there is no place for atonement ; the sufferings on the Cross are either those of a man Jesus who is the mere instrument of the redeeming Christ, or are unreal, since the body is but apparent. Redemption, indeed, in Valentinianism, takes effect primarily and really in the transcendental world, of which the lower world is the imperfect image, and into this transcendental world is introduced the true Cross, the Stauros which brings all existences out of separation into unity with the Absolute.[3] Marcion, however, laid more stress on the Crucifixion than is consistent with its being to him, in Baur's words, ' a mere appearance ' ;[4] while his disciple Apelles, breaking away from intellectualism and from soteriological ideas based on the threefold nature of man,[5] declared that those would be saved who set their hopes upon the Crucified and continued in good works.[6] Especially interesting is

---

[1] *Rechtfertigung und Versöhnung* [2], ii. 5.

[2] Dr. G. P. Fisher (*History of Christian Doctrine*, p. 60) truly says : 'Gnosticism stands on the page of history as a perpetual warning against all endeavours to substitute a physical or metaphysical for an ethical doctrine of sin and redemption.'

[3] Cf. Baur, *Lehre von der Versöhnung*, p. 24.   [4] *Op. cit., ibid.*

[5] Valentinus taught that a man's salvation was certain, doubtful, or impossible according as the spiritual, psychical, or bodily element predominated in him.

[6] Rhodon in Eusebius *H. E.*, v. 13.

Marcion's conception of the death of Christ as 'the price by which the God of love purchased men from the creator of the world,'[1] for though Baur's statement that the mythical conception involved is 'the foundation upon which the first theory concerning the reconciliation of man with God developed'[2] cannot be substantiated, as he believes, from Irenæus, yet the resemblance of Marcion's demiurge to the devil of Origen, Gregory of Nyssa and Gregory the Great, and the similarity of the parts they play, cannot be denied.   But to Irenæus we must now direct our attention.

Irenæus, like the Apologists, thought of men as enslaved by the powers of darkness, and of redemption as freedom from those powers : he goes beyond the Apologists by introducing the idea of the death of Christ as the act and power which liberates. But this is neither his most characteristic idea, nor, in the important passage, v. 11, is the devil looked on as the possessor of rights which must be satisfied. It is because it best becomes God that He uses no force against the apostasy, but redeems men from it by persuasion.[3] This is spoken of as just action, but it is just action as contrasted with violence—such as the devil used when in the beginning he seized what was not his own—not as recognising any rights of the devil. Irenæus' leading thought is that to which the word ἀνακεφαλαίωσις or *recapitulatio* gives expression ;[4] when the Son of God was incarnate ' He summed up in Himself the long roll of the human race, bringing to us a compendious salvation, that what we had lost in Adam, namely, being in the image and likeness of God, we might

---

[1] Harnack, *D. G.* i. 273 (E.T.); cf. Tert. *adv. Marc.* v.   [2] *Op. cit.*, p. 28.
[3] Shedd (*op. cit*, ii. 222) and Foley (*op. cit.*, p. 36) are probably right in interpreting the 'persuasion' as directed towards men rather than as towards the devil. Shedd, however, makes an impossible attempt to introduce into what Irenæus says about just action the idea of penal retribution, so that 'the omnipotence of the Deity shall not overthrow the justice of the Deity by arbitrarily remitting the penalty due to transgression without any satisfaction of law.'
[4] Justin had anticipated him here (*Haer,* iv. 6. 2).

regain in Christ Jesus.' [1]   First of all the Fathers Irenæus
tells us that Christ, because of His great love, ' became what
we are to make us what He is.' [2]   Particular stress is laid
on Christ's obedience ; what humanity as a whole lost
through Adam's disobedience that it regains as a whole
through Christ's obedience.[3]   From this standpoint there
is no essential difference between the Gospel of Creation
and the Gospel of Redemption, and between the Incarnation and the Atonement. ' The Incarnation effects the
Atonement. It brings to completion the original creation,
and is its perfecting as much as its restitution.' [4]   There
is another side to Irenæus ; he thinks of Christ as ' reconciling us to God by His passion,' [5] and as ' propitiating for
us the Father against whom we had sinned,' [6] though in
this last passage the reference is to the Incarnation and
to the life of obedience, not, at least verbally, to the Cross ;
elsewhere he speaks of the Son as given by God, of His
good-pleasure, as a sacrifice for our redemption.[7]   But,
as M. Rivière declares,[8] Irenæus does not bring these views
into connexion with his more general principles concerning
the necessity of the Incarnation ; and we must admit that
they are, in his case, more the effect of Scripture and
tradition than of what came naturally to his own apprehension of Christian truth.

From South Gaul we pass to Alexandria. In his more

---

[1] iii. 18. 1.   [2] v. *praef.*
[3] Cf. esp. v. 16. 3, ' In the second Adam we were reconciled, becoming
obedient unto death.'
[4] Bethune-Baker, *Introduction to the Early History of Christian Doctrine*,
p. 334, note 2. Cf. Moberly, *op. cit.*, p. 344 : ' Christ's atoning acts were not
so much acts done by Him instead of us as acts which, in His doing them,
we all did.'
[5] iii. 16. 9.   [6] v. 17. 1.   [7] iv. 5. 4.
[8] *Op. cit.*, p. 124. Cf. Baur (*op. cit.*, p. 34), who finds in Irenæus no
clear indication of the relationship between the death on the Cross and redemption from the devil: ' How the death of Jesus is connected with the
battle which He waged against the devil, and in what way the liberation
resulted, is not . . . explained.' Thomasius, *D. G.*[2], i. pp. 402, 405, presents Irenæus' thought as more of a unity. Disobedience against God and
subjection to the devil in Adam necessitated the Incarnation ; the obedience
of the God-man, in whom humanity endured unto death, vanquished the
devil, and, at the same time, discharged man's debt to God.

important works Clement's soteriology, when judged by any standard that tries to do justice to the New Testament, is seriously defective, and has more in common, now with Stoic, now with Gnostic, than with distinctively Christian conceptions. Christ is for him Saviour by being the Teacher who endows men with true knowledge, and leads them on to a love which has no desires, and a righteousness whose best fruit is contemplation.[1] But in the shorter treatise *Quis dives salvetur ?* much more importance is attached to Christ's death, and language is used which 'applies to the death of Christ the traditional principles of expiation and substitution, and comes near to the formulæ of vicarious satisfaction.'[2] He has paid the debt of death which men owed for their sins ; He gives Himself as a ransom, and lays down for each man His soul which outweighs all things.[3]

With Origen the case stands otherwise. No suggestion of indifference to the death of Christ, and of insensibility to its benefits, can be attributed to him ; but he sees its effects in so many different ways that it is never possible to be certain that any one passage, however strongly worded, represents his dominating idea ;[4] while it is equally difficult, or rather impossible, to make a synthesis of all the conceptions which he used. He is the first Christian theologian to teach clearly that the death of Christ is a ransom paid to the devil in exchange for the souls of men, forfeited by sin ; that the devil overreached himself in the transaction owing to the perfect purity of the Soul of Christ, which it was torture for him to try and retain ; while Christ, both for Himself and for all who will follow Him, triumphed over the devil and death.[5] It was as an exegete interested in finding an

---

[1] Cf. Bigg, *Christian Platonists of Alexandria*, pp. 91-96.

[2] Rivière, *op. cit.*, p. 133.   [3] *Quis dives salvetur !* xxiii., xxxvii.

[4] Cf. Harnack, *D. G.*, ii. 367, note 1 (E.T.), 'He propounded views as to the value of salvation, and as to the significance of Christ's death on the Cross, with a variety and detail rivalled by no theologian before him.'

[5] *In Matt. tom.* xvi. 8. Cf. *In Rom. tom.* ii. 13. Nothing like a deliberate act of deception on the part of God is implied.

answer to the question which may seem to arise from
Matt. xx. 28,—to whom is the λύτρον paid that Origen
formulated this theory ; but exegesis led him to other
conclusions also. Relying on Romans iii. 24 he speaks
of Christ making God propitious to men,[1] and elsewhere
he brings together the propitiation of God and the reconciling of men.[2] As Himself sinless Christ could take up
the sins of the whole world and destroy them in His death,
and the punishment which we deserved that we might be
corrected and gain peace fell upon Him.[3] Of the sacrificial
system of the Old Testament Origen made the fullest use.[4]
Sin must be expiated ; that is the message of the victims
offered under the Law, and for that end the Son of God
was incarnate, and, by the offering of Himself, the spotless
Lamb, put an end to all other sacrifices.[5] Yet for all his
fullness of exposition he does not attempt to show why
sin must be expiated, ‘ he has failed to explore the moral
realities which the words “ sacrifice ” and “ victim ” cover’ ;[6]
or perhaps it would be truer to say that when he asserts
the moral meaning of Christ’s sacrificial death he looks on
that death as a supreme but not unique example of self-
sacrifice, and as a stimulus to like conduct on the part of
men.[7] Moreover, he can think of the deification of human
nature without bringing in any reference to the Cross ;
it was begun by the union of divine and human in the
Incarnation, and continues ‘ in all those who, with faith,
follow the life which Jesus taught,’ and live according to
His commandments.[8] Highly as Origen prizes the thought
of Christ as the crucified Saviour, it is not, for him, final.
Van Eyck’s great picture of the Lamb, as it had been

---

[1] *In Rom. tom.* iii. 8.   [2] *In Lev. Hom.*, ix. 10.
[3] *In Joann. tom.* xxviii. 14. The thought and the words (κόλασις
παιδευθῆναι) are clearly of remedial punishment, but it is effected through
the vicarious substitution of Christ.
[4] Cf. Bigg, *op. cit.*, p. 210, ‘Under the touch of Allegory the whole ritual
of Leviticus becomes eloquent of Him, who bore our sins upon the tree.’
[5] *In Numb. Hom.*, xxiv. 1.   [6] Rivière, *op. cit.*, p. 141.
[7] Cf. *Exhort. ad martyr*, 30, 50 ; *in Matt. comment.*, p. 912.
[8] *c. Cels.*, iii. 28.

slain, receiving the adoration of the redeemed in heaven, is not spiritual enough for the Christian Gnosticism of Alexandria. 'Happy are they who no longer need the Son of God as physician or shepherd or redemption, but as wisdom and word and righteousness.' The Word made flesh draws men to Himself, that finally He may raise them ' to see Him as He was before He was made flesh.' [1]

The variety of the soteriological ideas of this great thinker explains the widely different judgments passed upon his influence on Christian doctrine in this connexion. Dr. Shedd thinks that the principles, especially as to punishment, from which Origen started are so contrary to any theory of real expiation of sin by Christ that we must give to some of his words a modified meaning, and acknowledge his conceptions to be 'very defective and erroneous.' [2] Baur represents the ransom to Satan as the dominant thought in Origen's idea of atonement,[3] whereas to Dr. Bethune-Baker this is ' quite a subordinate element.' [4] Thomasius represents his doctrine to be that of redemption through ransom, and propitiation through sacrifice, the two conceptions being by Origen most clearly distinguished ; [5] on the other hand, Dr. Moberly [6] has practically nothing to say about either. Such instances of divisions of opinion and diversities of treatment could easily be multiplied, and where there is so much to be said on every side, no one conclusion can be pronounced exclusively right. Whenever Origen dealt with any passage in Scripture, actually or conceivedly bearing on the redemptive Work of Christ, he did it the fullest possible justice on its own lines ; but how all these lines were to meet in one centre of unity was a problem that he never

---

[1] *In Joann.*, i. 22, *c. Cels.*, vi. 68. Of this deepest side of Origen's thought Harnack says, ' The historical work of Christ was to Origen no appearance but truth. But he did not view it as *the* truth, and in this he agrees with the Gnostics, but as *a* truth, beyond which lies a higher' (*D. G.*, ii. 369, E.T.).

[2] *Op. cit.*, ii. 237.
[3] *Op. cit.*, pp. 58, 62.
[4] *Op. cit.*, p. 338.
[5] *D. G.*, i. 405.
[6] *Op. cit.*, pp. 345-348.

set himself to solve, and which—for his writings at least—may be regarded as unsolvable.

The works of Athanasius are rich in passages which throw light upon his idea of the necessity and method of atonement. Unfortunately, the only treatise which deals with the subject at all systematically is his earliest—the *De Incarnatione*—and the tendency to expound Athanasius by almost exclusive reference to this work is deplorable.[1] Dr. Melville Scott, in a book just published,[2] makes out a case, which needs indeed critical examination, but is *prima facie* reasonable and strongly supported with quotations from the later writings, for holding that Athanasius progressed from his first view of the Atonement as an ' external transaction ' till it became for him an ' internal process,' a sanctification of human nature first in Christ, and so, potentially, in all men. His final doctrine was not one of substitution, but of a double metathesis, ' as Christ took what was ours, so we are to receive what was His, *i.e.* not His Divinity, which is incommunicable, but His perfected Humanity.' [3] Dr. Scott argues that according to this conception the human nature which the Logos took was fallen and ' inclined to sin,' ' corrupt,' and ' in bondage ' ; [4] but was preserved free from all actual sin, despite fierce temptations which culminated in the Passion, and was finally offered or restored to the Father as a perfect sacrifice in that death which was ' a final act of completion and of sanctification.' [5] Thus humanity as a whole, originally created after the image of the Logos, is restored in the Logos made flesh ; and that goal of deification (θεοποίησις) so dear to Athanasius is in sight, for ' the deification of humanity must be the perfection of humanity,

---

[1] It is only of the *De Incarnatione*, even if of that, that Dr. Lidgett (*op. cit.*, p. 450) can say with any truth, 'The redemptive meaning of our Lord's humanity is conceived in a very limited way. The bond of union between our Lord and mankind is found almost exclusively in the eternal Logos, and not in the divine humanity.'

[2] *Athanasius on the Atonement.*   [3] Scott, *op. cit.*, p. 66.

[4] Quotations from Ath. *in Ps.* xxii. 30 ; *c. Ar.*, iv. 33 ; *c. Ar.*, i. 43.

[5] *Op. cit.*, p. 81.

and this perfection must first be gained in Christ, and then must through Christ be transferred to us.' [1]

That such a view does justice to that which was of the deepest religious interest to Athanasius—the true divinity of Christ, and what man may become through Him—cannot be doubted. The conception involved is more ethical than physical ; according to it ' our Lord's saving work must be regarded as a continuous ethical process' ; [2] that is, it is not accomplished simply by the Incarnation, the uniting of the divine and the human in the person of Christ. If Dr. Scott lays the emphasis at all aright, it would be impossible to say of Athanasius what Harnack says of Methodius, the opponent of Origen, that for him ' salvation . . . came to light, already achieved for mankind, in the constitution of the God-man.' [3] Not only on what Christ is, but on what He does and endures, is the stress laid by Athanasius.[4]

At the same time we must recognise another side to his teaching, not confined to the De Incarnatione. It is concerned with the death of Christ as the payment of a debt which man cannot pay. The debt must be paid, because man has sinned and God cannot revoke His word, that sin shall be followed by death. It is not easy to see what exactly the debt is, for the death of Christ does not put an end to death, but only ' to death regarded as penal and as symptomatic of man's φθορά.' [5] But that full payment is made in Christ's death is clear, and neither from the De Incarnatione, nor from passages in later works,[6]

---

[1] Op. cit., p. 78. Cf. p. 66, ' What happened to Christ only happened to Him that it might afterwards be repeated in us. The successive steps by which humanity returned to God in the Person of Christ are to be reproduced in us . . . by a vital force emanating from His exalted Humanity.'

[2] Scott, op. cit., p. 62.   [3] D. G., iii. 107 (E.T.).

[4] Dr. Scott's work should be read along with Dr. Moberly's pages on Athanasius, though the thought of Christ's personal achievements is not prominent in Dr. Moberly, as, for instance, it is in Dr. Du Bose.

[5] Athanasius, ed. Robertson, p. lxx ; cf. de Inc., xxi.

[6] E.g. c. Ar., i. 60, ' The world, as liable, was being judged by the law ; but the Word took the judgment to Himself' ; c. Ar., ii. 66, ' The Logos took a body that, paying the debt in our stead, He might through Himself supply what man lacked ' ; i.e. ἀφθαρσία.

can we expunge the idea of substitution, impossible though
it is to agree with Dr. Shedd that ' he gives expression to
views which harmonise exactly with the modern Protestant
view of the doctrine ' : [1] to pay a debt is not the same as
to endure a penalty, and though the latter idea is not
wholly absent the former is much more prominent.[2]   On
the other hand, natural though the statement is, it is too
sweeping to say that Athanasius ' regards the incarnate
Logos as achieving all His work, or redemption as the
representative not the substitute of man ' ; [3] while true
exegesis is quite at a discount when Dr. Foley, commenting
on ἀνθ' ἡμῶν τὴν ὀφειλὴν ἀποδιδούς, restricts the sense to
Christ paying the debt ' with us,' and dogmatically decides
that ' nothing more than this can be meant by Athanasius.' [4]
The Cross may not stand out in the writings of Athanasius
as much as in some other theologians, but there is more
than a hint of substitution when he does deal with the death
of Christ.   It is a question of emphasis : the ideas of
representation and of the identity of Christ's humanity
with ours are more generally to the fore, and can be more
intimately connected with that insistence on process and
' becoming ' rather than on mere fact which, as Dr. Scott
says,[5] is characteristic of Athanasius.

The true successors of the Athanasian theology, in more
than one of its fundamental positions, were the three
great Cappadocians, Basil and the two Gregories.   But
first it should be said that in two of Athanasius' contemporaries, Eusebius of Cæsarea and Cyril of Jerusalem,
what is sometimes called the realistic,[6] as contrasted with

---

[1] *Op. cit.*, ii. 242.
[2] So Lidgett (*op. cit.*, p. 450).   He 'conceives death as a debt owing on
account of sin, rather than as a penalty inflicted in consequence of it.'
[3] Bethune-Baker, *op. cit.*, p. 347.
[4] *Op. cit.*, pp. 57, 58.   On the other hand, Harnack (vi. 55) speaks of 'the
noteworthy clearness' with which Athanasius spoke of 'the penal sufferings
which Christ took from us and laid upon Himself.'
[5] *Op. cit.*, p. 81.
[6] Tixeront (*Histoire des Dogmes*, ii. 149) thus describes the realistic view,
'The sinner must expiate his faults and satisfy divine justice.   Jesus Christ
substitutes Himself for all men. . . .   By His sufferings and death He pays

the physical or mystical, view of the Atonement, is strongly
asserted. Eusebius speaks of Christ as ' chastised for us,
and undergoing a penalty which He did not owe but we
for our sins, and so gaining for us forgiveness of sins.' [1]
Parallel expressions occur in Cyril, together with an
insistence on Christ's death as the free act of His love.
He speaks of the righteousness of Him who died far out-
weighing the iniquity of sinners,[2] since—and here he
anticipates his namesake of Alexandria [3]—He who died
was God made man. Jesus by giving Himself as a ransom
puts an end to God's wrath against men.[4] This is one of
the more rather than of the less distinct traces ' of the
thought of substitution in connection with satisfaction.' [5]
The testimony of Eusebius and of Cyril is important,
because, as neither is a great speculative thinker, their
teaching may correct possibly erroneous impressions
drawn from the writings of an Origen or even of an
Athanasius.

Of the Cappadocians, Basil of Cæsarea, though he won
much fame as a theologian in the fight against Arianism,
contributed but little to the doctrine of atonement. Such
references as there are to it in his works occur in letters
and in passages from his commentaries rather than in his
greater controversial treatises. There are evidences of
more than one point of view. In accordance with the
idea which goes back to Ignatius, salvation consists in the

---

our debt to God and ransoms us; He expiates our sins by undergoing the
penalty due to us; He satisfies justice, He appeases God's anger, and makes
Him favourable. In a word, He offers to God the expiatory and propitiatory
sacrifice, which blots out the sins of the world.'

[1] *Dem. Ev.*, x. 1. What precedes these words deals with the relation of
Christ to men, who are His body, so that He is able to bear our sins and
make His own our sicknesses. So Dr. Foley (p. 48) argues that Eusebius has
no theory of substitution, but of mystical union. But the sentence, Οὐ μόνον
δὲ ταῦτα πράξας . . . ἀλλὰ καὶ ὑπὲρ ἡμῶν κολασθείς, introduces a climax, in
which the thought is rather of the difference than of the resemblance between
Christ and man.

[2] *Catech.*, xiii. 33.   [3] Cf. Cyr. Al. on Gal. iii. 13.   [4] *Catech.*, xiii. 2.
[5] Harnack, *D. G.*, iii. 309 (E.T.), on the Greek Fathers of the fourth century. Didymus (*De Trin.*, iii. 27) also has the idea of Christ appeasing God
by His sacrifice, but the thought of penalty is absent.

gift of immortality; for this Christ came and died ' to deliver thee from mortality and make thee a partaker of heavenly life ' ; [1] if He had not come in our flesh, He could not have slain sin in the flesh and restored and reunited to God the humanity which fell in Adam and became separated from God.[2] Elsewhere he attaches a more specific meaning to the death of Christ, interpreting it in one of his homilies as at once a price paid to the devil, who held men captive, and an expiation ($\dot{\epsilon}\xi\dot{\iota}\lambda\alpha\sigma\mu\alpha$) made on behalf of all men, since they were powerless to give what God required.[3]

His younger brother, Gregory of Nyssa, is much more important. He follows Origen in explaining the death of Christ as a ransom paid to Satan, but elaborates the theory so that, though everything is done for the best, and every one, even the devil, profits, the means used to gain the desired end include and even necessitate an act of deceit on the part of God. Man deceived by the devil so as to mistake apparent for real good had fallen into captivity. God could not justly deliver him by force, and the devil would not give him up except in exchange for something better. In the incarnate Christ he saw what he preferred to all he possessed ; the Lord's body concealed His divinity, and the devil in grasping at Him thought he had nothing to fear, but the hook of the Deity was swallowed along with the bait of the flesh ; Christ entered into death and darkness as life and light and drove them away. Gregory then goes on to show how God's goodness, power, wisdom, and justice are all revealed, the last because the devil receives his due, is deceived as he had deceived, and actually himself benefits.[4]

---

[1] *Ep.* viii. 5. [2] *Ep.* cclxi. 2.

[3] *In Psalm,* xlviii. 3, 4. The transition from the thought of the devil to the thought of God is made quite arbitrarily. Basil relies on reason for his first point, on Scripture for his second. But he does not work out the idea of ransom so as to form a real theory.

[4] *Or. Cat.,* xxii.-xxvi. Apparently the devil is finally saved. Baur's criticism of the whole theory, and especially of the use Gregory makes of the idea of $\dot{\alpha}\nu\tau\dot{\alpha}\lambda\lambda\alpha\gamma\mu\alpha$, 'exchange,' is exceedingly acute (*op. cit.,* pp. 73 ff.).

Thus Christ delivers men from the devil : but this is, as it were, only the external side of man's salvation. Gregory is a true successor of Athanasius in the benefits which he sees accruing to humanity as a whole from the Word having taken to Himself human nature.[1] So much is this the case that Harnack is not guilty of misrepresentation when he says that 'underlying all the arguments of the " Great Catechism " we have the thought that the Incarnation was an *actus medicinalis*, which is to be thought of as strictly natural, and that extends to all mankind.'[2] At the Incarnation 'God joined Himself to our nature, that by union with the Divine it might become divine, being freed from death.'[3] The importance of the resurrection of Christ is that it ensures immortality and union with God for the human race. With Christ rose all men, since the part, that is Christ's body, which is consubstantial with ours, stands for the whole 'as though all nature were one living thing.'[4] Elsewhere, he explains the title 'redemption' (ἀπολύτρωσις), applied to Christ by St. Paul, as 'a gift to us of immortality as it were a price for the soul of each, so that He gained for His own possession those who through His life were bought by Him from death.'[5] With reference to the destruction of sin rather than its expiation, he describes Christ as the Good Shepherd going in search of men who had strayed far from God : 'He frees us from the curse, making our curse His own, and taking upon Himself our enmity against God, the result of sin, He slew it in Himself as St. Paul says (now sin was the enmity) ;[6] and becoming what we are He through Himself again united the human race[7] to God.'[8]

---

[1] Ritschl (*op. cit.*, i. 13) thinks that Gregory improves upon Athanasius by connecting the deification of human nature, not simply with the birth of Christ, but with the whole course of His life from birth to resurrection. As to Athanasius, Dr. Scott's book affords an able defence of his ethical interests.
[2] *D. G.*, iii. 297 (E.T.).   [3] *Or. Cat.*, xxv.   [4] *Or. Cat.*, xxxii.
[5] *De Perfecta Christiani forma* (Migne, *P. G.*, xlvi. col. 261).
[6] Eph. ii. 16.
[7] Or 'humanity,' which perhaps better expresses the abstract.
[8] *Contra Eunom.*, xii. col. 889.   Rivière speaks of the whole passage as 'an admirable summary of the whole economy of redemption' (p. 158). But,

Traces of other ideas may also be found, but hardly 'unequivocal expressions of the realistic theory.'[1]   In the *De Occursu Domini* the contrast is pointed between the Levitical sacrifices and the sacrifice of Christ, who, as the sinless high priest, offered His body to God in the place of (ἀντί) humanity.   But this humanity is not spoken of as sinful but as 'purified by faith in Him.'[2] And when we observe that Gregory has just been speaking of the purification of the whole human race through the assumption by the Son of flesh and a reasonable soul, we can hardly doubt that the word ἀντί is simply equivalent to ὑπέρ, 'on behalf of,' the idea being that Christ offers to God the pure sacrifice of His sinless human nature as the first-fruits and an earnest of purified humanity.[3]   Thus the notion is simply one of representation.   Nor can we in Gregory's writings find anything even as transactional as the conception of debt which we noted in the *De Incarnatione* of Athanasius.

Gregory of Nazianzus, friend as he was of his namesake of Nyssa, must first be noted as the second [4] Christian writer to repudiate with scorn and indignation the idea of a ransom paid to Satan.   It is an outrage to suppose that 'the robber' could receive God Himself in payment for us.[5]   Must we then say that the blood of Christ was paid to the Father as a ransom for us ?   But the Father neither held us captive nor, for Himself, demanded such blood-shedding.   Clearly then it was for our sakes, that humanity

despite the use of 2 Cor. v. 21 and Gal. iii. 13, the dominant idea is that of the moral power of humanity in and through Christ.

[1] Tixeront, *op. cit.*, ii. 152.

[2] *P. G.*, xlvi. col. 1165.   The last highly important words are omitted by Rivière (p. 157).

[3] He refers to Romans x. 16.

[4] The first is the third-century Pseudo-Origen (Adamantius) in his *De Recta in deum fide.*   He calls it 'blasphemous folly.'   See the long quotation in Harnack, ii. 291.

[5] *Or.*, xlv. 22.   Yet in *Or.*, xxxix. 13, though the idea of ransom in connexion with men's salvation from the devil does not occur, the idea of deceit does ; 'the sophist who deceived us is himself deceived by the covering of flesh, that hurling himself, as he thinks, upon Adam, he may rush against God.'

might be sanctified 'by the manhood (τῷ ἀνθρωπίνῳ) of God,' and the tyrant be put to flight. In other passages Gregory goes further in the direction of a doctrine of substitution and expiation. Christ 'gives Himself instead of us as a ransom which cleanses the world.'[1] He made the sins and offences of men His own, as being Head of the whole body.[2] Gregory's thought wavers between representation and substitution. On the Cross Christ was not deserted by the Father but showed our state, 'for it was we who had first been deserted, then saved by the Passion of the impossible.'[3] He became for us 'very sin and very curse,'[4] but the thought is at once given a moral turn, since the object is to produce in us true humility. Nor are the physical conceptions of other Greek Fathers absent. Christ is man 'to purify man through Himself, becoming like leaven to the whole lump, and, by uniting to Himself that which was condemned, to free the whole of it from condemnation.'[5] 'He is man by reason of thee, that by reason of Him thou mayest become God.'[6] The whole work of salvation can be used by Gregory in the interests of moral appeal, since the Incarnation and the Cross were not necessary to our redemption; 'by His will alone, as God, He could have saved us.'[7]

The death of Christ is more prominent in Gregory of Nazianzus than in Gregory of Nyssa. But Baur is right in saying that not yet had there appeared the problem of investigating 'the relation of the guilt that was bound up with sin to the idea of the divine holiness and righteousness.'[8]   And even though we may make too much of the passage where Gregory allows, as legitimate and without peril, speculation on (among other things) 'Christ's sufferings,'[9] such language clearly implies the absence of settled theory.

---

[1] *Or.*, xxx. 20.   [2] *Or.*, xxx. 5.   [3] *Ibid.*
[4] *Or.*, xxxvii. 1.   [5] *Or.*, xxx. 21.   [6] *Or.*, xl. 45.
[7] *Or.*, xix. 13; cf. Greg. Nyss., *Or. Cat.*, xvii., and even Ath., *c. Ar.*, ii.
68, 'God could simply have spoken and destroyed the curse.'
[8] *Op. cit.*, p. 89.   [9] *Or.*, xxvii. 10.

In the next evidence that we have to examine we shall find something rather more definite. John Chrysostom and Cyril of Alexandria, though they represent widely different schools of theology, are at one in the immense value they ascribe to the death of Christ, and not far removed in their interpretations. Chrysostom sees in Christ's Incarnation and sacrificial death the working of pity and love.[1] His work is a work of deliverance done for our sakes, but conditioned in its mode of operation by our sins. As sinners we were accused by the law and condemned by God, but Christ's coming and sacrifice of Himself stayed God's wrath.[2] God's action in giving His Son for men is compared to that of a king who gives his son to die in place of a bandit, and, moreover, ' together with the death transfers the charge ($\alpha i \tau i a$, almost " crime ") from the one to the other.' [3] Christ accepts the curse that was against us, so that we are no longer accursed.[4] But Chrysostom never forgets that Father and Son share together in the work of atonement.[5] The Father's love is the cause of that work of salvation which the Son freely takes upon Himself.[6] And with the characteristic religious interest, though without the exact dogmatic phraseology, of the Alexandrine theologians he can speak of the superabundant worth of Christ's sacrifice.[7]

Chrysostom is especially concerned with what M. Rivière calls ' the negative side ' of Christ's work ; Cyril of Alexandria is not less insistent on this, but he combines with it the idea of immortality and deification brought to men through the Incarnation. In no theologian, not even in Athanasius, do ideas of Incarnation and of Atonement

[1] *In Ep. ad Hebr. Hom.*, v. i.   [2] *In Ep. ad Gal.* (*P. G.*, lxi. col. 646).
[3] *In Ep. 2 ad Cor. Hom.*, xii. 4.   [4] *In Joann. Homil.*, xi. 2.
[5] *In Ep. ad Rom. Hom.*, vii. 2, ' When he says "God set forth," and points to the work as the Father's, he shows that it is the Son's also.'
[6] *In Ep. ad Rom. Hom.*, xv. 2, ' Think what goodness it was not to spare His own Son, but to give Him even for enemies and blasphemers.' And see in *Ep. ad Gal. Hom.*, iii. 3, where Christ is represented as voluntarily taking the place of one condemned to death.
[7] *In Ep. ad Rom. Hom.*, x. 2.

react so much upon one another, as is the case with Cyril.
For Christ to redeem us, all that He does must be the work
of one divine Person ; all the variations of Cyril's thought
return to this one point of departure.[1] His sufferings
have an infinite value, because the Word who cannot
suffer was ' in the suffering body,' [2] and that body is the
Word's very own.[3] Again and again Cyril insists that in
His death Christ appears as the equivalent, and more than
the equivalent (ἀνταξιώτερος), of man. ' He accepted the
punishment of sinners, and through the Cross put an end
to the decree of the ancient curse.' [4] Cyril's insistence
on Christ's Godhead, on the unity of His Person, coming
dangerously near to monophysitism,[5] and on the divine
character and value both of His flesh and of His acts, as
being the flesh and the acts of the Word, make it impossible
to stress, as Dr. Foley does, the passage where Cyril speaks
of men having paid in Christ the penalties due to sin.[6]
Cyril's dominant idea is rather of the satisfaction which
Christ as a divine Person makes to God, and Baur, commenting on the exegesis of Galatians iii. 13 in Cyril's
De recta fide,[7] where the thought is that only because Christ
is God does His acceptance of the penalties of sin suffice
for all men, can say that ' here to the full concept of satisfaction there lacks nothing except the express reference
of it to God and the divine righteousness.' [8]

There can be no doubt that the Nestorian controversy
turned Cyril's eyes to the Cross with a steadiness to which
earlier theology of an Alexandrine type has no parallel ;

[1] See the study of Cyril's Christology by Harnack, *D. G.*, iv. 174-180.
[2] *Ep. dogmatica ad Nestor.*
[3] ἴδιον, a word used with obvious emphasis by Cyril in the anathemas
against Nestorius.
[4] *De Incarn. Domini*, xxvii.
[5] As to whether monophysitism should be imputed to Cyril, see Harnack,
iii. 178, and Loofs, *Leit-faden* [4], pp. 293 f.
[6] Foley (*op. cit.*, p. 69) on *de adorat. in Sp. et ver.* (*P. G.*, lxxviii. col.
296).
[7] *P. G.*, lxxvi. col. 1344.
[8] *Op. cit.*, p. 103. Thomasius (p. 408) holds that not even the reference to
God's righteousness is absent, since the curse was that ' which the *divine law*
pronounces against transgressors.'

not less necessarily did one aspect of the Cross reveal itself more clearly. Very seriously does Cyril take the words of Ignatius three centuries earlier, ' The Passion of my God.' There can, of course, be no question of the importance he attaches to the Incarnation in itself, when, in the humanity of Christ, human nature as a whole was transfigured and deified : yet the Incarnation is not for him itself the Atonement. What M. Rivière says of one passage in his works may be given a wider reference : ' The strictest notion of the atoning death can keep its place side by side of the broadest speculation as to the benefits of the Incarnation.' [1]

From Cyril of Alexandria to John of Damascus the history of doctrine in the East is concerned with the subtleties of the monophysite and monothelite contro- versies, the real issues involved being often almost smothered in endless logomachies. Soteriology, in parti- cular, was not advanced, though the case of Petrus Fullo, monophysite Patriarch of Antioch, who propounded the Trisagion, ' Holy God, Holy the Strong one, Holy the Immortal one, who was crucified for us,' and the more moderate formula of the Scythian monks in 518, ' One of the Trinity was crucified—suffered in the flesh,' approved in the fifth General Council of 553 in the yet more moderate form, ' Our Lord Jesus Christ, who was crucified in the flesh, is true God and Lord of Glory, and One of the Holy Trinity,' show an anxiety to secure a divine value for Christ's sufferings and death—but more as a means of precluding anything in the nature of a Nestorian Christology than as an end in itself. Yet it must be remembered that the more insistence was laid by monophysites and dominant Eastern thought as a whole upon the deification of humanity through the human nature assumed by the Son, the more necessary was it to find an adequate explanation of the

[1] *Op. cit.*, p. 201. Dr. Foley's judgment on Cyril is that he ' may be regarded as evidencing the deterioration in thought and language of the Greek Fathers of the fifth century ' (p. 70).

death on the Cross, since the idea of it as an example was altogether too rationalistic. Similarly, though from a different standpoint, in earlier times Antiochenes, who were inclined to uphold the exemplary value of Christ's human experiences, and had no sympathy with the mystical tendencies of Alexandria, found it necessary to do justice to Scriptural testimony concerning Christ's death, which their literal principles of exegesis forbade them to explain away, but which undoubtedly presented the Cross as something other than even the most stupendous object-lesson.[1]

Greek patristic thought culminates in John of Damascus, ' the teacher of scholasticism for the after-centuries of the Greek Church.'[2] He devotes no particular attention to the Atonement ; he does not formulate an orthodox doctrine. But views that we have met before all appear in his works, while he himself regards the death of Christ as a sacrifice offered on our behalf and in our stead to the Father against whom we had sinned, for ' it was necessary that He should receive the ransom on our behalf, and so we should be freed from condemnation : God forbid that the Lord's blood should be offered to the devil.'[3] Writing on the Epistle to the Ephesians [4] he speaks of the cause of grace being the goodness of God, the way into it redemption

[1] Cf. Theodoret on Isaiah liii. 5, 'We, having sinned, were exposed to punishments ; but He . . . endured them on our behalf.' Baur's remarks on the connexions of Nestorianism and Monophysitism with soteriology are interesting, 'The more the Nestorian separation of the two natures allowed the human element to have its rights, thereby assuring actual reality to the sufferings and death, the more doubtful did it make the divine-human significance of the same ; while the more the monophysitic unity of the natures, to which the orthodox theory approximated, established the objective significance of the infinite work of the sufferings and death, the more doubtful was the actual reality of the same bound to become, and the docetism which affected the whole theory showed with special prominence at this point' (p. 105). Recent investigation has put out of court confident statements as to what 'Nestorianism' did or did not involve, but the Aphthartodoketae, 'whose point of view was determined solely by the thought of redemption' (Harnack, iv. 237), are good evidence for Baur's final remarks.

[2] Loofs, *op. cit.*, p. 323.

[3] *De Fide Orth.*, iii. 27 ; cf. *P. G.*, xcv. col. 1004, 'Men were to be punished for their sins, but instead of them He gave His own Son.'

[4] *P. G.*, xcv. col. 821.

through the blood of Christ. Exactly like Chrysostom he compares Christ's action to an innocent man's readiness to step into the place of one condemned to die.[1] Less specifically, but in full agreement with his predecessors, he views the object of the Incarnation as the restoration of humanity after the image of God, the teaching of and provision for a virtuous life, liberation from corruption by the resurrection, and the call to knowledge of God.[2]

When we turn West, we shall find ourselves in a world of very different premises and conceptions. But our necessarily brief study of some of the greatest Greek Fathers may perhaps have shown the fallacy of supposing either that there is a 'Patristic Theory' of Ransom to Satan, especially dominant in the East, or that these theologians, considered as a whole, see in the death of Christ no other benefits for man than those already secured by His birth. Doubtless there is something in the cry 'Back to Greek Theology,' just as there is something—and more than that—in the cry 'Back to the Christ of the Gospels.' But those who raise such cries do not always understand what they involve.[3]

[1] *P. G.*, xcv. col. 796.   [2] *De Fide Orth.*, iv. 4.
[3] Modern Eastern Teaching on the Atonement may be seen in Question and Answer 208 in *The Longer Catechism of the Orthodox, Catholic, Eastern Church* (Schaff, *Creeds of the Greek and Latin Churches*). The question is, 'How does the death of Jesus Christ upon the Cross deliver us from sin, the curse, and death?' The answer first compares Christ with Adam. 'Adam is by nature the head of all mankind . . . Jesus Christ, in whom the Godhead is united with manhood, graciously made Himself the new almighty Head of men, whom He unites to Himself through faith. Therefore as in Adam we had fallen under sin, the curse, and death, so we are delivered from sin, the curse, and death in Jesus Christ.' To this Irenæan conception is attached a more definite view, 'His voluntary suffering and death on the Cross for us, being of infinite value and merit, as the death of one sinless, God and man in one person, is both a perfect satisfaction to the justice of God, which had condemned us for sin to death, and a fund of infinite merit, which has obtained Him the right, without prejudice to justice, to give us sinners pardon of our sins, and grace to have victory over sin and death.'

CHAPTER

THE ATONEMENT IN LATIN THEOLOGY

TERTULLIAN has won the title of ' Father of Latin Theology,' and, though he embraced the teachings of the ' new prophecy ' and became the great champion of Montanism, was held in reference as ' the Master ' by that fervent opponent of schism—Cyprian. But in neither of these two great African Fathers do we find anything like a philosophy of the Atonement, though in this as in many another department of theology words introduced by Tertullian were destined to have a far-reaching influence. Especially does this apply to the term *satisfactio*. His legal outlook naturally led him to emphasize the necessity of reparation when an offence had been committed, and he transferred the idea from law to theology. Only he applies it not to the work of Christ, but to repentance and good deeds.[1] In this he is followed by Cyprian.[2] Nevertheless, Tertullian lays great stress on Christ's death, more indeed than his contemporary Irenæus : denial of the reality of Christ's body means denial of ' the whole weight and fruit of the Christian faith (nomen)—the death of Christ.'[3] Christ was ' sent to die,'[4] and this death is sacrificial, springing from Christ's love and the Father's

---

[1] E.g. *De Poenitentia*, v., '*qui per delictorum poenitentiam instituerat Domino satisfacere.*'

[2] *de Lapsis*, xvii., ' *Dominus nostra satisfactione placandus est.*' Yet in the same chapter Cyprian says that He alone can forgive our sins, 'who bore our sins, who grieved for us, whom God delivered up for our sins.' Harnack (ii. 294, note) seems to be wrong in attributing to Cyprian the idea that Christ satisfied God. See note 3 on page 84 in Dr. Foley's book.

[3] *Adv. Marc.* iii. 8.   [4] *De Carne Christi*, vi.

will.[1] Only by His death could our death be destroyed.[2]
While, therefore, we are debarred from ascribing to
Tertullian later juridical theories, and it is even going too
far to speak of his conception as that of ' an expiation
provided by Jesus Christ dying for us,' [3] we cannot rule
out entirely from his meaning the idea of substitution.
and of Christ's death as determined by moral necessities,
whether real or imagined, and therefore not to be described
as simply object-lesson or self-sacrifice.

From Tertullian and Cyprian we may pass to Hilary
and Ambrose, for Arnobius and Lactantius who intervene
are no more representative in their soteriological outlook
than in other respects.[4] Hilary of Poictiers is especially
interesting. As the first Latin Father to interpret Greek
thought to the West, he shows himself influenced by the
typically Greek conception of the restoration of humanity
in the human nature of the Son of God. That nature had
a universal character,[5] and thereby there existed in Christ
' a purified body of the whole human race '; [6] this mystical
conception, together with his anti-Arian insistence on
Christ's Godhead, leads him at times dangerously near to
docetism ; like Clement of Alexandria he can say that
Christ needed not to eat and drink, but did so only to
refute docetic ideas by proving His body to be real,[7] and,
as Professor Gwatkin says of Clement, to refute them in
vain.[8] But this does not prevent Hilary from attaching
the most definite importance to Christ's death. The
Passion was voluntarily accepted to satisfy a penal

---

[1] *Adv. Jud.* xiii., xiv. ; *Scorp.* vii. ; *adv. Marc.* iii. 18. Of the curse in
Deut. xxi. 23 he speaks in *adv. Jud.* x. ; *adv. Marc.* v. 3 ; *adv. Prax.* xxix. ;
and interprets with strict reference to the law. To its curse He was
surrendered, and so made a curse for us, but no curse of God fell upon Him,
though in the passage against Marcion he speaks of the curse as God's own
(*sua*).

[2] *de Bapt.*, xi.   [3] Tixeront, *Histoire des Dogmes*, i. 344.

[4] They do not rise above the idea of Christ's death as a supreme example
of virtuous endurance. Arnob., *adv. Gentes*, i. 40 ; Lactantius, *Inst. div.*,
iv. 26.

[5] *Tract. in Psalm.* li. 16, '*naturam in se universae carnis assumpsit.*'

[6] *de Trin.*, ii. 24.   [7] *de. Trin.*, x. 23, 24.

[8] *Early Church History*, ii. 175.

necessity;[1] through Christ propitiation is made to God;[2] in His death we see a guiltless sufferer paying the penalty for sins He had not committed.[3]   Hilary thinks of Christ as expiating by His death sins for which others should have suffered ; so far, at least, a penal significance is ascribed to the Cross, though he has not gone so far as to see in it a satisfaction exacted by and rendered to God or God's attribute of justice.

Ambrose represents a very similar point of view, though with more pointed stress on the Cross as the means of man's salvation.[4]   Through it we gain remission of sins ; for this end Christ came.[5]   His death both satisfied and destroyed the penalty of death to which sinners were subject.[6]   When we owed our blood because of the bond of sin, Jesus came and offered His blood on our behalf.[7] Quite like one of the Greek Fathers, Ambrose connects redemption with the value of Christ's divine nature ; 'since the Son was above all He could offer Himself for all.'[8]   But Christ's humanity means more to him than to Hilary.   It is as man, the second Adam, that He succeeds where Adam fails ; there can be no change in the divine decrees, but there can be a change of person.[9]   Ambrose also speaks of 'sin' and 'our sins' being nailed to the Cross,[10] expressions which seem to refer to the guilt rather

[1] *In Psalm.* liii. 12, '*officio ipsa satisfactura poenali.*'   [2] *In Psalm.* lxiv. 4.
[3] *In Psalm.* lxviii. 8.   Hilary, later on in this section, introduces the idea of the devil's demands and defeat in a moderate form.   The devil had no right to put in force the law of death against the innocent author of life : so he is judged.
[4] Of rhetorical rather than dogmatic value is the statement, 'The tears of that infancy washed away my sins,' *in Luc.* ii. 41.
[5] *In Psalm.* xxxix. 17.
[6] *de fuga saeculi*, vii. 44, '*suscepit mortem ut impleretur sententia satisfieret iudicato.*'
[7] *de inst. virg.*, xix. 126.
[8] *In Luc.* vi. 10, cf. *in Psalm.* xlviii. 15, 'He alone reconciled the Father.'
[9] *In Luc.* iv. 7, '*ut . . . persona magis quam sententia mutaretur.*' Harnack (iii. 313) calls this 'the genuine idea of substitution.'   This is true since the representative character of Christ's humanity is not suggested.   It is strange that Harnack thinks it bold of Ambrose to say that 'because He took our sins He was called sin.'
[10] *de Poen.*, i. 3, 13 ; *Ep.* lxiii. 112.

than the power of sin ; though at a time when our distinctions were not worked out, the destruction or crucifixion
of sin implied that in every respect sin had lost power—
to bind for the future as well as to condemn for the past.

The student of doctrine, whatever be the object of his
researches, approaches Augustine with the expectation of
finding both richness of material and definiteness of
conclusion. Yet on the subject of atonement he has
exercised no special influence. It can truly be said of his
soteriology, what would be a flagrant contradiction of the
facts in connexion with the doctrine of the Trinity or
anthropology, that his view ' is essentially that of the
Fathers who had preceded him ; neither falling short, nor
making any marked advance, in scientific respects.' [1]   He
has devoted no single treatise to the question, so that in
his case as in that of other Fathers we have to rely mainly
on incidental references ; but in the thirteenth book of his
work *De Trinitate* there is something like a formal present-
ment of his opinion. He begins by arguing that the
Incarnation—with its outcome in the death on the Cross—
was not the only, but the fittest, method of healing human
misery and conferring immortality. He goes on to speak
of God's gifts as depending on no merits of ours, and to
ask the meaning of ' justified in His blood ' and ' reconciled
through the death of His Son.' Relying on Romans viii.
31 f., he concludes that God the Father's love for men
preceded, and was not the result of, the Son's death ; also,
we must think of the Son as of His own free will giving
Himself for men. For an interpretation of these phrases,
Augustine starts from one aspect of the Fall. Though
man then did not cease to belong to God, yet God justly
allowed him to fall into the power of the devil. How then
was he to be saved from the devil and reconciled to God ?
An act of power was possible, but power should come
second to justice. Accordingly, not by power but by the
righteousness of Christ was the victory won. The devil

[1] Shedd, *op. cit.*, ii. 253.

over-stepped his rights when he killed Christ, though
unable to find in Him anything worthy of death ; ' and
so it is just that the debtors in the devil's power should
go free, believing on Him whom the devil slew, though
owed nothing by Him.' Augustine then shows that it
was necessary for Christ to be both God and man, man in
order to die, God to have been able not to die and so to
make the death an act of free choice. The divine power
which succeeds the divine justice was shown in the
resurrection.[1]

Thus Augustine's doctrine, like Origen's, is conditioned
by his view of the devil's rights.[2] But along with this he
can think of Christ's death as a sacrifice to God and an
expiation of guilt, and of Christ as man's substitute, though,
according to Dr. Loofs,[3] he has never used the word *satisfactio* of the work of Christ. In the *Enchiridion*, the
important work which contains Augustine's interpretation
of the creed, the need of a mediator who can offer a
unique sacrifice and thereby appease God's just wrath
against sin is distinctly asserted, and we are further told
that God made Christ sin, that is a sacrifice for sin, ' through
which we could be reconciled.' [4] With this may be compared a chapter in the *De Trinitate*,[5] where Christ is shown
to be the perfect victim, ' since in every sacrifice four
things have to be considered—what is the offering, and to
whom, by whom, and for whom it is made. So He is the
one true Mediator, reconciling us to God by the sacrifice
of peace, remaining one with Him to whom He made the
offering, making one in Himself those for whom He offered,
Himself alike offerer and sacrifice.' Elsewhere, the penal
significance of Christ's death is brought out. Every sin

---

[1] *de Trin.*, xiii. 10-15. The same argument appears in *de lib. arbitrio*. x.

[2] No '*pia fraus*' is attributed to God in Augustine's statement. Ambrose,
on the other hand, allows this, though it is not quite clear in what the fraud
consists—probably in Christ's mortal body being that of an immortal Person
(*in Luc.* iv. 12, 16). He also seems to think that the devil had some right
to the blood of Jesus, for he says (*Ep.* lxxii. 8), 'The blood of Jesus had to be
paid to him to whom we had been sold by our sins.'

[3] *Op. cit.*, p. 400.   [4] *Ench.*, xxxiii., xli.   [5] iv. 14.

is accursed, and death is the penalty of sin. 'Let him' says Augustine, 'deny that Christ was accursed who denies that He died.' The explanation is that 'Christ took our punishment without guilt that He might thereby do away with our guilt and end our punishment.' 'He is ever blessed in His own righteousness, but accursed because of our sins in the death that He submitted to because it was our punishment.' [1] There was a debt to pay, and an expiation to make; Christ does voluntarily for us, and we must also say instead of us, what we ought to have done.[2] The office of Mediator, on which Augustine lays such stress, is combined with the thought that Christ must be man, and mediate as man: 'In so far as He is man He is Mediator, but in so far as He is the Word He is not Mediator.' [3] Nor are the mystical ideas of the Greeks absent from his writings: the Word by sharing in our mortality made us to share in His divinity.[4] One feels that had the occasion of a great controversy been present, Augustine might have anticipated Anselm, and given to Western Christendom such a synthesis of all the various elements of his thought as would have constituted an authoritative soteriology; but the battle with Pelagianism, though really involving questions of vital moment in connexion with the value and effects of the death of Christ, concentrated on other points; while even if, as M. Rivière contends,[5] he succeeded not in adopting but in adapting the widespread theory of a ransom to the devil, he is also a witness to the necessity for a complete discarding of the theory if soteriology was not to be continually estopped from its true line of advance by the introduction of irrelevant considerations.

Of the numerous contemporary and later theologians who owed themselves in large measure to Augustine, only one or two of the more famous need be noticed. Leo the

---

[1] *contra Faustum Manich.*, **xiv. 3-7.**

[2] Cf. *in Psalm.* lxi. 22, 'The blood of a just one was needed to wipe out the handwriting of sin.'

[3] *Confess.*, **x. 68.**   [4] *de Trin.*, iv. 2.   [5] *Op. cit.*, p. 408.

Great makes many allusions to the devil, his relative rights and his loss of them through his injustice in killing Christ.[1] Though he thinks of the devil as not recognising the Son of God beneath the veil of flesh, and so as deceived there is much less crudity in his exposition than in the metaphor of the bait of the flesh and the hook of divinity employed by Rufinus [2] and Gregory the Great.[3] He also makes use of ideas of sacrifice and propitiation. Christ ' offered Himself to the Father as the new and true sacrifice of reconciliation ' ; [4] the Son makes propitiation, the Father is propitiated.[5] It is on Christ's work as man that he insists ; if the devil's kingdom over man was to be overthrown, it was only right that this should be done by man ; [6] similarly, if God was to become gracious again to humanity there was needed a Mediator between God and man to plead the cause of all men.[7] Of mystical ideas of the transformation of humanity through the Incarnation there is no lack ; thereby humanity is brought back to a new beginning ; [8] in Him all died and rose again.[9] More definite in the expression of his views is that other great Pope of the first six centuries—Gregory I. The Godward aspect of Christ's death is clearly indicated by him. In one passage we are given what has legitimately been called ' the completest synthesis of [ancient] Latin theology on the Atonement.' [10] Man of his own choice passed under the dominion of the devil and death ; only a sacrifice could blot out such a sin, but what sacrifice could be found ? An animal could not serve as a true sacrifice for man endowed with reason, and no man, though a man was needed, could be found without sin. Therefore the Son of God was incarnate : ' He took our

[1] E.g. *Serm.* lx. 3, '*antiquae fraudis iura non perderet, si se a Domini Jesu sanguine contineret.*'

[2] *In symb. apost.*, xiv.-xvii.   [3] *Moralia*, xxxiii. 7.
[4] *Serm.* lix. 5.   [5] *Serm.* lxxvii. 2.
[6] *Serm.* xxii. 3.   [7] *Epist.* clxv. 4.
[8] *Serm.* xxii. 5; cf. Paulinus of Nola on harmony of human nature resulting from Christ's destruction of sin (*Ep.* xii. 6).
[9] *Serm.* liv. 3.   [10] Rivière, *op. cit.*, p. 276.

nature, not our sinfulness; He made sacrifice for us, giving
His body a victim free from all sin for sinners, a victim
that could die in virtue of humanity and cleanse in virtue
of righteousness. . . . He paid for us a debt of death
which He had not deserved, that the death which was
our due might not harm us.' [1] Certainly, Dr. Shedd had
no business to translate *sacrificium* 'penal offering to
justice,' [2] but Dr. Foley's protest cannot be so extended
as to eradicate from Gregory's writings a doctrine which,
without implying that Christ was punished, is, nevertheless,
a doctrine of substitution, and of the enduring of that
which in the case of men would have been punishment.[3]
Gregory's concern with the problems of sin, guilt, and
redemption leads him to an appreciation of the expiatory
value of the Cross, with which other elements of his
theology may indeed clash, yet do not overthrow it.

The five centuries which separate Gregory from Anselm
were not of a character to promote theological learning
and penetrating thought. The only writer of outstanding
genius to illuminate these dark ages was John Scotus
Erigena—though to ascribe to his works the quality of
illumination is scarcely correct. But soteriology is not
a chief concern of his, at least in reference to the death
of Christ, for his system as a whole might be described
as a mystical soteriology, inclining towards pantheism.
When he does refer to the Cross he expresses himself in
more ordinary fashion than might have been expected.[4]

If any one Christian work, outside the canon of the
New Testament, may be described as 'epoch-making,' it
is the *Cur Deus Homo* of Anselm. It has affected, though
in different degrees, and by way now of attraction, now
of repulsion, all soteriological thought since his time; while

---

[1] *Moralia*, xvii. 30.   [2] *Op. cit.*, ii. 263.
[3] Cf. *Moralia*, xiii. 30, 'Our Redeemer . . . bore the punishment of our sin,
Himself sinless.' Harnack, in his account of Gregory's doctrine (v. 263 ff.),
makes too much of what may be a 'candid,' but is none the less a merely
formal, 'avowal that the death of Christ was not absolutely necessary.'
[4] See the references given by Rivière (p. 287), who, however, seems to
exaggerate Erigena's *réalisme*.

I

opinions of the work itself vary from Professor Denney's tribute to it as ' the truest and greatest book on the atonement that has ever been written ' [1] to Harnack's judgment ' no theory so bad had ever before his day been given out as ecclesiastical,' [2] and Dr. Stevens' severe words ' it would be difficult to name any prominent treatise on atonement, whose conception of sin is so essentially unethical and superficial.' [3]

A brief account of the arguments and conclusions of the treatise may now be given.[4] The form is that of dialogue, in which Boso, the pupil representing people with difficulties, or even unbelievers, asks questions—not always with the rigour of the Socratic Elenchus, and Anselm the master answers.

Why has God assumed the weakness of human nature ? To retrieve by man's obedience the life which had been lost through disobedience. The deliverance which thereby results must be the work of God, or man will belong to an undivine Redeemer and not to God. But could not God have redeemed as He created by a word, especially as we must entirely discard all ideas of ransom or satisfaction to be made to the devil ? Moreover, even if Christ died freely in the cause of righteousness, was it right that He should die ? Here Anselm changes the form of the discussion ; he puts revelation on one side, and starts from the agreed principle that man was made for blessedness, but cannot attain to it unless his sins are forgiven. What then is sin ? Not to pay to God what is owed to Him. Now this does God dishonour, so that when payment is made, over and above the actual debt, something more

---

[1] *The Atonement and the Modern Mind*, p. 116.   [2] vi. 78.
[3] *The Christian Doctrine of Salvation*, p. 242.
[4] All histories of dogma and treatises on the Atonement pay attention to Anselm. Special reference may be made to Shedd (ii. 273-286), who is highly favourable ; Foley, *Anselm's Theory*, a book with which I find myself often disagreeing, but which is undoubtedly a valuable contribution to the subject ; and J. S. Lidgett (*op. cit.*, 132-139), whose discussion is singularly sane and balanced. Harnack's lengthy review is unduly subtle and tries to prove too much, and Rivière is over-concerned with making points against Harnack.

must be given as a satisfaction. But if this is not done God will punish ; to forgive unatoned sin would be unjust, and though God is free and subject to no law He will not do something that conflicts with His dignity ; we, on the other hand, are told to forgive, because it is not our right to take vengeance.

God, therefore, cannot let an offence against His honour go unpunished if no reparation is made. It is true that no dishonour can really affect God, but as far as rests with him the sinner takes away God's honour. Now punishment gives God honour by proving the sinner's subjection to God. And so ' it is necessary that every sin should be followed by satisfaction or punishment' (i. 15).

Then, after some discussion to show that from among men are to be replaced the fallen angels, though more men will be saved than angels perished, Boso is led to see that man cannot make satisfaction for sin. Everything good is owed to God ; therefore nothing can serve as compensation. Moreover, even if good works were not owed they would be useless. For since the smallest sin, as an act committed against the infinite God, outweighs the whole world and all that is not God, the amends must be proportionate. Such amends are beyond men's power. One or two further considerations bring us to this conclusion at the end of the first book, that reason shows how impossible man's salvation is, since he cannot pay what he must. And yet that will mean a thwarting of God's purposes, since beatitude was that for which God made man, and no man can attain to it.

The second book begins with a reiteration of the statement that man was made to enjoy God. Then, after an exposition of the meaning of necessity in relation to God, we are brought back to the thought of the value of the reparation to be made for sin. Clearly, as sin outweighs everything that is not God, the gift made to God in compensation must transcend in value all that is not God.

But such a gift, surpassing all that is not God, can only be God. Therefore, God alone can make reparation ; but as the reparation must be made by man, God must become man, and God the Word—for it is most reasonable that it should be He—be united with humanity in One Person. Now of the God-man obedience could be required, for obedience is the supreme duty of man towards God ; but not death, since death is the penalty of sin, and in virtue of His own nature, and not of compulsion, He could not will to sin, and therefore could not sin. So when He dies He surrenders His life as a debt that is not due ; it is a gift surpassing in value all that is not God, and therefore more than a compensation for all sins. Such a free gift must in justice be rewarded ; but there is nothing which the Father can give the Son for Himself ; hence, what is due to the Son is by Him, with the Father's good pleasure, passed on to men, and takes the form of forgiveness of sins and future beatitude, if men live according to the commandments of the Gospel. Thus, in the end, justice and mercy, which once seemed to be separated by a great gulf, are found to be harmonious, and even those who committed what is, strictly speaking, the ' infinite ' sin of slaying Christ can be forgiven, because they did it in ignorance.[1]

It is well to note one or two salient facts about the *Cur Deus Homo* before any attempt at appreciation is made. Negatively, the outspoken repudiation of any rights of the devil is enough to mark a turning-point for Latin thought ; positively, ' the necessity for the death of Christ becomes for the first time absolute . . . as a satisfaction to God.' [2] We cannot but perceive, in the working out of the theory, the influence of contemporary feudal ideas as to the relation of king and subject, together

[1] In this short résumé the exact order has not always been kept, but, as far as possible, justice has been done to the vital moments in the discussion. In the second book, after the rational necessity for the appearance of the God-man is reached, reference is freely made to the facts of revelation.

[2] Oxenham, *Catholic Doctrine of the Atonement*, p. 171.

with juridical conceptions drawn from the customs of Germanic law and the penitential system of Latin theology.[1] And further, whatever be thought of its value, the doctrine is not one of vicarious punishment, and to that extent differs widely from some later notions.[2]

The outstanding merit of the theory is its sense of the seriousness of sin and its issue in guilt. This is true, however inadequate the actual concept of sin may be. And this inadequacy may be unduly pressed. There is truth in M. Rivière's contention that the juridical formulæ are but a clothing, ' a more rigorous expression of high moral realities.' [3] Further, the insistence upon guilt and upon the need of forgiveness is an ethical advance as compared with the Patristic stress upon death, and upon the necessity for the almost physical antidote of deification.[4] Nor should the self-sacrifice predicated of God be lost sight of as by Baur when he ascribes the atonement simply to an inner necessity of God's nature, and as not wrought for man's sake.[5] Undoubtedly, Anselm's feeling that God's purpose in creating man cannot be overturned greatly obscures the element of self-sacrifice, but chapter twenty of the second book points in another direction, to a free grace and mercy which must arouse gratitude.[6]

[1] Ritschl, in his discussion, exaggerated the Germanic element as is made clear by Harnack (iii. 311, vi. 57) and by Loofs, who speaks (p. 511) of Anselm's theory as ' an appraisement of the work of Christ with conceptions drawn from the doctrine of penance.' The antithesis *aut satisfactio aut poena* goes back, almost verbally, to Tertullian and Sulpicius Severus.

[2] Harnack criticises it on this account, among others, ' In the idea that sin can be compensated for by something else than penalty, there lies an under-estimate of its gravity that is extremely objectionable' (vi. 69). Rivière (p. 310) tries, not very successfully, to preserve the penal notion, since satisfaction as a painful work is itself a penalty, and in Christ's case can only be the penalty of our sins.

[3] *Op. cit.*, p. 313.

[4] Cf. Thomasius, *D. G.*[2], ii. 114, ' His significance consists in his viewing the whole work of atonement from the standpoint of guilt, and attempting to explain it from that, while his predecessors had reflected on the consequences of sin—death and the curse—and so had regarded redemption as liberation from death.'

[5] *Op. cit.*, p. 170.

[6] Dr. Shedd (ii. 284) speaks of the compassion of God as seen ' in its most tender, because its only *self-sacrificing*, form.'

It is no small part of Anselm's heritage to us that he has given us the thought which, even if not thoroughly ethicised by him, has all the promise of a rich moral interpretation, that the redemption of man is a work which none save God can do, and that its achievement taxes God Himself.

On the other hand, the defects are not small. The internal inconsistencies have been made too much of by some writers, but there are two which cannot be passed over in silence. There is no clear expression of the relation between God's honour which must be vindicated, and God's justice which necessarily punishes unatoned sin. And if, as seems to be the case, God's honour is the primary consideration, it is not obvious why repentance should not be accepted as a satisfaction to that honour. Secondly, the idea of forgiveness though prominent as a need in Book I. is ultimately deprived of all relevance ; a satisfaction which more than pays a debt that is owed leaves no room for forgiveness on the part of the Creditor. God the Father does not forgive men ; He pays them a great reward because the Son wishes it, and as the Son's just due it cannot be refused Him.[1]

Besides such not unimportant lacunæ there are four grave faults. In the first place, God the Father and God the Son represent, in the main body of the work,[2] almost to the point of sheer dualism, different moral qualities, justice and love or mercy ; the theological and moral weakness of this needs no explanation. Secondly, the problem of sin is conceived of, and its solution determined, in so external a way that the adjectives 'commercial' and 'mathematical' are fairly applied to it.[3]   There is

---

[1] Cf. Foley, p. 165, who quotes the frank admission of the Calvinist theologian, Dr. Charles Hodge, 'It is a simple matter of commutative justice, a *quid pro quo*.' In i. 19 Anselm teaches that the prayer for forgiveness is part of what is due from man, and indicates man's submissiveness to God.

[2] ii. 20 brings the Father and the Son together, but it is not enough to correct the main idea.

[3] Dr. Moberly (*op. cit.*, pp. 370 f.) says, 'The problem caused by sin is exhibited as if it were a faulty equation, which by fresh balancing of quan-

a perfectly sound moral force in Anselm's idea of debt,
but if this idea is treated as exhausting the meaning of
sin—and except in i. 23 Anselm comes very near to so
doing—then sin must tend to be regarded quantitatively
rather than qualitatively, with most unfortunate results.
Thirdly, and in close connexion with the last objection,
though men are called Christ's ' kindred and brethren,'
there is no inner relationship between Christ and them
despite Ritschl's subtle argument that such a relationship
is indicated by the idea of the merit of Christ's act, in
which merit His followers share, though not by the
idea of satisfaction.[1] And, fourthly, the rational method
employed, though defensible for purposes of apologetic,
entails the construction of a dogmatic edifice built up in
complete independence of Holy Scripture, so much so
that the only important use of Holy Scripture is for Boso
to raise objections which Anselm answers by purely
rational considerations.[2] So we have sin as debt, and
atonement as satisfaction, which more than covers the
debt. These are conceptions which do not misrepresent
Scripture, but by no means do it full justice.[3]

Anselm's theory preserved a particular significance
for the death of Christ, which, while it ceased to be a
ransom to the devil, was looked upon as influential with
God.[4] His work revived interest in soteriology in the

tities is to be equated aright,' and of the solution, ' Nothing could be more
simply arithmetical, or more essentially unreal.'

[1] *Op. cit.*, p. 33 (E.T.). Dr. Lidgett truly says (p. 138), ' The sense of
solidarity between Him and those He represents is well-nigh destroyed.'

[2] *E.g.* i. 8-10, 12, 19.

[3] A translation of the *Cur Deus Homo*, and of some of the letters, is published by Grant, Edinburgh, 1909. Rivière quotes from the prayers and
meditations passages which deserve study alongside of the greater work.
There is in them much of that religious feeling which the dialectics of rational
theology forbid. The beautiful admonition to a dying man who fears too
much because of his sins (Migne, *P. L.*, clvii. 686) should be read by all who
would gain an insight into St. Anselm's heart.

[4] That Christ's death influences, and indeed changes God's conduct towards
men, is so manifest that it is surprising that Anselm's formal notion that God
cannot really be dishonoured should have brought Dr. Simon (*The Redemption of Man*, p. 58) to the paradoxical conclusion that Anselm's conception
of the influence or action of the work of Christ ' is not properly objective.'

early days of scholasticism, and though it is impossible
to describe the views of all the writers who fall within this
period, the opinions of the more eminent must be indicated.

The argument of the *Cur Deus Homo* did not at once
carry all before it, and, as we shall see, when the notion
of *satisfactio* as supremely regulative for the death of
Christ was accepted, its full rigour was reduced. But
first there must be noticed a doctrine widely different
from Anselm's and of little consequence in the days when
it was propounded, both on account of its own character
and of the suspicions which gathered round all the work
of its author : its vitality and attractiveness were left
for future ages to disclose. It is in his commentary on
Romans that Abelard develops his theory that Christ
died, neither because a ransom had to be paid to the devil,
nor because the blood of an innocent victim was needed
to appease the wrath of God, but that a supreme exhibition
of love might kindle a corresponding love in men's hearts,
and inspire them with the true freedom of sonship to
God.[1] In accordance with this, Abelard elsewhere views
the purpose of the Incarnation as the instruction of men
by the preaching of the Incarnate Wisdom, and the example
of His earthly life.[2] All that is left of the Anselmic scheme
is the thought of Christ's merit reckoned to us on account
of His continuous intercession.[3]

We find indications of other points of view in other
parts of Abelard's works,[4] but there can be no doubt that
the moral, or perhaps we should say the emotional,[5]
influence of the Cross is his real interest. Appreciation

---

[1] *P. L.*, clxxviii. 833-836.

[2] *Theologia Christiana*, Pl. clxxviii. 1278.

[3] But the idea of merit has changed. For Anselm merit is what Christ has
to dispense because of the superabundance of His satisfaction ; for Abelard,
'Christ's merit is His service of love' (Harnack, vi. 79), and its fruit is
simply responsive love.

[4] In the twelfth sermon the notion of vicarious penalty is strongly expressed,
while in his retractations he says that Christ died to deliver us from the yoke
of the devil.

[5] As Dr. Moberly points out in his sympathetic exposition (pp. 372 ff.), the
Cross is too much of an exhibition.

of this aspect of Christ's death was needed as a counter-weight to the somewhat forbidding dialectics which fortify Anselm's treatise, and Abelard did most valuable service in proclaiming love as the motive, method, and result of God's work of reconciliation.   But as an answer to the question, Why was it necessary that Christ should die ? Abelard's argument must be pronounced quite uncon-vincing ; and as the love of Christ is brought into no real relationship with human sin and guilt, there is a certain superficiality of treatment even in connexion with this leading idea.[1]

Bernard of Clairvaux, though he attacked Abelard both for his rationalistic spirit and for his particular conclusions, never adopted the soteriology of Anselm. He neither gave up in its entirety the idea of ransom from the devil,[2] nor did he make use of the conception of *satisfactio*.   On the other hand, his mystical tendencies, strikingly manifested in his commentary on the Song of Songs, led him to lay stress on the love revealed in Christ's redemptive work, and on the union between Christ the Head and His members.[3]   But Bernard is not really anxious to arrive at a theory.   In the letter to Innocent II. (*Ep.* 190), which is a lengthy treatise concerning Abelard's errors, the piety which accepts a fact, but is not careful to explore its meaning, is in possession of the field.   Yet one phrase of Bernard's has lived : *non mors sed voluntas placuit sponte morientis*—it was not the death that was

---

[1] Cf. Harnack (vi. 79), 'He has not clearly perceived that *that love* is the highest . . . which, by taking the *penalty* upon itself, reveals at the same time the greatness of the absolution *and the greatness of the cancelled guilt.*'

[2] Bernard did not go even as far as Augustine in recognising 'rights' of the devil, but he allowed that the devil had a dominion over men, which was a just penalty for men's sins.

[3] This should be borne in mind as against Harnack's assertion that Bernard incautiously emphasized the example of Christ (vi. 80).   Of Bernard's difference from Anselm Dr. Shedd (ii. 291) says, 'Anselm was a metaphysician, and could not stop until he had traced back his faith to the eternal and necessary principles of the divine nature and government, while Bernard could hold the doctrine at a middle position, without subjecting it to the rigorous tests and conclusions of science, to whose methods he was somewhat disinclined, from his mystical tendency.'

well-pleasing, but the will of Him who died of His own accord.

Anselm's influence is, however, apparent in the writings of the two theologians of the school of St. Victor—Hugo and Richard. Both conceive of Christ's work as satisfaction, while conjoining with that the idea of penalty. But like the earlier Fathers and the greatest of the Schoolmen they teach, in opposition to Anselm, that God could have redeemed man by other means, while they approach Abelard in arguing that the method chosen was best because it afforded the highest example of humility and love.[1] Peter Lombard, the Master of the Sentences, brings together all preceding conceptions of the Atonement, with the single important exception of the theory of satisfaction. Abelard's influence is clearly seen in one passage ; since, by the death of God's Son for us,' a pledge of such mighty love toward us has been shown, we also are moved and kindled to love God.'[2] But the Lombard has no unified doctrine. Penal and sacrificial notions are found along with ransom from the devil through the ' mouse trap ' of the Cross, an old metaphor of Augustine's. Though he says nothing of satisfaction, he says much of the merit of Christ's death ;[3] by no other offering could we have been saved, though that does not imply that no other way of salvation was possible for God. Like Hugo of St. Victor he clearly defines God's work of reconciliation as the effect, not the cause, of His love.[4] The great theologians of the thirteenth century make use of the materials provided by his labours to construct a definitive soteriology, after the manner of Anselm, but with some important alterations of his guiding principles. Alexander of Hales closely follows Anselm in his doctrine of the supremacy of the attribute of justice in God, and of the impossibility

---

[1] *P. L.*, clxxvi. 306-312 ; cxcvi. 1002-5.   [2] *Sent.*, iii. ; *Dist.*, 19. 1.
[3] In connexion with the idea of merit the whole of His life comes into view (*Sent.*, iii. ; *Dist.*, 18. 2).
[4] Hugo put this epigrammatically, 'non quia reconciliavit amavit sed quia amavit reconciliavit ' ; for Peter see *Sent.*, iii. ; *Dist.*, 19. 6.

of satisfaction except through the passion of a God-man ; on the other hand, the necessity for the redemption of mankind is less clear in him than in Anselm.[1] His great pupil, Bonaventure, decides this question in the negative ; it was fit rather than necessary that man should be restored ; the method of satisfaction was the fittest though not the only available one ; such satisfaction was beyond the power of any save a God-man. But the Death of Christ was not necessary to such satisfaction ; Bonaventure, in fact, does not bring the need of satisfaction and the fact of the Passion into intimate correspondence, but falls back, in connexion with the latter, on the thought of penalty and on the influence of so great a proof of love.[2]

Scholasticism reached its climax in the *Summa Theologica* of Thomas Aquinas, and the conclusions which he reached in soteriology have held their ground in Roman Catholic theology as supplying the true rationale of the Atonement. He treats of it in the third part of the *Summa, Quaestio* i. and *Quaestiones* xlvi.-xlix. ; also in his commentary on the Sentences. His teaching may be summarised as follows : fallen man could have been allowed to die in his sins, therefore there was no absolute necessity for redemption to take place ; but, as most fitting, whichever of the divine attributes was considered, God determined to redeem man. This He could have done without demanding an adequate satisfaction or any satisfaction at all, since as Supreme Judge He was able, without any injustice, to remit sins committed against Himself. But as God decided that adequate satisfaction should be made the Incarnation became necessary, for sin which possessed ' a certain infinity from the infinity

---

[1] See the passages in Rivière, pp. 361 ff.
[2] Bonaventure's soteriology is found in his commentary on Peter Lombard's Sentences. Dr. Shedd (i. 292-304) gives a long account of his position. The departure from Anselm is seen in Bonaventure's words, ' We could have been liberated by the way of mercy, nor thereby would God's justice have been prejudiced had He willed so to act. For He could have blotted out all demerits and restored man . . . and nothing in the universe would have remained unordered or unpunished.'

of the divine majesty' could not be atoned for by man, but only by a God-man. Therefore the Son of God was incarnate, and Thomas like Bonaventure inclines to the view of Athanasius and Augustine, that if there had been no sin there would have been no Incarnation. But the Passion was not equally necessary; full satisfaction could have been made by Christ without it; nevertheless, it was the most suitable of all methods; the rights of justice and mercy were thereby harmonised, and the greatest possible effect was produced, since men could realise the greatness of the love of God, and possess the most perfect example of obedience, humility, constancy, and other virtues. In four ways does the Passion effect our salvation; by merit, since the merit which Christ acquired is rightly passed on to the members whose Head He is; by satisfaction, since by His loving and obedient sufferings Christ pleased God more than men's sins had displeased Him. So His Passion 'was not only a sufficient but even a superabundant satisfaction for the sins of mankind,' and that satisfaction is reckoned to all the faithful in virtue of their mystical unity with Christ. Thirdly, by sacrifice, for Christ's Passion was a true and voluntary sacrifice, most pleasing to God; fourthly, by redemption, since man, reduced to slavery by the devil, and liable to punishment according to God's righteousness, was liberated, by Christ's gift of Himself, from both conditions; this price was paid not to the devil, but to God, for the devil had no rights whatever to be considered; only God allowed him for a time to keep man a slave and to punish him. The reason why Christ's Passion, though a superabundant satisfaction, does not save absolutely apart from baptism and penance is found in the necessity for the 'configuration' of the members to the Head.[1]

Taken as a whole it is Anselm's doctrine less rigidly expressed. This, however, has not saved it from severe

---

[1] There is a good short account of Thomas's doctrine in Labauche, *Théologie Dogmatique*, i. pp. 334-338; to it I am much indebted.

criticism. On the contrary, he has been accused of pre-
paring the way for the rationalism of Duns Scotus, who in
the opinion of Ritschl [1] and Harnack [2] carried the admissions
of Aquinas to their logical conclusion. According to this
subtle thinker there was no necessity of any kind, apart
from the mere will of God, for atonement or satisfaction ;
nor was the Incarnation in any way necessary ; an angel
or a sinless man could have redeemed mankind had God
so willed. Everything is referred to the *acceptatio* of
God. 'Hence the value of Christ's death was as high as
God chose to rate it.' [3] One must agree with Dr. Dale
that the principles from which Duns started involved
'the degradation of the idea of the Atonement,' [4] but
one need not therefore follow those who look on this as
the natural outcome of the Thomist position. There is
a very great difference between the formal acknowledgment of Aquinas that God might have dispensed with
satisfaction and redeemed by a word, which in no way
conflicts with the excellent reasons he gives against such
a course of action, or rather in favour of a very different
one, and the conclusion grounded in the metaphysics of
Duns Scotus, that whatever has redeeming value has it
simply because of God's absolute, and, we must say,
unmoral will. It is possible, but not in the least necessary,
to make a dialectical passage from the one to the other,
and it is not even possible to deny that the actual differences of moral and religious values render the passage
undesirable as well as unnecessary, and also suggest that
whatever similarity there may be in the bases of the two

[1] *Op. cit.*, p. 59 (E.T.).
[2] vi. 196. Cf. Shedd (ii. 316), 'It would be difficult to see how the followers of Aquinas could in the end avoid the conclusions of Duns Scotus, if
they started from that doctrine of a *relative* necessity of satisfying justice,
which we have seen Aquinas held.'
[3] Harnack, vi. 196. Duns strongly opposed the idea of infinity of sin or
of merit. So his scheme, as Oxenham (*op. cit.*, p. 193) says, 'for an infinite
merit substitutes a voluntary acceptance, while the denial of an infinite debt
removes any plea for the necessity of an infinite satisfaction.'
[4] *The Atonement*, p. 286. For Scotus' theory see his commentary on the
Sentences, iii. ; *Dist.*, 19, 20.

schemes, the schemes themselves have been built up in such different ways that no true resemblance remains between the one finished product and the other.[1] Similarly we have heard, without being impressed, that the only logical outcome of Ritschlianism is Feuerbachianism.[2]

Thomas, apparently, does not keep to the Anselmic distinction *aut satisfactio aut poena*. Rather does he think of ' satisfaction by the legal penalty merited and duly borne,' [3] and so of penal expiation. But the idea of penalty is not prominent, and M. Rivière rightly speaks of the Passion as being to Thomas above all ' a sublime act of obedience and love.' [4] Certainly Thomas does not describe Christ's satisfaction as punishment in the plain words of Innocent III., who speaks of Christ's assumption of punishment as the mode whereby He might satisfy mercy and justice.[5]

The Council of Trent in its soteriology closely followed Aquinas. The ideas of merit and satisfaction were brought together in the statement that Christ merited justification for us, and by His most holy passion on the wood of the cross made satisfaction to God the Father.[6] At an earlier session His work had been viewed as reconciliation,[7] while

---

[1] What Thomasius (ii. 144) says most truly of the Scotist doctrine would be absurd if applied to the Thomist, 'The fact of atonement through the suffering and death of Christ is entirely removed from human understanding.'

[2] The New Testament so distinctly regards the Incarnation and the Passion as acts of free grace that there can be no doubt that Thomas is right as against Anselm in denying that the redemption which followed from these acts had any necessity consequent to the fact of sin. Therefore the only real objection which can be taken to his doctrine is that he admits the possibility of redemption without a *condigna satisfactio*. And this objection has weight only through the assumed possibility of first isolating the divine righteousness or justice from other attributes, and then laying down as irrefragable dogma what that justice must do or demand under a given state of things. Athanasius (*c. Ar.*, ii. 68), Cyril Al. (*De Incarn. Dominic.*, 18), and Augustine (*de Agone Christ.*, 11) are all Thomists on this point.

[3] Sabatier, *The Atonement*, p. 76 (E.T.). On the other hand, Harnack (vi. 193) writes, ' A vicarious penal suffering, in the strict sense of the terms, is not recognised by Thomas.'

[4] *Op. cit.*, p. 367.   [5] Quoted by Foley, p. 215.

[6] *Sess.*, vi. c. 7.

[7] *Sess.*, v. c. 3. Christ is the one Mediator, ' Who reconciled us to God in His blood.'

later it was to be presented as a sacrifice.[1] In modern
Roman Catholic theology the category of satisfaction is
still the most prominent, though the meritorious character
of Christ's death allows of a close connexion between it
and good works, the sacrificial aspect of an intimate
relationship with the Mass. Thus Father Pesch entitles
his first soteriological proposition *nulla erat necessitas
incarnationis nisi in suppositione satisfactionis condignae
pro peccato praestandae*,[2] and reasons from sin to satisfaction—though satisfaction could have been dispensed with
—and from that to the Incarnation with its climax, though
not absolutely necessary climax, in the Passion. Less
is made of the conception of penal substitution, but if
penalty is not linked up with satisfaction in such a way
that the latter is effected through the endurance of the
former, still less is there any thought of the latter excluding
the former by a strict application of *aut satisfactio aut
poena*.[3]

Despite our lack of sympathy, not always perfectly
informed, with Latin theology in its doctrine of the work
of Christ as the one means of human deliverance from the
power of the devil, and the sense of strangeness which
we cannot but feel when confronted by the subtleties,
dialectical rather than spiritual, with which the Schoolmen
adorned the notion of satisfaction, we ought to be able to
realise, underneath all this, the moral austerity and the
dependence upon God which are the foundations of the
whole western point of view. The Greek is by nature the
better theologian if by theology we mean the science which
aspires to speak of God as He is, and to pierce into the
mystery of the Trinity in Unity. But the Latin better
understands that other mystery, the secret of God's
noblest handiwork—man. And if Christianity is to be

---

[1] *Sess.*, xxii. *c.* 1. 'Our Lord on the altar of the cross . . . was about to
offer Himself to God the Father.'

[2] *Compendium Theol. Dogmat.*, iii. 61.

[3] The penal aspect is treated at length, and independently of satisfaction
and merit, by Professor Laminne in his treatise *La Rédemption*.

CHAPTER VI

REFORMATION AND POST-REFORMATION DOCTRINE

'However much Roman Catholics and Protestants differed as to the *causes* and *consequences* of Christ's death (sin and justification), they were in perfect accordance respecting its object.' [1] The Atonement, regarded as God's redemptive act in the death of Christ, was a belief held in common by both sides of the great sixteenth-century cleavage, though the Anselmic principle of satisfaction was made more drastic in the Lutheran and Reformed Churches by the penal interpretation attached to it; whereas the Schoolmen as a whole had shaken the coherence of Anselm's scheme by admitting that it had been in God's power to dispense with satisfaction, in which admission they were generally followed by later Roman Catholic theologians.[2] Yet the number and the extent of the differences of opinion on the Atonement, characteristic of later theological thought, can be traced directly to the Reformation both because of the prominence which the whole soteriological question then acquired, though at first with special reference to the application of Christ's work to men, and also as a result of that critical spirit which, though it did but rear its head in days when men rejected the authority of the mediæval Church in favour

[1] Hagenbach, *History of Doctrines*, iii. 210 (E.T.). He goes on to quote Baur (*op. cit.*, p. 344), 'It is the common doctrine of Protestants and Roman Catholics, that the sufferings or merits of Christ possess an infinite objective value.'

[2] *E.g.* Bellarmine, *De gratia et libero arbitrio*, ii. 9. The Lutheran theologian John Gerhard instances this as one of the errors whereby the 'Pontificii,' as he terms the Roman theologians, rendered the doctrine of Christ's atoning work insecure (*Loci Theol.*, xvii. 2, 54).

of the mightier authority of the Bible, was destined to
put to the most rigorous tests of inquiry, both scriptural
and rational, a doctrine which had not, like others, won its
way to precise form by a series of triumphs over dangerous
oppositions.   An exhaustive account of post-Reformation
soteriology would need a work on a vastly larger scale
than the present treatise.   All that I shall attempt to do
in this chapter is to describe briefly the doctrine of the
leaders of the Continental Reformation, the main points
in the criticism of Faustus Socinus and the answer of
Grotius, and to follow that up with some account of
individual theologians chosen either for their representative
character or for the originality and interest of their theories.
Where it is impossible to survey minutely the whole field,
the provision of an aperçu must suffice.[1]

The Reformers, says Ritschl,[2] ' made it their aim to
deduce the *absolute* unavoidable necessity of Christ's
satisfaction from that moral order of the universe, which
is *solidaire* with the essential will of God.'   True though
this is of the tendency of Protestant theology, and of the
systems of seventeenth-century scholastics such as Gerhard,
Quenstedt, and Turretin, it is too sweeping an assertion
when applied to the earlier Reformers ; while Calvin, far
the greatest theologian of them all, uses expressions which
recall Duns Scotus, whom he resembled in founding his
doctrine upon the thought of the sovereign will of God.   The
classical statement of Luther on the Atonement is found
in his commentary on Galatians iii. 13.[3]   There he insists
in highly rhetorical language that Christ was the greatest
of all sinners, ' because He assumed in His body the sins
we had committed, to make satisfaction for them by His
own blood.'   Though Luther does not shrink from supply-

---

[1] Far the best account of the work of American and English divines since
the Reformation is to be found in Dr. Stevens' *Christian Doctrine of
Salvation*, part ii.   The treatises of Dr. Lidgett and Dr. Foley are also
useful.

[2] *Recht. und Versöhn.*, i. 197 (E.T.).

[3] This is a work of the year 1535, not to be confused with the commentary
of 1519.

ing in Galatians iii. 13 the words St. Paul omits, and so boldly represents Christ as *maledictum Dei*, he attributes the coming of Christ to the compassion of the Father, who saw us oppressed by the law's curse. In this respect Luther has an advantage over Anselm, who does not indeed dispense with the thought of God's love for men but keeps it in the background.[1] That Luther gives very extreme expression to the idea of penal substitution cannot be denied, but for him it was a piece of religion, not merely of theology ; it was the way in which, relying on a literal exegesis of Scripture, he could realise most clearly the fact of forgiveness of sins through Christ. The word *Genugthuung*—satisfaction—he was prepared to dispense with altogether,[2] and his sense of the value of Christ's sufferings did not blind him to the value of Christ's life of active obedience ; he 'rather regards Christ's obedience to the law as the *genus* under which is included as a species His vicarious endurance of the curse of the law.'[3] Christ's obedient life could have no value in the Anselmic Soteriology, since it was but the payment of the due which, as man, He owed to God ; but Luther conceived of so close a union between the two natures in Christ that in his appreciation of the value of all that Christ did he passed outside the bounds of typical Latin thought.[4] Something less than justice has at times been done to the Reformers in this connexion, so that it is worth while to point out that their soteriology is not concentrated to such an extent upon Christ's death that His life ceases to have any redemptive value.[5] The idea of the imputation

[1] Ritschl (p. 201) thus describes the order of Luther's ideas, 'God's love as the ultimate motive of the Sinner's redemption is the superior determination of His will, while penal justice or wrath . . . is considered as the subordinate motive of His action in carrying out the work of redemption.'

[2] Quotation from the *Kirchenpostille* in Sabatier's work, p. 152. Yet Loofs (p. 778) says that his thought in general moved 'within the limits of the mediæval doctrine of satisfaction.'

[3] Ritschl, *op. cit.*, p. 210.

[4] Cf. Baur, p. 303.   Harnack (vii. 174) compares him to Cyril of Alexandria.

[5] Dr. Foley exaggerates the passive aspect when he writes (p. 216), 'The Reformation doctrine was chiefly, and tended to be exclusively, passive.' Calvin (*Inst.*, ii. 16. 5), while ascribing special importance to the death of

of Christ's righteousness to men should not be regarded as
simply the obverse of the imputation of men's sins to
Christ, but as expressing the importance and, indeed, the
necessity of Christ's active obedience ; since, as Quenstedt
says (de Christi Officio, xxxvii.), man needed, in order to
stand before God, not only freedom from God's wrath,
but also a righteousness ' which he could not gain except
through the fulfilment of the law. . . . So Christ satisfied
the law in all things, that this His fulfilling and obedience
might be reckoned to us for righteousness.'

Melanchthon devoted no special Locus to the question
of the Atonement, and Zwingli, while he paid attention to
the exemplary side of Christ's work, was substantially
in agreement with Luther.[1] Calvin, on the other hand,
lays down his doctrine in two important chapters of
the Institutes. He begins by addressing himself to the
question of the compatibility of God's love for sinful man,
from which flowed the work of redemption, with that
hatred which cannot be denied a place in God's just vengeance upon sinners, and endorses Augustine's words, ' In

Christ, allows to 'the whole course of His obedience' a place in His reconciling activity. 'From the moment when He assumed the form of a servant
He began, in order to redeem us, to pay the price of deliverance.' Salvation
is completed in the death and resurrection, 'Still there is no exclusion of the
other part of obedience which He performed in life.' His later successor, the
eminent divine Francis Turretin, in his Institutio Theologiae Elencticae, Loc.
xiv., Quaest. 13, decides that Christ's satisfaction must not be restricted to
the Passion, but 'extended to the active obedience, whereby He perfectly
fulfilled the law in His whole life.' Gerhard, Loc., iv. 15, 323, not only
speaks of the active satisfaction of obedience, but tries to transcend the
formal antithesis of active and passive ; 'we must note,' he says, 'that active
and passive obedience are most closely linked together in Christ's satisfaction,
since His passion was active and His action passive.' So also Quenstedt
and the Formula Concordiae. Hagenbach (iii. 213) says the advocates of
orthodox Protestantism weakened the Anselmic doctrine 'by adding the
Obedientia activa, since the redeeming element was then no longer exclusively connected with the pouring out of the blood, and the agony
endured, but diffused through the whole life, and only concentrated in the
sacrificial death.'

[1] Nevertheless, Ritschl holds Melanchthon to be 'the true author of the
subsequent orthodox doctrine,' since the fundamental conception in the idea
of God was for him 'forensic punishment-demanding justice' (p. 202). As
to Zwingli, Ritschl speaks with apparently justifiable severity of those critics
who would drive a cleavage between him and Luther. Cf. also Thomasius,
ii. 403, for Zwingli's adherence to the objective necessity of Christ's death.

a manner wondrous and divine He loved even when He hated us.' Christ's work is then, as we have seen, referred generally to His whole obedience, particularly to His death, wherein He ' was offered to the Father as a propitiatory victim ; that, expiation being made by His sacrifice, we might cease to tremble at the divine wrath.' When Christ is said in the Creed to have descended into hell, that is to be interpreted of the necessity for Christ to engage ' as it were at close quarters with the powers of hell, and the horrors of eternal death.' ' There is nothing strange in its being said that He descended to hell, seeing He endured the death which is inflicted on the wicked by an angry God.' But this does not mean that God was angry with Him. ' How could He be angry with the beloved Son, with whom His soul was well pleased ? ' To the resurrection the greatest importance is attributed ; by it ' righteousness was restored and life revived.' In the seventeenth chapter Calvin proceeds to argue that the merit of Christ depends entirely on the free grace of God, to which it is related as accessory to principal. The central thesis of the chapter, which is then defended from scripture, may be found in the words, ' There is nothing to prevent the justification of man from being the gratuitous result of the mere mercy of God, and, at the same time, to prevent the merit of Christ from intervening in subordination to this mercy.'

Merit dependent on God's good pleasure is a very different conception from satisfaction demanded by justice, and Calvin's anxiety for the complete revelation of God's sovereignty at every point has undoubtedly led him back to Duns Scotus and the doctrine of *acceptatio*.[1] Otherwise Calvin's view is the same as Luther's, and differs from Anselm's in that ' satisfaction *by* punishment ' is

---

[1] Ritschl (p. 208), while admitting this, regards the chapter as ' only a casual appendage to Calvin's system of doctrine.' But even in the sixteenth chapter the necessity of a satisfaction to God's justice through Christ's death is not clearly stated. Baur (p. 335) draws attention to the difference at this point between Calvin and the Lutheran theologians.

substituted for 'satisfaction or punishment.'[1] Not only is there imputed to Christ the guilt which makes men liable to punishment, but Calvin goes beyond every one of his predecessors in teaching that Christ 'bore in His soul the tortures of a condemned and ruined man.' One is not surprised that Bellarmine spoke of this as 'a new and unheard-of heresy,' though I think it possible that both Bellarmine and, after him, Gerhard misunderstood Calvin on the descent into hell.[2] But apart from the reference to the clause in the Creed, Calvin was followed in this opinion by Gerhard and Quenstedt in the following century. The latter's statement, 'Christ felt the torments of hell, though not in hell, and not for ever,'[3] sums up their belief.

The penal view of the Reformers, which can be seen in its completest form in the *Institutes* of Turretin, has been thus described : 'Though it is a matter of indispensable justice to punish sin, it is immaterial whether or no the punishment be endured by the sinner.'[4] This is not put with perfect accuracy, for the word 'immaterial' conveys

---

[1] Stevens, *op. cit.*, p. 152.

[2] Bellarmine, *de Christo*, iv. 8, and Gerhard, *Loc.*, xvii. 2. 54, clearly think that it was Calvin's belief that Christ after His death descended into hell and experienced in His soul the tortures of the damned, and Bellarmine suggests that Calvin conceived of Christ as in hell till the resurrection. But Calvin's language (ii. 16. 10) is not quite free from ambiguity. Certainly he speaks of Christ as made to enter the abode of wicked men, but he seems to think of Him as enduring on the Cross rather than in hell the torments of the lost.

[3] *de Christi Officio*, i. 39. There is a curious passage in the Tenth Book of the *Excitationes* of Nicolas of Cusa, the fifteenth-century Spanish cardinal, which certainly points towards the 'new and unheard-of heresy.' After a not very comprehensible statement as to the relations of death and hell, Nicolas continues, 'Than Christ's Passion no passion can be greater ; it was as the suffering of the damned, whose damnation cannot be increased, even to the pain of hell. He is the only one who by such a death passed to His glory, and willed to suffer that pain of sense, similar to the damned in hell, to the glory of God His Father, to show that He must be obeyed even to the final punishment. . . . We sinners in Him paid the penalties of Hell, which we justly deserve.'

[4] Oxenham, *op. cit.*, p. 215. Turretin, *Loc.*, xiv. ; *Quaest.*, x. 10, records the opinion of theologians, 'Punishment must necessarily be inflicted *impersonally* for every sin, but not at once *personally* on every sinner, since God by His singular grace can exempt some from it by substituting a surety in their place.'

a somewhat false impression, as though some one had to
be punished, but it did not matter who. But as the
question was never about punishment in itself, but about
punishment as the means of satisfaction, the final need
for the Reformers, as much as for Anselm, Augustine, or
Athanasius, was for some one of such a nature that the
punishment which fell upon him could be reckoned as
satisfaction. The arguments whereby Turretin defends
the penal substitution of Christ for sinners may not be
adequate, but they do at least prove that a blind infliction
of punishment was not regarded as sufficient to safeguard
the righteousness of God and secure the salvation of men.[1]

The Reformers' doctrine [2] soon gave rise to opposition.
We need not pause to consider the Lutheran Osiander's
protest, since that was concerned directly with justification,[3]
and only incidentally with the character of Christ's atoning
work ; though his semi-mystical speculations, and his
adoption of the Scotist view that the Son of God would
have been incarnate even if man had not fallen, pointed
outside the limits of orthodox Protestant Soteriology.
Nor does any theological importance belong to the Ana-
baptist movement, which, in such leaders as Thomas
Münzer, hardly passed beyond the idea of Christ as an
example. But the work of Faustus Socinus is of classic
importance as an attack upon every point in the conception
of the death of Christ as a satisfaction to God, and of
living interest in that its arguments and conclusions are
widely adopted.

The Socinian position can be best seen in the *Praelec-
tiones Theologicae* of Faustus Socinus, cc. xv.-xxix., and,
more shortly, in the *Christianae Religionis Brevissima*

---

[1] In *Loc.*, xiv., x. 14, Turretin lays down five necessary conditions if the
substitution is to be free from every trace of injustice. Two of these are the
substitute's free consent, and his power not only to bear but also to take
away punishment.

[2] The relevant clauses in Schaff's *Creeds of the Evangelical Protestant
Churches* may be consulted with advantage.

[3] He strenuously argued that justification must imply a making, and not
simply a pronouncing, righteous. See Ritschl, pp. 215-218.

Institutio.[1] It may be summarised as follows from the
former work : the sentence pronounced by God against
sin can be changed, and man granted a blessed immortality
in contrast to eternal death only if man is justified, that
is, pronounced righteous. Now since all men are sinners
this involves the blotting out of sin. In two ways this
is possible: 'by compensation or satisfaction or by remission
and forgiveness.' Socinus proceeds to attack the first
method and champion the second. As sin is an offence
against God's majesty, God can forgive the offence without
requiring satisfaction, or He has less power than man.[2]
God's righteousness is not to be identified with punitive
justice, nor are justice and mercy to be viewed as opposite
qualities in God ; each is only an effect of His will ; mercy
does not prevent Him from punishing, nor justice from
forgiving. The Old Testament is then called in to show
that on the one condition of repentance God forgives sin
without demanding satisfaction and without reference to
any future satisfaction ; while in the New Testament
nothing is said of God demanding satisfaction, which
would, indeed, have been incompatible with the higher
revelation of God's favour to men under the new covenant.
Socinus now passes to his rational thesis, ' to forgive sins
and to receive satisfaction for sins are plainly contradictory and cannot exist together.' It is idle to reply
that the sinner can be forgiven, since satisfaction is made
by a third party ; ' where there is no debt there is no
forgiveness, where now full satisfaction has been made
there is no debt.' The consequences of this are drawn
out at some length, after which the mediating view that
God could have dispensed with satisfaction, but thought
it better to demand it in order to reveal His generosity

---

[1] Pp. 664-668 in the Irenopolis edition of 1656, tom. i.
[2] Cf. Stevens, *op. cit.*, p. 243, 'Socinus had but to substitute a differently
disposed private Deity for Anselm's in order to show that he might waive
the punishment of man's offence if he chose.' There is point in this remark,
though regard for private rights is not the only motive impelling Anselm's
God to demand satisfaction.

and the heinousness of sin, is examined and rejected.
Neither through Christ's endurance of the punishment
due to us, nor by the imputation to us of His righteousness, could satisfaction have been made ; for apart from
vicarious punishment of the innocent being unjust and
unscriptural, eternal deaths would have had to be endured,
and that to the number of guilty sinners ; similarly as
to the observation of the law ; righteousness could be
imputed to one person at most.   The doctrine of satisfaction cannot be deduced from the Person of Christ.   He
did not die eternal death ; satisfaction cannot be made
to hinge on the value of His Person, for even supposing
He was God He did not suffer in His divine nature, and
therefore His sufferings could not possess infinite worth ;
as to His obedience, it was owed to God, and so could not
be imputed to even one man.   Long reviews of Scriptural
passages prepare the way for more positive conceptions.
It was not on the Cross but in heaven that Christ's perfect
oblation was made.   Christ does expiate our sins, not by
any satisfaction directed towards God, but by saving us
from sin's penalty and entail, that is, from death.   This
expiation becomes effective when we accept mercy and
grace from or through Him, so that we may not be left
without help in time of need.   Accordingly, expiation is
to be connected not with the Cross but with the resurrection, and above all with His eternal priesthood and oblation
in heaven, where 'He continually intercedes with God for
us, that is, by the authority and power given to Him by
God ever frees us from all ills, and so makes perpetual
expiation of our sins.'   With this agrees the *Institutio*.
Christ's priesthood is His prerogative and desire to expiate
our sins, and this He does ' because He frees us from our
sins' penalties,' a power visible in the fact that God for
His sake freely forgives our sins.   The particular character
of His death was necessary if the example of His life was
to have its full effect, since what His followers may suffer
from trying to live like Him He suffered first, and further

that He by knowing the worst of human ills might be the
more anxious to help others. Finally, we may note the
definition in the first chapter of the *De Jesu Christo Serva-*
tore ; 'I think,' says Socinus, 'that Jesus Christ is our
Saviour, because He proclaimed to us the way of eternal
life, confirmed it and clearly showed it forth, both by the
example of His life and by rising again from the dead,
and because He will give eternal life to us who have faith
in Him.'

There is an acuteness in Socinus' arguments and a regard
for moral values which recall Pelagius, or perhaps, even
more, Julian of Eclanum. Nevertheless—and again like
Pelagianism—the system is not favourably judged even
by some theologians, who profess no adherence to the
doctrines which Socinus assailed. Ritschl, though he
admits the strength of Faustus' ethical position,[1] implies
that the Socinian community was not a church but a school
composed of 'those acquainted with the saving doctrines
of Christ.' [2]   Harnack, while paying high tribute to its
courage, methodical criticism, and freedom from prepossessions, regards Socinianism as 'simply a step backwards' in the history of religion. 'That the Christian
religion is *faith*, that it is a relation between person and
person, that it is therefore higher than all reason, that it
lives, not upon commands and hopes, but upon the power
of God, and apprehends in Jesus Christ the Lord of Heaven
and earth as Father—of all this Socinianism knew nothing.' [3]
It is noteworthy that Socinus in his positive doctrine of
the saving work of Christ does not mention the forgiveness
of sins ; one might have supposed that his strong opposition
to any satisfaction, partly, at least, as being incompatible
with forgiveness, would have caused a prominent place
to be given to the latter in his own scheme ; in point of
fact this is very far from being the case, so that Socinianism

---

[1] Cf. Sabatier, *op. cit.*, p. 84.   The Socinians 'forced Christian thought
. . . to take its stand at last on the firm ground of moral realities.'
[2] P. 129.
[3] *D. G.*, vii. 167 (E.T.).

is as religiously inferior to what its own logic demands
as its opponents are religiously in advance of their own
dialectic. Socinianism was from the first a book-religion ;
Lutheran and Reformed Protestantism did not become so
till the seventeenth century, and even then it had inner
resources to draw upon for a counteractant, as the rise of
Pietism shows.

'The Socinian doctrine forms such a contrast to that
of the Church, that of itself a mediating theory could not
but arise.' [1] There is, as Ritschl suggests,[2] an Hegelian
ring about these words of Baur, though the latter theologian,
no less than the former, is aware that the great jurist
Hugo Grotius had no intention of holding a middle course
between 'orthodoxy' and Socinianism.[3] The title of his
work, published early in the seventeenth century, reveals
his intention. It is *Defensio Fidei Catholicae de Satisfactione Christi*. But a brief outline of his argument will
ensure our understanding why, by the year 1618, it was
necessary for J. Vossius to undertake a defence of Grotius
against Herrmann Ravensperger, 'who represents that
bold adversary of the Socinians as agreeing with their
sentiments,' [4] and why most modern critics regard his
defence of orthodoxy as rather calculated to remove the
buttresses and imperil the foundations of the edifice which
had arisen since the Reformation than to reveal the
insecurity of the opposing fabric.

Grotius begins by expounding the Catholic view : ' God
being moved of His goodness to be signally beneficial to us,
but our sins, which deserved punishment, standing in the
way, He appointed that Christ, who was willing of His
love towards men, should, by enduring grievous torments
and a bloody and ignominious death, pay the penalties
due for our sins, that, without prejudice to the demonstra-

---

[1] Baur, *op. cit.*, p. 414.   [2] P. 309.
[3] On the other hand, the later Arminian theologian Limborch speaks of his
own doctrine, which in many respects is akin to that of Grotius, as a mean
between two extremes. See Sabatier, p. 91.
[4] Vossius, *Responsio*, ix.

tion of the divine righteousness, we, by the intervention
of true faith, should be freed from the penalty of eternal
death.' Questions of causation are then considered. Sin
is the ' impulsive ' and ' meritorious ' cause of punishment ;
hence there is an antecedent cause of Christ's death besides
His will and God's. As to the satisfaction which Christ
made, the material cause is suffering, and especially, death ;
the formal cause is the enduring of punishment for men's
sins ; ' to bear sins by suffering, and so that others may be
delivered from it, can indicate nothing but the undertaking
of another's punishment ' ; ' God inflicted punishment on
Him that deserved it not.' The end of Christ's Passion
is twofold : the demonstration of the divine righteousness,
here to be understood as ' that property of God which moves
God to punish sins,' and man's freedom from punishment.
It is now necessary to see what is God's ' rôle or office ' in
this matter. Granted that He is not to be thought of as
a judge under law, may we think of Him as an offended
Party, or as a Creditor ? This is what Socinus does,
adding to these two terms the term Lord, and treating the
three as meaning the same thing ; and this is his πρῶτον
ψεῦδος. It is not as an offended Party or as a Creditor
that God punishes or forgives, but as supreme Governor.
So when He punishes He has the common good in view,
' the preservation and example of order,' for ' except from
this end punishment has not the character of being desirable.' Now punishment points back to law, but not to
natural, immutable law, but to positive law, which is ' a
certain effect of God's will,' therefore obviously mutable.
Of such a character is the all-important decree that death
shall follow sin in Genesis ii. 17. Positive penal laws are
therefore dispensable ; that a sinner should deserve
punishment is ' properly natural,' but that ' any sinner
should be punished with a penalty which corresponds to
the offence is not simply and universally necessary ; it
is not properly natural, though agreeable to nature ;
hence it follows that nothing prevents the law which

commands this from being relaxable.' Two weighty
causes induced the relaxation of the law of Genesis, as
otherwise 'two most beauteous things would utterly have
perished—on the part of men religion towards God, on
the part of God the proof of His special benevolence
towards men.' But punishment was not simply cancelled,
since Christ was punished for man's sins. This is not
unjust, for the essence of punishment does not consist
in its relation to a man's own sin, and it is agreed that the
innocent can be afflicted by God ; therefore it is not unjust
that an innocent person should be punished for another
man's fault by such affliction, especially if he has voluntarily offered himself for such punishment, and has power
in himself to undertake it. This is especially true of
Christ, since He was appointed by God ' to be the Head of
the body of which we are members.' But why did God
think fit to punish Christ ? As a proof of His hatred of
sin, and that the law's authority might not be endangered
by the entire abrogation of punishment. This is secured
by so notable an example, just as His goodness, 'which
of all the Properties of God is most proper to God,' is
revealed in His remitting of eternal punishment.[1] There
is no opposition between satisfaction and remission, since
satisfaction is antecedent to remission, and not to be
confused with it, as is made very clear by the law of
deliverance from debt, according to which only ' the
payment of something wholly the same with what was in
the obligation frees *ipso facto* ' ; satisfaction, therefore,
must not be simply identified with payment. The Catholic
faith gives better reasons for Christ's death than any that

---

[1] A brief statement of the doctrine of the Atonement which has much in
common with Grotius is given by the Cambridge scholar, Henry More, in his
work, *An Explanation of the Grand Mystery of Godliness*, i. 5. 4.   'The
Divine complotment was this : that the Eternal Son of God should be made
flesh, and to testify the hatred of God to sin, and His love to mankind,
should be sacrificed for an Atonement for the sins of the world, than which
a greater engine cannot be imagined to move us to an abhorrence of sin ; and
to the love of His law that thus redeemed us, and wrought our reconciliation
with the Father.'

Socinus can give, and does more justice to the words of
Scripture. When it speaks of the appeasing of God's
wrath, of Christ's death as the price of man's deliverance,
of substitution, of an expiatory sacrifice for past sins, it
is giving full value to language which Socinus wrests to
unnatural meanings.

Grotius' Defence 'exhibits that subtlety in analysis,
acuteness in rebuttal, and ample learning, which we should
expect to find in the trained jurist.' [1] His pages are full
of precedents, both Scriptural and pagan, with which he
overwhelms his adversary. A Calvinistic theologian could
hardly say more often and more strongly that punishment
was inflicted on Christ, and is rightly to be regarded as a
satisfaction. But that his position is irreconcilable with
that of Anselm, and with that of the Reformers, is apparent
at point after point. There is no dominant quality of
distributive justice in God which demands satisfaction by
punishment, or satisfaction as an alternative to punishment. The satisfaction itself is not the strict equivalent
of the debt, it is 'some payment.' The punishment is
simply an affliction which serves the ends of punishment,
and, in any case, looks towards the future as a deterrent
rather than towards the past as an expiation. Grotius
stands to the Reformers rather as the later Schoolmen do
to Anselm; as they explicitly deny that God cannot
dispense with satisfaction, so he implicitly denies what
Dr. Stevens satirically describes as the doctrine that
'the necessity to punish is Heaven's first law.' As compared with Anselm he has a worthier idea of God, while
he neither appals us as do the Epigoni of the Reformation
by the cast-iron character of his scheme, nor leaves a mere
impression of argumentative skill which characterises some
of the pages of Socinus; yet there is an artificiality about
his theory which is hardly to be found in any other doctrine
of the Atonement. The root evil is that Grotius sets out
to give an explanation of the death of Christ as a penal

[1] Stevens, *op. cit.*, p. 162.

satisfaction, and merely involves it in greater obscurity. His conclusion is a penal example, and what one must call ' a sort of ' payment. What meaning are we to attach to the latter, and how are we to justify the former, considering its actual character ? What is the relation between penal example and expiation ? Grotius contends vigorously against Socinus that expiation looks backwards rather than forwards ; the reverse is undeniably true of his ' notable example.' He accuses Socinus, quite unfairly, of applying the word *acceptilatio* to the remission of sins, whereas his own theory has no coherence at all apart from the Scotist idea, to which the term acceptilation is technically applied, that God can fix a value as He will.[1] And this entirely corresponds to the patent fact of this soteriology that the final cause of the work of atonement is external to God ; what the interest of the universe requires, not what the nature of God demands. The weakness of the Grotian doctrine is best summed up in the wise words of Hagenbach : ' It could not satisfy either the feelings or the reason of Christians, while the theory of Anselm accomplished the former, and that of the Socinians the latter, though both were one-sided and imperfect.' [2]

The Grotian Soteriology was adopted by the Arminian theologians Curcallæus and Limborch, who made more prominent in it the idea of the death of Christ as a sacrificial

[1] Baur (p. 428) says, 'There is no theory to which the idea of acceptilation could more rightly be applied than that of Grotius.' Grotius (c. vi.) argues that *acceptilatio* is inapplicable to punishment, since in punishment God receives nothing, and is inconsistent with any payment, whereas Christ gave His life as ' some payment.' Such arguments are inconclusive as not establishing fundamental variety of principle. But Grotius does not go to the length of making justice simply dependent on the divine will. Justice is a true attribute of God, but, as Dr. Stevens says (p. 168), 'the actual exercise of " punitive justice " is dependent on the Divine will.'

[2] iii. 216 (E.T.). Turretin in *Locus* xiv., *Qu.* 10 of the second part of his *Institutio* deals at length with the question of satisfaction, with the Socinian objections in mind. He defends the compatibility of satisfaction and forgiveness by the argument that sin is a crime as well as a debt. Satisfaction consists in the bearing of punishment, forgiveness in the admission, and acceptance of Christ as a substitute. The proper penalty was not paid, but a vicarious penalty. Even Turretin comes perilously near a doctrine of *acceptilatio*. See the section on Turretin and Grotius in Lidgett, *op. cit.*, pp. 476-481.

offering whereby more justice could be done to the God-ward aspect of the Atonement. But both of these divines approximate to the Socinian position in important respects, especially in denying that the 'satisfaction' of Christ had 'the value of a prestation made to God's strict justice.' [1] Grotius' own work escaped detailed consideration and attack till, early in the eighteenth century, the Lutheran theologian Buddæus fastened on the crucial point that the Church doctrine of satisfaction was entirely under-mined if Christ could be said to have satisfied God *aliquid pretii dando*; moreover, a mere man could have done this. [2] But seventeenth-century controversies between Arminians and Calvinists were directed rather to the alternatives of a 'universal' or a 'limited' atonement, as to which one must say that granted the belief that Christ had endured the amount of punishment which was due to men, and granted further that all men would not be saved, the Calvinistic restriction of 'men' to 'some men' was strictly logical and just. An atonement made for all men is quite inconsistent with a doctrine of reprobation, and a mathe-matically penal view of the value of Christ's death. [3]

In England, with one exception, no one of the many eminent theologians of the seventeenth century contri-buted anything fresh towards a rationale of the Atonement. This is true both of Anglicans and Puritans. Hooker, who died in the year 1600, speaks as formally of satisfaction as Quenstedt or Turretin. Sin against the infinite God is an infinite wrong, therefore 'justice . . . doth necessarily exact an infinite recompense, or else inflict upon the offender infinite punishment.' [4] Pearson has precisely the same thought of Christ needing to die for the satisfac-

---

[1] Ritschl, p. 316.   [2] Baur, p. 455 f.
[3] Cf. M'Leod Campbell, *The Nature of the Atonement*[6], p. 47 f. Dr. Stevens (p. 185) quotes the modern American Calvinist, Dr. Charles Hodge, as pointing out 'the absurdity of supposing that Christ should die to save those whom God never intended to save; nay, had from eternity 'for the manifestation of His glory,' as the Confession says, 'fore-ordained to ever-lasting death.'
[4] *Eccl. Polity*, vi. 5. 2.

tion of God's Justice;[1] while Bull, who was engaged in prolonged controversy on the subject of justification, regarded it as almost a mark of insanity for any orthodox person to doubt that the remission of sins depended on ' the righteousness and meritorious satisfaction ' of Christ.[2] Of the Puritans, John Owen expounds with great precision the Calvinistic doctrines, and argues against Grotius that Christ's satisfaction, while it is the payment of the very same thing as was owing, is yet consistent with the idea of forgiveness.[3] Baxter, on the other hand, though cautious in his statements, holds the Grotian rather than the strictly penal view ; he denies that Christ paid the same penalty as was due from men, and contends that the idea of satisfaction can be preserved only if Christ paid an equivalent, but not the same, penalty, with avowed approval of the Grotian *satisfactio non est solutio eiusdem*. To speak of sins being imputed to Christ is a ' tolerable ' but not a ' proper ' phrase, and Luther's language of Christ as the greatest of sinners may be allowed but not approved.[4]

But from one quarter a new note sounded. The Quaker theologian, Robert Barclay, in his *Apology*, diverges sharply from the Protestant doctrine of justification by teaching that it is ' by the inward birth of Christ in man that man is made just and therefore so accounted by God, and that since good works naturally follow from this birth . . . therefore are they *of absolute necessity to justification* as *causa sine qua non* ' : this is reminiscent of Osiander, but he goes beyond Osiander in distinguishing between ' the Redemption performed and accomplished by

---

[1] *Exposition of the Creed*, Art. iv., ' Dead.'
[2] *Examen Censurae in Animadv.* xiii.
[3] See the 1852 edition of Owen's works, x. 268 f. (on *The death of death in the death of Christ*), ' Freedom of pardon hath not its foundation in any defect of the merit or satisfaction of Christ ' (he says God bated Christ not one farthing), ' but in, first, the will of God freely appointing this satisfaction of Christ.   Secondly, in a gracious acceptation of that decreed satisfaction in our steads ; for so many, no more.   Thirdly, in a free application of the death of Christ unto us.'
[4] See his *Methodus Theologiae Christianae*, iii. 1, 5-15.

Christ for us, in His Crucified Body, without us,' and ' the Redemption wrought by *Christ in us*, which no less properly is called and accounted a Redemption than the former.' Now apart from the twofold use of the word redemption, there is at first sight nothing very remarkable in a proposition which puts in the forefront Christ's historic act of atonement.   But when one remembers that, in Barclay's opinion, salvation was not dependent on conscious knowledge of and response to that act, but on man's submission to the guidance of the light or seed which God had implanted in every one, it is obvious that a conception of the Atonement in its relations to man had been formed, which was not only alien to the thoughts both of Calvinists and of Arminians, but was certain to grow into a form of doctrine beyond anything that Barclay could have imagined or approved.[1] The distinction between the fact and the principle of the Atonement, contrasted as historic and eternal, follows close upon such twofold application of the idea of redemption, and not far off is that treatment of such expressions as ' Son of God ' and ' Incarnation ' which characterises the religious philosophy of the German idealists, Fichte and Hegel.   With Barclay and the Quakers may be compared German mystics such as Schwenkfeld, in the middle of the sixteenth century, Weigel and Böhme in the seventeenth. They carry on the tradition of Osiander in opposition to the Lutheran doctrines of justification and imputation.[2]

The eighteenth century was a time of severe strain for Protestant orthodoxy in Europe, especially in Germany.

---

[1] See Barclay's *Apology, Prop.* vii. *concerning Justification*, especially §§ 1-7.   Baur (p. 469) says that it is clear in Quakerism in what subordinate relation the external historical Christ stands to this inner Christ.   The history is a mere ' pictorial image ' of what develops in the individual and in mankind as a whole. So Ritschl (p. 292) speaks of the impossibility, on the Quaker principle, of ' attaching any real significance to Christ's work, either in doing or in suffering.' Weingarten (*Revolutionskirchen Englands*, p. 359) says that ' no doctrine was more offensive to the Quakers than that of vicarious satisfaction, which was to them a mark of the church of Babylon.'   He refers to a (?) Tract *Morning-watch*.

[2] For detailed account of the various reactions from exact Lutheran orthodoxy at this time, I must refer those interested to the pages of Baur and Ritschl.

The spirit of rationalism characteristic of the age combined with the theology of what is known as the *Illumination* [1] to challenge the authorised, confessional statements, not least in connexion with the doctrine of the Atonement. The movement met no important check, till Kant, by his destructive analyses and his rebuilding on the foundations of moral certainty, caused metaphysicians and theologians, orthodox and rationalists, to look and see whether their own edifices rested on rock or sand. But, in America, this same century saw the rise of the most notable theological school for which the New World could as yet claim credit, its founder a man of quite extraordinary capacity as philosopher and divine, who, to mention only one of the many activities of his life, attempted to raise the Calvinistic doctrine of determinism to the level of an inevitable metaphysic,[2] by arguments easier to disagree with than to refute. Jonathan Edwards, senior, was President of New Jersey College, and from him the school known as Edwardean takes its name. The soteriology both of President Edwards himself and of his followers is of interest, since the natural expectation that in it would be reproduced the most rigid penal conceptions of seventeenth-century orthodoxy is not fulfilled. It is not easy to classify with exactness Edwards' treatise *Of Satisfaction for Sin.* His idea of justice as requiring the punishment of sin, and of sin as infinite deserving infinite punishment, prepares us for a strictly penal view. But Grotian conceptions immediately follow ; it is fit or suitable—the words are frequent—that sin should be punished as it deserves : ' It belongs to God, as the

---

[1] The standpoint of the Illumination is, according to Ritschl, 'the standpoint of individuality, guided by the reason, striving after relative virtue' (p. 344). He traces its individualism back to Pietism and to the Wolfian philosophy.

[2] Whereas Augustine, and most of the Calvinistic theologians who followed him, allowed to Adam, before he sinned, freedom of choice, Edwards refused to allow any place, at any time, for freedom in created beings. As to the will 'he teaches a determinism belonging to its very nature. Freedom is as predicable of men now as of Adam before he sinned.' ' He encloses in the network of philosophical necessity all intelligent beings.' (Fisher, *History of Christian Doctrine*, p. 401.)

Supreme Ruler of the universality of things,[1] to maintain order and decorum in His Kingdom.' In the work of satisfaction Christ intervenes as mediator, as the patron who seeks in love the welfare of his client man, while He shows His disapproval of that client's offence by suffering ' the whole penalty due to the offender.' Christ bears the wrath of God ' in such a way as He was capable of,' by His clear sense of the punishment due to sin, and by enduring the effects of God's wrath. He bears man's sins by His clear view of sin and its hatefulness. After this Edwards insists on the maintenance of God's honour in quite Anselmic fashion, while at the end of the treatise the idea of satisfaction is distinguished from that of merit, since ' Christ's bearing our punishment for us ' as a fulfilment of the law has not properly anything to do with merit.[2]

Edwards' thought has obvious affinities with more than one type of theory.[3] But before we pass from him and from his school two points in his teaching deserve to be noticed. The first is that whatever substitution of Christ for man takes place in his doctrine, the legal idea of arranged transference is quite subsidiary to the moral idea of sympathetic identification. Christ's action is illustrated by that ' strong and lively love and pity toward the miserable ' which ' tends to make their case ours,' so that we can actually suffer ' in their stead by strong sympathy.' [4] The second is the admission that an

---

[1] A. V. G. Allen (*Jonathan Edwards*, p. 91) speaks of his ' mediæval and feudal conception of Deity as an absolute sovereign,' but his conception is Grotian rather than Anselmic, despite the importance ascribed to God's honour in § 37.

[2] In his *History of Redemption*, ii. 2. 1, Edwards defines the effects of satisfaction and merit thus, ' The *satisfaction* of Christ is to free us from *misery*, and the *merit* of Christ is to purchase happiness *for us*,' but he does not insist on hard and fast usage. Christ's satisfaction for sin was carried on throughout His life; all His sufferings—those of His death pre-eminent in degree alone—were ' propitiatory or satisfactory.'

[3] Dr. Stevens (p. 421) speaks of the treatise as ' a Grotian edifice built upon a penal basis, with Anselmic and ethical embellishments'; M'Leod Campbell classes Edwards with Owen as a strict Calvinist, but this is to overlook important elements in his exposition.

[4] § 32.

adequate repentance for sin would render punishment unnecessary. God's outraged majesty must be vindicated by punishment, ' unless there could be such a thing as a repentance, humiliation, and sorrow, proportionable to the greatness of the majesty despised.' Edwards denies the possibility ; ' there can be no infinite sorrow for sin in finite creatures.' [1] But M'Leod Campbell and Moberly, in conceiving of such sorrow or penitence on the part of One who was not a ' finite creature,' are following in a path which Edwards had seen but left untrodden.[2]

As this chapter began with some account of the original Reformation doctrine, a brief survey of the progress of thought in Germany from the time of Kant to the present day may be interesting, and is certainly an obligation upon the writer. The German theologian always has his eye fixed on the Reformation, however much he may dissent from the immediate positions taken up in that epoch of forced theological marches. Accordingly, to this day, theological schools of thought flourish in Germany to a far greater extent than in England, each school claiming to be the true representative of the Reformation spirit, if not of the Reformation's standardised dogmatic. Not unnaturally German theology has for the English reader too much of a ' school-character,' though this should not blind us to the fact that, regarded as a science, it is subjected to a minuteness and care in investigation which makes it, within limits, an admirable example to follow.

Kant and the idealists who came after him have much to say of the conditions of atonement, that is, of the reconciliation of the finite, whether regarded as the universe itself or as the finite spirit to God ; indeed, it is for Schelling, Fichte, and Hegel the very essence of religion. Kant's influence on soteriology, which, as Baur most truly says, could not fail to be immense, sprang inevitably from the

[1] §§ 7 and 2.
[2] The Edwardean school, on the whole, developed the Grotian element in President Edwards. The younger Edwards explicitly denied the doctrine of penal equivalence. See Foley, op. cit., p. 242.

primacy which he assigned to the ethical over the speculative interest. In his opposition to the optimistic view
of human nature which rationalism had popularised, in
defining punishment as essentially requital, in representing
an atonement for past guilt as at once necessary and possible,
he occupied the same ground as the Church, and, in the
last point, passed beyond morality to religion. His
position is worked out in his treatise on *Religion within the
bounds of mere reason*, and the relationship of his point
of view to that of orthodox Church teaching made clear.
Original sin is accepted as an evil bias, which is yet compatible with human freedom, and therefore with responsibility for evil acts and guilt consciousness. Within man
there is a conflict of good and evil principles. This good
principle, which metaphysically regarded is 'humanity
(the rational being as such) *in its complete moral perfection*,' [1]
has been truly personified by Christianity as the only-
begotten Son of God. Moreover, this ideal of perfected
humanity cannot be conceived save under the idea ' of a
man who has borne the greatest suffering and death itself
for the good of men and even of his enemies.' And by
the help of such conceptions the possibility of an atonement for apparently infinite past guilt is revealed. When
a man abandons an evil and adopts a good life, ' the change
from the corrupt to the good mind involves the sacrifice
of self and the acceptance of a long series of the evils of
life, which the new man takes upon himself in the spirit
of the Son of God ; *i.e.* merely for the sake of the good ;
evils which, however, properly should have fallen upon
the old man (who is morally another) in the shape of
punishment. . . . It is, then, this new personality as the
guiltless Son of God which bears the penalty of sin ; or
(if we personify the Idea) the Son of God, as *Substitute*
for him and for all who (practically) believe on Himself,
bears the guilt of sin ; as their *Redeemer*, makes satisfaction

---

[1] The quotations are from Dr. E. Caird's translations of passages in the
treatise in his *Critical Philosophy of Kant*, ii. 566 ff.

to the highest justice for it by suffering and death ; and,
as their Representative, secures to them the hope of
appearing as justified before their Judge.'

In Kant's religious philosophy we see the use made by
a great thinker, for whom existence is to be interpreted
along ethical rather than along speculative lines, of ideas
which carry the moral values he requires, but must themselves be treated as representative symbols (*Vorstellungen*).
But because he ' cannot admit that moral evil or moral
good are to be referred to anything which lies beyond the
individual will,' [1] his theory is thoroughly subjective in
character. The life of the individual must be worked
out in isolation face to face with the categorical imperative
of the moral law, and in such a conception there is no
place for, in Dr. Caird's words, ' that very idea which gives
its great moral power to Christianity, viz. the idea of a
real objective mediation, by which the individual is raised
above himself.' [2] Ritschl therefore speaks the exact
truth, a truth illustrated by his own work and that of
many other theologians, when he says ' the high importance
of Kant's contributions to the right understanding of the
Christian idea of Reconciliation lies less in any positive
contribution to the structure of doctrine than in the fact
that he established critically—that is, with scientific
strictness—those general presuppositions of the idea of
Reconciliation which lie in the consciousness of moral
freedom and of moral guilt.' [3]

Schelling, Fichte, and Hegel did much more justice to
the notion of objective reconciliation. But their speculative interests rendered their theories more incompatible

---

[1] Caird, *op. cit.*, ii. 596.

[2] P. 619. Cf. Baur (p. 581), 'The ground-thought is that the regenerate
man may in virtue of his mind, which is good in itself and beheld as a unity,
know himself to be reconciled and justified.' Baur points out that the
objectification of the idea of the good principle as the Son of God is no real
way of escape, since this objectivity ' is only the objectivity of the ideal,
which always appears only in an unbridgeable distance, in which it is
impossible ever to reach true objective reality.'

[3] *Op. cit.*, p. 387.

with historic Christian doctrine than Kant's had been, and tended towards notions of cosmic and pantheistic rather than ethical reconciliation. For Schelling Christian doctrine is the symbol of the falling away of the finite from the infinite, and of its return.[1] Fichte has even less place for anything approaching the Church doctrine in his conception of the distinction of the universe from God as necessitated by the very act of knowledge. By Hegel ' the idea of reconciliation is restricted to the return of the finite spirit to God, but not brought to bear upon the universe as a whole.'[2] Because Man is potentially the Good reconciliation is possible ; that is, it rests upon ' the implicit unity of divine and human nature.'[3] This is involved in the doctrine of Christ as the God-Man. But thereby no concession is made to finitude as such ; on the contrary, the principle of finitude, though it is revealed in its most extreme form in Christ's death, is by that death slain. ' It is a proof of infinite love that God identified Himself with what was foreign to His nature in order to slay it.'[4] Nevertheless, Hegel can sum up the whole matter as follows, ' This is the explication of the meaning of reconciliation, that God is reconciled with the world, or rather that God has shown Himself to *be* by His very nature reconciled with the world, so that what is human is not something alien to His nature, but that this otherness, this self-differentiation, finitude, as it is sometimes expressed, is a moment in God Himself, though, to be sure, it is a vanishing moment.'[5]

Contemporaneous with these great thinkers who, for

---

[1] Cf. Ritschl, p. 582. ' Christ offers to God the Finite in His own person, and thereby works reconciliation. As He was appointed thereto indeed from all eternity, yet passes by as a phenomenon in time, Christianity as history is founded upon that spirit which carries back the Finite to the Infinite . . . the Son of God is the Finite itself (as that exists in the eternal intuition of God), which makes its appearance as a God who suffers, and is subject to the inflictions of time, who, in the climax of His manifestation in Christ, closes the world of Finitude, and opens up that of Infinitude or of the dominion of the Spirit.'

[2] Ritschl, p. 597.   [3] Hegel, *The Philosophy of Religion*, iii. 71 (E.T.)
[4] iii. 93.   [5] iii. 99.

all their theological and religious interests, were primarily metaphysicians, lived the theologian D. F. Schleiermacher. His systematic theology, till lately unduly neglected in England,[1] is controlled by the thought of redemption. ' In the idea of redemption through Christ,' says Ritschl,[2] he made the form of Christianity to consist. But Schleiermacher's constructive work bears little resemblance to the theories of the past, except when his dwelling on Christ's sympathetic suffering and its effect upon men recalls Abelard. Redemption is the impartation of Christ's God-consciousness to men,[3] whereby they come into life-fellowship with Christ. In this connexion the conception of the Church is made much of, since through the Church is mediated that life-fellowship. Discarding the doctrine of penal satisfaction [4] he describes Christ in language which echoes Irenæus as ' our satisfying representative in that He presents human nature in perfection by the manifestation of His archetypal worth in His redemptive activity, so that God regards in Him the totality of believers, and sees in His free devotion to death such a perfection of redeeming power as is sufficient to bring the whole race within His communion.' [5] For anything like an objective expiation there is no place in his system, since, while exception may be taken to the statement that in it ' Sin is a lower stage in human development,' [6] it is true that for more reasons than one Schleiermacher is unable to make any such connexion of the ideas of sin, guilt, punishment, atonement, as is visible in Kant.[7]

---

[1] Dr. Cross's *Theology of Schleiermacher*, with a condensation of his chief work *Die Glaubenslehre*, and Dr. Selbie's *Schleiermacher* are valuable works of the last four years.

[2] P. 451.   [3] Cross, p. 213.

[4] ' In His passive obedience Christ suffers for our sins not in bearing the punishment of them, but because through them He is brought into contact with evil and misery.' Selbie, p. 176.

[5] Cross, p. 223.

[6] Fisher, *History of Christian Doctrine*, p. 507.

[7] One must remember that his inadequate idea of Personality in God leads Schleiermacher at times to conclusions verging on pantheism, so that his doctrine of reconciliation is mystical rather than ethical. Baur (p. 628) says of his theory, ' The necessary presupposition, in accordance with which

' The work that has been devoted, since Schleiermacher,
to the doctrine of reconciliation displays an incredible
want of co-operation on the part of theologians ; so much
so that memory is unequal to the task of mastering all
the variations, even of views which follow only one type.'
So writes Ritschl towards the end of the first volume of
his own great work—and the pages which precede justify
the feeling which informs the remark.   Merely noting that
between 1834, when Schleiermacher died, and 1870, when
Ritschl published his first volume, almost the last attempt
in modern Germany was made by theologians such as
Philippi and Hengstenberg to maintain in all its rigour the
doctrine of penal satisfaction,[1] while, on the other hand,
one of the most individual and attractive of religious
thinkers, Richard Rothe, developed Schleiermacher's
mystical view of redemption, and gave it a deeper ethical
content, we may pass to Ritschl's own doctrine.

That Ritschl's theology, as he says himself, ' has no
place in the ordinary classification of theological parties ' [2]
is shown to be true, both by the internal evidence of his
own work with its unwonted combination of ideas, set,
as it were, in battle array against assailants from every
quarter, and by the external evidence of the judgments
as to what he meant, which vary as widely as possible,
both in Germany and in England. Since for him the
religious focus [3] of Christianity is the idea of justification
or the forgiveness of sins—for he identifies the two—and
forgiveness is not based with the Socinians on the equity
of God, or with the theologians of the ' Illumination ' on
His love, but upon the work and Passion of Christ,[4] one
might expect to find him developing some doctrine of

alone the individual can be united with God or redeemed and reconciled, is
that man in himself is one with God.'

[1] See quotation from Philippi in Ritschl, p. 551.

[2] In the preface to the first edition of his third—the constructive—
volume.

[3] *The Christian Doctrine of Justification and Reconciliation: the Positive
Development of the Doctrine*, p. 11 (E.T.[2]).

[4] *Op. cit.*, pp. 536 ff.

satisfaction, though it were neither the Anselmic nor the Reformation doctrine. In fact, he does nothing of the sort, and only the closest study of one of the profoundest but at the same time most intricate and perplexing works of modern theology allows his positive meaning to appear. The interpreter of Ritschl must never forget, at any part of this theologian's dogmatic scheme, that second, ethical focus of Christianity, the idea of the kingdom of God. It is of vital moment to his soteriology, since forgiveness of sins or justification applies primarily to the community [1] which Christ founded that in it His relation to God might be reproduced ; but it was necessary for Christ as the Founder of the community to preserve unfailingly His loyalty to His vocation, in which His violent death was an unavoidable element. Because He did this ' God's forgiving love is thereby secured beforehand to those who belong to Christ's community. Their guilt is not taken into account in God's judgment, since they are admitted in the train of God's beloved Son to the position towards God which was assumed and maintained by Him.' [2] The ethical character of Ritschl's thought is made clear by his identification of Christ's priestly office with His loyalty to His vocation, so that he actually affirms that ' if His Priesthood is to be regarded as availing for others, it can only be in virtue of this fact.' [3] Ritschl certainly approaches one side of the older theory in his valuation of Christ's meritorious obedience, but any attempt to combine this with the idea of substitutionary punishment he rejects. One not unimportant line of division between him and the older Lutheran dogmatists may be noted. Everywhere he lays stress on activity rather than on endurance. What Christ endured He endured in the interests of His active following of that vocation which He had from His Father, not because of some mysterious virtue in endurance as such.[4] But it

[1] Pp. 109 ff., 549.   [2] P. 547.   [3] P. 484.
[4] Cf. such statements as ' The human life of Christ must be viewed under the category of His consciously pursued personal end ' (443) ; ' The suffering of Christ, through the patience with which it was borne, becomes a kind of

is almost impossible to isolate Ritschl's doctrine of the work of Christ, and present it as a department of his dogmatic. Admirable as Dr. Stevens' classifications seem to be in general, I cannot but think that it was rather as a counsel of despair that he gave Ritschl's doctrine a place among Modern ' Subjective ' Theories.

Ritschl enormously influenced German theology, and while he made theological enemies, whom it cannot be said that he ever spared in the slightest degree, he rallied round him supporters of outstanding ability. To-day, questions concerning the environment of Christianity and the nature and value of its credentials are more prominent than those which concern the systematisation of its inner content. Nevertheless, the question of the Atonement continually comes up, and it is possible to gain a fairly clear idea of current thought on the subject. Members of the so-called ' religious-historical ' school touch upon it in their Biblical Theologies and their studies of special subjects. Their general conclusion is that while Christianity is truly to be thought of as a religion of redemption, no attempt must be made to conserve in any way the old dogma. Thus Wernle writes, ' How miserably all those finely constructed theories of sacrifice and vicarious atonement crumble to pieces before the faith in the love of God our Father, who so gladly pardons. The one parable of the prodigal son wipes them all off the slate. Sin and its burden lie far away from the disciples of Jesus, and still further is the theology of sin and propitiation.' [1] Bousset represents the enlightened moral sense as declaring, ' The sin which you have committed no one can atone for instead of you, neither man nor God. . . . Sin and guilt can only be removed by the voluntary moral and personal act of one God, who forgives sin and remits guilt.' [2]

---

doing. For this is the only way in which an ethical value can be got out of suffering at all' (444); 'He bore His sufferings as the accident of His positive fidelity to His vocation ' (566).

[1] *Beginnings of Christianity*, i. 109 (E. T.)
[2] *What is Religion ?* p. 282 E.T.)

Theologians who carry on, with whatever modifications, the tradition of Ritschl make much less sweeping assertions. Herrmann approves the reluctance ' to let go the thought that redemption has been won by the vicarious suffering of Christ,' and the instinct which makes the believer say, as he looks back on Jesus' work, ' He suffers what we should have suffered.' Only the doctrine of substitutionary satisfaction must not be made a starting-point, ' and the ground of our certainty of the forgiveness of our sin.' [1] Harnack strikes the same note in more than one place. He finds fault with Anselm's theory because, among other things, there is no recognition of ' the deep proposition that the innocent suffers for the guilty, that the *penalty* lies upon him that we might have peace.' [2] He urges that a distinction be drawn between ' a vicarious penal suffering ' and ' a satisfaction demanded by God.' [3] History has decided in favour of the idea of Christ's death as an expiatory sacrifice, since it has shown that the blood-sacrifices, which responded to a religious need, were ended by the Christian message of the death of Christ : this could have resulted only from His death having the value of an expiatory sacrifice.[4] In his essay in the volume, *The Atonement in Modern Religious Thought*, Harnack considers Christ's death in its power to calm the terrified heart, which is bound by its sin to regard God ' as a wrathful judge,' and to show that *there is something mightier still than Justice—Mercy*. And further, ' if they, the sinners, have escaped justice, and He, the Holy One, has suffered death, why shall they not acknowledge that that which He suffered was what they should have suffered ? In presence of the Cross no other feeling, no other note, is possible.' [5] Kaftan's teaching is reminiscent of Ritschl. Decisively, though rather more sympathetically, he rejects the idea of satisfaction ; his own position is not quite easy

---

[1] *Communion with God*, pp. 135 f. (E.T.).
[2] *D.G.*, vi. 69 (E.T.)   [3] vi. 81.
[4] *What is Christianity?* pp. 159 ff. (E.T.).
[5] *The Atonement*, etc., pp. 122 ff.

of comprehension, and he leaves the impression of trying to maintain the values of the ecclesiastical doctrine while lacking an adequate apparatus. Jesus could not have fulfilled His vocation without enduring ' all evils which, as the result and penalty of sin, had come into the world ' ; [1] ' what as our punishment lay upon us that has He borne, and thereby reconciled us with God and brought us to new life'; only we must not think of this as a satisfaction paid to God's justice, as a punishment inflicted by God on the Innocent instead of the guilty, for, if we do, the real truth in the idea of Christ's substitutionary penal suffering (*Stellvertretenden Strafleiden*) will be endangered.[2] It is when Kaftan faces the question of the necessity of the death of Christ in the work of salvation that a certain obscurity clouds his thought. Christ's death had nothing to do with the wrath of God ; [3] nor did it induce God to forgive ; but the Socinian view which sees no necessary connexion between Christ's death and salvation must be refused, since it starts from God's absolute power, not from His righteousness.[4]   Our starting-point must be the words in which Jesus declared His death to be necessary for the fulfilment of His mission, that is as a means for an eternal end.   It is certain that the historic conditions of that mission necessitated His death, ' the holy love of God on the one side, on the other the sin of men ' ; [5] the Bearer of the divine revelation was inevitably killed, since the content of that revelation, the Kingdom of God, had been degraded through sin to an external, political form ; but His death is the necessary means for the accomplishment of salvation, since by it men are convinced of God's love, ' which is holy and yet forgives sins, which is gracious to man while it judges him.' [6]   But more than this, Christ's

---

[1] *Dogmatik* [6], p. 543.   [2] *Op. cit.*, pp. 544 f.
[3] Pp. 573 f.   [4] P. 577.
[5] P. 586 ; cf. p. 591, 'The death of the Mediator of salvation could have been avoided . . . only if God's love had ceased to be holy, or sinners ceased to be sinners.'
[6] P. 592.

saving death was a necessity for God, though not as stated in the ecclesiastical theory of satisfaction : ' It was necessary for God, provided that He wished to make men blessed, despite their sin ' ; not otherwise could God reveal Himself to sinners, not otherwise could sinners be brought to faith. The necessity for the work of redemption is to be found in God's nature of holy love, for the means to that end in man's moral state.[1]

Thus Kaftan preserves the idea of Christ's penal suffering, though, as Dr. Stevens would say, only ' in a sense,' while he tries to show that, the fact of sin being posited, Christ's death was absolutely necessary; yet I doubt whether one can think that his argument really carries so far.

Over against the religious-historical and the Ritschlian theologians stands the ' positive ' school. We have seen that its representatives in the study of New Testament theology, Feine and Schlatter, find strong exegetical support for the general idea that Christ's death is the saving fact by its Godward as well as its manward influence, that by it God is reconciled to man as well as man to God, though, at the same time, they do not neglect the New Testament affirmation of redemption as set in motion by the love of God.[2] These conclusions are formulated in the dogmatic writings of such men as Kähler and Seeberg. Kähler regards the work of Christ as God's act of reconciling the world to Himself, as a vindication of the true moral order of the world, which stands in causal relationship to God's dealing with the individual as the Pardoner of his sins. ' A reconciliation with God is for sinners morally impossible and for the God of holy love impossible, if the barrier of guilt is not taken away, if the wrath of the Holy One has not been expressed and the immutability of His world-order maintained.'[3] The death of Christ has a sacrificial and a penal aspect. The

---

[1] Pp. 594 f.
[2] Crucial passages are John iii. 16 ; Romans v. 8, viii. 32.
[3] *Zur Lehre von der Versöhnung*, p. 367.

essence of sacrifice is obedience ; in the Old Testament sacrifices are Israel's obedient fulfilment of what God Himself has ordered.[1] Thus the sacrifice of Jesus is His life-long obedience, which culminated in the Passion.[2] This sacrifice avails us neither as a satisfaction to God according to Anselm's idea, nor simply as a revelation of God's love and an awakening of ours, but as the punishment of our sins. Christ's death has a penal character, because for the Bible death is essentially separation from God,[3] and the death of Jesus was ' our death ' because He died, not for Himself, since He was guiltless, but for others.[4] So ' He has shared in our fate,' [5] He has died ' to suffer the consequences of sin in death ' ; [6] His sympathy with human weakness culminates in His understanding of man's deepest trial, of the crushing load of self-judgment.' [7] Punishment, for Kähler, is an idea of high religious significance ; it is ' the religious judgment of the kingdom of wickedness,' [8] and so through Christ's penal sacrifice, and as its result the world is once for all reconciled with God,[9] since in it man is seen wholly surrendering himself to God's will. God's order is acknowledged in and through man's will ; judgment and penalty prove the means for the restoration of fellowship with God.[10]

Kähler presents a doctrine of Christ's work in highly moralised terms of sacrifice and punishment. Seeberg sets himself to answer the question how it is possible that ' in communion with Christ we see and condemn our sins most strictly, and yet at the same time we feel them forgiven.' [11] The explanation is the Cross, which reveals at once God's love and His judgment on sin. On the Cross Christ, in whom ' humanity had again become the organ of God and

[1] P. 380.   Cf. Forsyth, *The Cruciality of the Cross*, p. 178, ' We go . . . to the obedience of faith, answering God's will of grace.   The value of the sacrificial rite lay wholly in the fact of its being God's will, God's appointment, what God ordained as the machinery of His grace for national purposes.'
[2] P. 383.   [3] P. 393.   [4] P. 395.   [5] P. 396.   [6] P. 397.
[7] P. 398.   [8] P. 405.   [9] P. 407.   [10] P. 409.
[11] *The Fundamental Truths of the Christian Religion*, p. 246 (E.T.).

precious to Him,'[1] is seen as men's representative and surety. 'He bore sufferings for them which He had not deserved, and He did for them what they did not do.'[2] Thus His work is one of 'vicarious atonement and vicarious surety.'[3] In Him and pre-eminently in His sufferings humanity becomes obedient again, while His divine power is the surety for our new life. 'And now our heart may be certain that in Christ, and in virtue of our inward connection with Him, we really have forgiveness of our sins, are graciously accepted by God, and live in a new relation of reconciliation and under a new covenant.'[4]

We must now turn to modern English and American writers. The difficulty of a fair and representative selection immediately confronts us, since the number of those who have treated of the doctrine of the Atonement is so large that anything like individual attention is an impossibility, so much so that theologians of real note must be dismissed silently or with a word. Fortunately, there are three types of soteriological theory which can be distinguished with more or less accuracy, though hardly any theologian avoids a certain crossing and mixture of types, and every theologian makes his individual contribution by viewing some aspect of the doctrine from an angle of his own, or varying some chord by a single note. The three types are represented in the past, the first by Anselm and the Reformers, the second by Irenæus and Athanasius, the third by Abelard. The characteristic expression to describe the crucified Christ is, in the first type, our Substitute, in the second our Representative, in the third our Example, or perhaps better, our Inspirer. For the first type the atoning Christ acts on God for man, for the second He acts on God as man, for the third, He acts on man for God. And as thinkers illustrative of the three types[5] I have chosen—with more diffidence as to my

---

[1] P. 250.   [2] P. 254.   [3] P. 255.   [4] P. 256.
[5] Readers of Dr. Stevens' book may feel surprised and critical at my omission of the 'Ethical Satisfaction' type, with its notable expression in the works of Dr. Scott Lidgett, Mr. W. L. Walker, and others. I would

exclusions than my inclusions—of the first, Dr. Dale, Professor Denney, and Dr. Forsyth ; of the second, Dr. M'Leod Campbell, Dr. R. C. Moberly, and Dr. Du Bose ; of the third, Dr. G. B. Stevens, Dr. W. N. Clarke, and Dr. Vincent Tymms.[1]

It will be best to begin with some description of the doctrinal position of the last-named theologians, for it stands in very decisive opposition to the orthodoxy of previous centuries, and the members of the other two groups have been greatly affected by this ' moral influence ' theory—to give it its usual name—both in adopting some of its positions, and in reaction from what they would consider its extremes.

The third part of Dr. Stevens' work is devoted to the constructive development of the doctrine. We must start from the Christian conception of God as holy love, of which wrath is an aspect. Next we see in Jesus the Saviour in virtue of His character, rather than of any metaphysical estimate of His Person : ' in Him, for the first time, we see humanity at its climax.' [2] Since sin is the opposite of love, salvation from sin is ' recovery to right relations with God, to the life of love, obedience, and sonship.' [3] Punishment is primarily disciplinary, and Christ died ' not to meet the ends of punitive justice, but

refer in justification of myself to what Dr. Stevens himself writes (p. 240) of the difficulty of distinguishing between ' ethical satisfaction ' and ' subjective ' or ' moral influence ' theories.   Writers representing the ' ethical satisfaction ' point of view hardly form a distinct school, and the fact that Dr. Stevens classes Dr. Moberly among them shows that this classification has been specially constructed for otherwise unclassifiable theologians.   On the other hand, Dr. Moberly and Dr. Du Bose seem to me to represent an influential and distinctive movement which gravitates towards the Incarnation itself as controlling idea, and to the expression of the religion controlled by that idea in sacramental categories.   In this connexion Dr. M'Leod Campbell is less their representative among older thinkers than is Dr. Milligan.

[1] Had Dr. Horace Bushnell's *The Vicarious Sacrifice* remained in its original form, I should certainly have taken its author as the first representative of the third group.   But he himself substituted *Forgiveness and Law* for parts iii. and iv. of the previous work, and the obscurity of this later treatise is to me so great that I feel it wiser to choose another representative of the third type.

[2] *Christian Doctrine of Salvation*, p. 295.   [3] P. 321.

to save man from the sin which makes justice punitive.' [1]
Forgiveness is not simply acquittal, a preliminary to
salvation, but, ' as a name for the beginning or restoration
of right personal relations, denotes the first step on the
divine side, in the development of the saved life.' [2] Christ's
relationship to mankind is that of the representative man,
and by ' sympathetic identification ' with us He shared
the curse of sin. His death was ' providentially necessary
. . . as being an indispensable part of a divine life purpose
and life-work of love.' [3] His work can be termed a satisfaction, not as a propitiation or penal substitution, but as
satisfying God's total nature ' by revealing it and realis-
ing in humanity its gracious and holy requirements.' [4]
Salvation is brought home to the individual by union
with Christ through moral kinship. Dr. Stevens' conclusion is that ' the ultimate choice among theories of
atonement reduces, at last, to the alternative between
the penal satisfaction and the moral theory.' [5]

Dr. Stevens' work is without any doubt an exceedingly
powerful exposition and defence of the theory he adopts,
while there is no lack of acuteness in his criticisms of
antagonistic positions. In particular one should note
his constant protest against the idea that representatives
of the moral theory make light of sin, and are committed
to what Professor Warfield calls ' benevolencism,' the
doctrine of the indiscriminate love of God, and that they
teach that Christ's death was a mere exhibition of love,
for which there was no moral necessity.[6]

Very similar is the teaching of Dr. Tymms.[7] His
premisses for a theory are two, that God must do all He
rightly can to exterminate sin, and do all He rightly can
to save sinners.[8] Forcible suppression of sin would be
useless as involving the suppression of human personality.
Penal satisfaction conflicts with Scripture, and with all

[1] P. 339. [2] P. 356. [3] P. 406.
[4] P. 432. [5] P. 531. [6] See pp. 268, 392, 400-1.
[7] In *The Christian Idea of Atonement*. [8] P. 81.

that we can suppose of God's feelings and purposes. Only
in *the reconciliation of man to a state of voluntary obedience
to the Divine will*[1] is there remedy for sin and a satisfaction of God. But this can be secured only through a
revelation of God's love. This revelation reaches its
climax in Christ's death, which reveals at once God's
hatred of sin, since He gave His Son to die that it might be
destroyed, and God's power to forgive, since, even to those
guilty of the sin of crucifying Christ, pardon was offered.[2]
Christ's death ' does prove the love of God to all who
appreciate its meaning . . . in this proof lies the redemptive power of the Cross.'[3]

Dr. Tymms says hardly anything of the doctrine of
Christ's Person in connexion with the Atonement, while
Dr. Stevens' lack of regard for the Chalcedonian Definition
is manifest when he speaks of ' the cold and bloodless
categories of metaphysics.'[4] Dr. Clarke, on the other
hand, sees the possibility of atonement grounded in the
unique constitution of Christ's Person.[5] By His perfect
sympathy with God and man Christ sought and was able
to bring God and men together. It was the depth of the
unity which He felt with sinful men that caused Him on
the Cross to think Himself forsaken by the Father.[6] The
Cross is, above all, the expression of God's attitude towards
sin and sinners, and the revelation of His bearing of sin
as a burden.[7] We may speak of the satisfaction of God
in Christ's death if by this we mean pleasure, not in the
infliction of punishment, but in the sight of love suffering
for sinners.

---

[1] P. 167.
[2] Dr. Tymms gives several other reasons why Christ's death was necessary
for man's redemption—to convince men of Christ's understanding sympathy
with them in the most dreaded of experiences, etc.
[3] P. 450.   [4] *Op. cit.*, p. 298.
[5] *Christian Theology in Outline* [6], p. 298. Dr. Clarke's Christology is not
easy to define. The stress falls on the idea of a creation of a new humanity
through which the Logos is able to function in a particular way.
[6] P. 352.
[7] This is Dr. Bushnell's view; Christ bore sins on His feeling; His
sacrifice represents God's eternal feeling (*The Vicarious Sacrifice*, pp. 11, 30).

These writers and others who may be classed with them [1] repudiate all attempts to keep the penal idea in any form whatever. The next group of writers are concerned to retain it. But they are equally concerned to present it ethically rather than forensically, or in mere dependence upon selected passages of Scripture. It would be a profound mistake, therefore, to correlate them with the Protestant scholastics of the seventeenth century, or to confuse them with the rigid American school of half a century ago. The great names of this last-named school must not be passed over without mention. The *Systematic Theology* of Dr. Charles Hodge recalls Turretin or Calvin himself, and the corresponding works of Dr. A. A. Hodge. Dr. W. G. Shedd and Dr. A. H. Strong reveal similar qualities of learning, grasp, and power. Given their premisses as to the inspiration of Scripture, and the validity of a perfectly precise method of deduction with the use of hard and fast ideas, and their conclusions afford little scope for logical disintegration. But those conclusions are morally so disquieting that the slightest suspicion as to premiss or method is fatal to the system as a whole.[2] Briefly, one may say that the doctrine of these theologians is that Christ in His death bore the punishment of those men whom God had predestined to salvation. The finite punishment of an infinite Person outweighed the infinite punishment of finite persons, and the inevitable demands of God's distributive justice were satisfied.

The first writer of our modern group to be noticed is Dr. Dale. His work [3] is probably the best known of all English treatises on the Atonement, and its reputation

---

[1] Dr. J. M. Wilson in his book, *The Gospel of the Atonement,* gives forcible and popular expression to this denial.

[2] See Dr. Stevens' account and discussion, pp. 174-187, 244-252. Dr. Strong's later work shows signs of other influences. Thus, in the 1907 edition of his *Systematic Theology,* he inserts a page which is dominated by mystical conceptions. 'Christ . . . as incarnate, rather revealed the atonement than made it. The historical work of atonement was finished upon the Cross, but that historical work only revealed to man the atonement made both before and since by the extra-mundane Logos.' ii. 762.

[3] *The Atonement.*

is immensely and worthily enhanced by the grave and
noble spirit which reveals itself on every page, not least
when the writer applies himself to the refutation of the
arguments of others. The great strength of the book lies
in the handling of the New Testament. As Dr. Moberly
says, ' He has shown quite convincingly that no conception
of the work of Christ, or of the hope of Christians, is really
compatible with the New Testament, which would sweep
aside the fact, or minimise the transcendent significance,
of the death on Calvary, regarded as the unique atoning
sacrifice for the sins of mankind.' [1] In the final chapters
of the book Dr. Dale develops his own theory. Relying
largely on the cry of desolation from the Cross, which, he
insists, must represent ' the actual truth of our Lord's
position,' [2] and reasoning from the conception of punishment which ' represents it as pain and loss inflicted for the
violation of a law,' [3] Dr. Dale reaches the conclusion that
in the death of Christ ' the principle that suffering is the
just desert of sin is not suppressed.' On the contrary,
Christ, in whom, as Moral Ruler of the human race, there
is the closest relationship to the Law of Righteousness,[4]
asserts this principle, ' not by inflicting suffering on the
sinner, but by enduring suffering Himself.' [5] Thus satisfaction is rendered to the apparent necessity that ' if in
any case the penalties of sin are remitted, some other
Divine act of at least equal intensity, and in which the ill
desert of sin is expressed with at least equal energy, must
take its place.' [6] So in the Cross remission of sin follows
upon admission of the justice of sin's punishment ; Christ
' endured the penalties of sin, and so made an actual
submission to the authority and righteousness of the
principle which those penalties express.' [7] And this He
could do in the name of the human race, because of His

---

[1] *Atonement and Personality*, p. 389.   [2] P. 61.   [3] P. 383.
[4] See the preface to the seventh edition, pp. xxvii.-xxxvii. for Dale's defence
of his argument at this point.
[5] P. 392.   [6] P. 391.   [7] P. 423.

original and ideal relationship to the race.[1] Dr. Dale's position may be summed up in the following words of his : ' The Death of Christ was a propitiation for the sins of men, because it was a revelation of the righteousness of God, on the ground of which He can remit the penalties of sin ; because it was an act of submission to the justice of those penalties on behalf of mankind, an act in which our own submission was really and vitally included ; and because it secured the destruction of sin in all who through faith are restored to union with Christ.' [2]

Sin deserves punishment ; to this desert justice was done in the death of Christ. This is Dr. Dale's belief, and to this extent he preserves the penal element. Nevertheless, his doctrine is not the orthodoxy of the past. No sin was imputed to Christ, such imputation is ' a legal fiction.' [3] There can be no such antithesis of qualities in God as to enable us to say that a ransom was paid by the Divine mercy to the Divine justice : ' that hypothesis is mere rhetoric.' [4] And though it is said that Christ ' submitted to the actual penalty of sin,' [5] which would imply that His sufferings were in the truest sense penal, yet there is much in the treatise which recalls Grotius [6] rather than post-reformation orthodoxy, and the theory of *acceptilatio*, that Christ's sufferings were not the actual penalties of sin, but were accepted by God in place of, or as of equal value with, those penalties. In any judgment of Dr. Dale full value must be given to the grandeur of his conception of the eternal Law of Righteousness, upon the demands of which his theory, whether it be estimated as strictly penal or Grotian, depends ; while, at the same

---

[1] The tenth lecture is devoted to a discussion of this relationship. Both Dr. Moberly, *op. cit.*, p. 395, and Dr. Stevens, *op. cit.*, p. 330, regard it as inconsistent with the preceding lectures. I think they exaggerate the inconsistency.

[2] P. 434.   [3] Preface to seventh ed., p. lxiii.

[4] P. 357.   [5] P. 424.

[6] Dr. Stevens (p. 190) thinks that the Grotian element is the dominant one in Dale. The latter (p. 294) refers curiously to the true character of the Reformation theory being ' most perfectly expressed in the exaggerated and degraded form which it received from Grotius.'

time, his theory of the relation of this Law to God, that in Him ' it is *alive* ; it reigns on His throne, sways His sceptre, is crowned with His glory,' needs more rigorous investigation than is to be found in his pages.

In Professor Denney's works a substantially similar view is presented with equal ability but with an occasional narrowness and harshness [1] towards the supporters of other conceptions which is noticeably absent from the pages of Dr. Dale. His exegesis is illuminating for, among other things, his exposure of the false antithesis between ' historical ' and ' dogmatic ' interpretation, while, in the constructive portions of his writings, we may notice the following as leading principles : (i.) the often-made distinction of ' fact ' and ' theory ' in connexion with the atonement is neither reasonable nor scriptural ; ' the work of Christ in relation to sin is not a naked fact, an impenetrable, unintelligible fact ; it is, in the New Testament, a luminous, interpretable, and interpreted fact.' [2] (ii.) In the work of Christ His distinction from men rather than His likeness to men should be in the foreground ; accordingly ' substitution ' is a better word than ' representation,' if only because the latter word might suggest that Christ was ' ours ' to begin with, and was put forward by us : ' but a representative not produced by us, but given to us—not chosen by us, but the elect of God, is not a representative at all, but in that place a substitute.' [3] (iii.) The atonement was, originally, ' outside of us,' ' a finished work in which God in Christ makes a final revelation of Himself in relation to sinners and sin ' ; union with Christ, a moral rather than a mystical union, ' is not a presupposition of Christ's work, it is its fruit.' [4] (iv.) The essence

[1] Those who read his review of *Foundations* in the *British Weekly* will understand my use of these terms.

[2] *Studies in Theology*, p. 106.

[3] *The Atonement and the Modern Mind*, p. 99. Cf. Forsyth, *The Cruciality of the Cross*, p. 85. 'He saved us by His difference from us. He did not redeem us because He represented us ; rather He represents us because He redeemed.'

[4] *Op. cit.*, pp. 101, 102.

of this work, which must be interpreted as action—' Our Lord's Passion *is* His sublimest action '[1]—is to be found in Christ's bearing God's condemnation of man's sin, and ' dying that death of ours which is the wages of sin,' [2] so that, since He died for our sins, '*that death* we do not die.'[3] There is a real moral connexion between sin and death,[4] and in His death Christ bore our sins, and through His death forgiveness is mediated. (v.) The antithesis often supposed to exist between love and propitiation has no relevance for the New Testament, according to which the propitiation that God provides in Christ is the final proof of His love.[5] (vi.) Sin and atonement confront one another as the world's one religious problem, and the one religious solution of that problem.[6] A doctrine of the atonement which seeks to be in accord with the New Testament must treat sin ' with the seriousness with which it is treated in the New Testament.' [7] And, in accordance with this, ' propitiation, in the sense of an absolutely serious dealing with God's condemnation of sin for its removal, is essential to forgiveness, as long as we regard God's condemnation of sin as an absolutely real and serious thing.' [8] Only it is wrong to suppose that this involves a ' forensic ' or ' legal ' doctrine of atonement, resting on similar conceptions of man's relation to God.[9]

I doubt whether Dr. Stevens is justified in the somewhat sharp contrast he draws [10] between *The Atonement and the Modern Mind* and Professor Denney's earlier works. In the two earlier books, especially in the *Studies*, it is easier to grasp Dr. Denney's meaning ; but there was no particular reason for thinking that he taught a ' forensic ' doctrine, though he did teach a doctrine of penal substitution, meaning by this that Christ died the sinner's death. In

[1] *Op. cit.*, p. 109.   [2] *Studies*, p. 112.   [3] *Op. cit.*, p. 126
[4] See the discussion in *The Atonement and the Modern Mind*, pp. 63-76.
[5] *Studies*, p. 133.   *The Death of Christ*, p. 275.
[6] *The Death of Christ*, p. 327.
[7] *Studies*, p. 143.   [8] *Op. cit.*, p. 133.
[9] *The Atonement and the Modern Mind*, p. 46.
[10] *Christian Doctrine of Salvation*, p. 196.

the last of the three books he takes special care to defend the connexion which St. Paul makes between sin and death, so that, though there is a certain toning down of the colours and less sharpness of outline, the picture is not radically altered. As compared with Dr. Dale, there is less of the Grotian spirit in Professor Denney's work.

Professor Denney generally leaves on a reader the impression of having something very definite to say, together with the power that flows from the correspondence of word with thought. This is by no means the case with Dr. Forsyth. The student of this remarkable thinker feels that language is taken by force, and strained to its utmost capacity for the expression of the conceptions which raise themselves from the great deeps of a mind wherein the Christian has triumphed over the philosopher, and then served himself of his adversary's weapons. Systematic is not a word that one would naturally apply to Dr. Forsyth ; yet I know of no theologian of the day who has fewer loose ends to his thought. To adopt a phrase of his own he never attempts to set up in his theology a subsidiary centre, but at every point which he reaches in the gradual development of a position, or by some bold *coup de main*, one knows that there is a straight line back, as from any point on the circle's circumference to its centre, to that which is the moral and therefore the only possible centre of the world—the Cross of Christ.

Philosophically he stands with the voluntarists who trace themselves ultimately back to Kant, but there is no sign of the unsettling scepticism of the intellect, which modern pragmatism too often engenders. The stress laid on the moral sense by Butler and Kant, and latter-day psychological insistence on the primacy of the will among the faculties, combine to give Dr. Forsyth the formula by means of which he envisages reality. Moral Action— and one cannot over-emphasise either the adjective or the noun—on this everything turns, and the mightiest of all moral actions is the Death of Christ, for in it we see

God acting decisively, and—if we understand the word aright—finally.

To any one acquainted with his works there must be a suggestion of artificiality in any attempt at compendium or résumé made by another. Something of the spirit is inevitably lost in the course of a formal presentation of ideas which have nothing of that abstract quality which we are accustomed to associate with that word. If I quote somewhat fully it will be to obviate, to some extent at least, this disadvantage.

The starting-point is not a doctrine or a report but a verifiable reality ; ' the need of atonement does not rest on an historic fall, but on the reality of present and corporate guilt.' [1] It is to such a situation that salvation must come, and come in a moral manner with moral power equal to the situation.[2] But this means action, not process : ' a process has nothing moral in it,' [3] and religion is apt to become subjective self-culture if it does not dwell upon ' the objective reality of the act of God.' [4] Such an act is necessary for the treatment of a world guilty and by its guilt estranged from God, and it will be an act of reconciliation involving—and this was St. Paul's thought—' the fundamental, permanent, final changing of the relation between man and God, altering it from a relation of hostility to one of confidence and peace.' [5] Such reconciliation must, in view of all the moral issues, rest on atonement.[6]

But this does not mean that we have learnt nothing, and must pledge ourselves to the old dogmatic interpretations. On the contrary, we must stand quite free from many notions which have fastened on to the idea of atonement.

---

[1] *The Atonement in modern religious thought*, p. 63.

[2] ' We can only be saved by the moral ; that is, the grand sheet-anchor of our modern theories ' (*The Work of Christ*, p. 81).

[3] *Op. cit.*, p. 67.   [4] *Op. cit.*, p. 70.

[5] *Op. cit.*, p. 54.   Cf. p. 105.   ' God's feeling towards us never needed to be changed.   But God's treatment of us, God's practical relation to us—that had to change.'

[6] *Op. cit.*, p. 57.

Any idea of the atonement as ' a deflection of God's anger ' must be discarded. There was no strife of attributes in God the Father, adjusted by the Son. ' Procured grace is a contradiction in terms. The atonement did not procure grace, it flowed from grace.' Again, ' we must not think that the value of the atonement lies in any equivalent suffering ' ; we must never speak about the transfer of guilt so as to suggest that it was ' a ledger amount which could be shifted about by divine finance ' ; and though we cannot renounce the idea of penalty ' we have to be cautious in using the word,' and must abandon any thought that on the Cross Christ ' was punished by the God who was ever well pleased with His beloved Son.' [1]

The clearing-away of misconceptions prepares the way for a positive view. The first thing to grasp about the atonement is that it was the act of God. ' The real objectivity of the atonement is not that it was made to God, but by God. It was atonement made by God, not by man.' [2] This cuts at the root of all conceptions which explain the atonement along the lines of the progressive development of human nature. For Dr. Forsyth there is a difference not of degree but of kind, a difference of plane. ' When Christ did what He did, it was not human nature doing it, it was God doing it. . . . It was not human nature offering its very best to God. It was God offering His very best to man.' [3]

The Cross is what it is, that is, God's saving act in Christ, by virtue of two moral elements which go to make up its total value. The first is expressed by the words sacrifice and obedience, the second by the words confession and judgment. Let us see how each is handled in turn.

Obedience is the truth of sacrifice ; it was so in the Levitical praxis, and it is so in the Cross. There, in the

---

[1] *The Cruciality of the Cross*, pp. 78, 79.   [2] *The Work of Christ*, p. 92.
[3] *Op. cit.*, p. 24. Cf. *The Cruciality of the Cross*, p. 27. ' The prime doer in Christ's Cross was God. Christ was God reconciling. He was God doing the very best for man, and not man doing his very best before God. The former is evangelical Christianity, the latter is humanist Christianity.'

work that God had given Him to do, Christ shed His
blood, that is, made absolute consecration and sacrifice
of His will.   That was the interior side of the giving of
His life, for ' our will alone is our ownest own, the only
dear thing we can and ought really to sacrifice.' [1]   ' We
move up the moral scale . . . when we discard the idea
of equivalent penalty in favour of Christ's obedient
sanctity as the satisfying thing before God.' [2]   So we pass
right away from any thought of atonement as dependent
on sufferings containing a certain—prescribed—degree of
pain.   ' The suffering was a sacrifice to God's holiness.
In so far it was penalty.   But the atoning thing was not
its amount or acuteness, but its obedience, its sanctity.' [3]

We must go still deeper than this to gain insight into
the Cross, and pass ' from the idea of *sacrifice* to the graver
and more ethical idea of *judgment*.' [4]   The Cross reveals
God reconciling, reveals not only His love, but His holy
love.   But ' holiness and judgment are for ever insepar-
able.' [5]   Hence there is a penal side to the Cross.   ' God
must either punish sin or expiate it, for the sake of His
infrangible holy nature.' [6]   Now we can begin to understand St. Paul's language, ' God made Christ to be sin on
our behalf.'   ' In being " made sin," treated as sin (though
not as a sinner), Christ experienced sin as God does, while
He experienced its effects as man does.   He felt sin with
God, and sin's judgment with men.' [7]   ' There is a penalty
and curse for sin ;   and Christ consented to enter that
region. . . .   Christ, by the deep intimacy of His sympathy
with men, entered deeply into the blight and judgment
which was entailed by man's sin, and which must be
entailed by man's sin if God is a holy and therefore a judging God. . . .   You can therefore say that although Christ
was not punished by God, He bore God's penalty upon

[1] *The Cruciality of the Cross*, p. 192.
[2] *Positive Preaching and the Modern Mind*, p. 294.
[3] *The Work of Christ*, p. 157.
[4] *The Cruciality of the Cross*, p. 204.
[5] *Op. cit.*, p. 205.   [6] *Ibid.*   [7] *Op. cit.*, p. 212.

sin. That penalty was not lifted even when the Son of God passed through.' [1]   But Christ's part was not a passive one, an obedient endurance of the punishment of sin which fell upon Him.   It was Christ's active confession of God's holiness from within the sphere of sin's penalty which was the satisfaction to God.   'We speak of His confession of God's holiness, His acceptance of God's judgment, being *adequate* in a way that sin forbade any acknowledgment from us to be.' [2]   In deliberate contrast to M'Leod Campbell and Moberly, Dr. Forsyth speaks of the holy law being satisfied 'by practical confession of God's holiness far more than man's guilt.' [3]   So the positive result of Christ's work, in which is to be seen 'the energy and victory of His own moral personality,' [4] is 'the establishing and the securing of eternal righteousness and holiness,' [5] the forgiveness of the world which 'can only be accomplished by the judgment of the world.' [6]

So far it has not been made clear how this act can benefit the race, what vital connexion binds together the Cross and man's salvation.   Dr. Forsyth is not forgetful of what is needed at this point.   If Christ represents God on the one hand, He represents Humanity on the other.   'Our repentance was latent in that holiness of His which alone could and must create it, as the effect is really part of the cause—that part of the cause which is prolonged in a polar unity into the sequential conditions of time.   Not only, generally, is there an organic moral connection and a spiritual solidarity between Christ and us, but also, more particularly, there is such a moral effect on Humanity included in the work of Christ, who causes

---

[1] *The Work of Christ*, p. 147. Cf. *Positive Preaching*, p. 314, 'The judgment of God was on Christ, and not only through Christ on us.' This line of thought is pressed to its furthest conclusion in the important 'Addendum' at the end of *The Work of Christ*. Its object is to answer in the negative the question, 'If God's direct displeasure and infliction is the worst thing in sin's penalty, did the displeasure totally vanish from the infliction when Christ stood under it?'

[2] *The Work of Christ*, p. 126.   [3] *The Cruciality of the Cross*, p. 206
[4] *The Work of Christ*, p. 183.   [5] *Op. cit.*, p. 135.
[6] *Positive Preaching*, p. 300.

it, that that antedated action on us, judging, melting, changing us, is also part of His offering to God. He comes bringing His sheaves with Him. In presenting Himself He offers implicitly and proleptically the new Humanity His holy work creates.'[1] Thus representation is a better word than substitution, provided we understand that 'it is representation by One who creates by His act the Humanity He represents and does not merely sponsor it.'[2]

So the reconciliation effected in the Cross is the reconciliation of the world, and not primarily of individuals. 'It is a reconciliation of *the world as a cosmic whole*.'[3] 'God did so save the world as to carry individual salvation in the same act. The Son of God was not an individual merely; He was the representative of the whole race, and its *vis-à-vis*, on its own scale.'[4] In this sense the reconciliation is 'final in Jesus Christ and His Cross, done once for all; really effected in the spiritual world in such a way that in history the great victory is not still to be won; it has been won in reality, and has only to be followed up and secured in actuality.'[5] The relations of race and individuals to the work of Christ, and the uniting of what still remains to do with what Christ has finally done, are finely brought out in a passage with which this attempt to give Dr. Forsyth's meaning mainly in his own words may fittingly end. 'Christ, in His victorious death and risen life, has power to unite the race to Himself, and to work His complete holiness into its actual experience and history. He has power, by uniting us with Him in His spirit, to reduce Time to acknowledge in act and fact His conclusive victory of Eternity. When you think of what He did for the race and its history, you must on no account do what the Church and its theology has too

---

[1] *The Work of Christ*, p. 192; cf. the fine phrase (p. 193), 'He stretches a hand through time and seizes the far-off interest of our tears.'

[2] *Op. cit.*, p. 182.

[3] *Op. cit.*, p. 77; cf. p. 129, 'What Christ presented to God for His complete joy and satisfaction was a perfect racial obedience. It was not the perfect obedience of a saintly unit of the race. It was a racial holiness.'

[4] *The Work of Christ*, p. 116.   [5] *Op. cit.*, p. 77.

often done—you must not omit our living union with Him. It is not enough to believe that He gained a victory at a historic point. Christ is the condensation of history. You must go on to think of His summary reconciliation as being worked out to cover the whole of history and enter each soul by the spirit. You must think of the Cross as setting up a new covenant and a new Humanity, in which Christ dwells as the new righteousness of God. " Christ for us " is only intelligible as " Christ in us," and we in Him. By uniting us to Himself and His resurrection in His spirit He becomes the eternal guarantee of the historical consummation of all things some great day.' [1]

Two facts must strike every reader of these books : the first is the concentration upon the necessity for the moralising of such a doctrine as the Atonement. He may differ from Dr. Forsyth's ethical judgments, but he must recognise that they are ethical judgments and not, primarily, bits of Biblical or ecclesiastical traditionalism. And if he is also a student of Ibsen he will understand the respect in which Dr. Forsyth holds that gloomy moralist. The second fact is the social as opposed to the merely individual outlook, not only by the recognition of ' a common and universal responsibility,' and the discarding of the ' atomic conception of personality,' [2] in which Professor Denney is at one with him, but in the subordination of the redemption of the individual to the redemption of the world and the new redeemed society, the Church, which is the great witness-bearer to Christ's atoning work. If, for once, one of our controversial phrases may serve its true purpose, Dr. Forsyth is a High Churchman. Only he comes to his High Churchmanship through the Atonement, whereas it is generally arrived at through the Incarnation, in the case of the *Lux Mundi* school, for instance.

The real obscurity in his work relates to his preservation

[1] *Op. cit.*, p. 130.
[2] Denney, *The Atonement and the Modern Mind*, p. 22.

of the penal idea and terminology, in connexion with the idea of judgment. One must ask what exactly is means to say that God ' judged sin upon Christ's head,' and ' took Him in the place of sin, rather than of the sinner, and judged the sin upon Him.' [1] That the withdrawing of the light of communion with God on the Cross was a necessary expression of that judgment is clearly indicated,[2] but how that is to be integrated into the victorious side of the Cross,[3] of which Dr. Forsyth makes so much, is not clear. There are other debatable points which his controversy with the theological liberalism [4] of scholars like Wernle, and the man-in-the-street generally, brings to the front. Many will hesitate to see nothing moral in process ; is nothing ethical revealed in the process of creation ? And many—with, I think, justification—will feel that in saving love from the trivial associations which too often have gathered round it, Dr. Forsyth never quite does it full justice as a controlling idea and power. Such a statement as ' nothing but holiness can forgive. Love cannot,' [5] is one of a number of statements which, taken together, lead me to conclude that Dr. Forsyth's insight into love is not quite equal to his insight in other respects. But even though points of disagreement were multiplied, it would be impossible for any one with knowledge and understanding of the modern theological position to deny the importance of his work, and the far-reaching character of the issues which he challenges.

The theologians of the final group which we have to deal with are bound together by the general idea that Christ as man made an adequate satisfaction to God, not

[1] *The Work of Christ*, p. 83.　　　　　[2] *Op. cit.*, p. 243.

[3] 'The blood of Christ stands for . . . the scourge of God on sin. . . . It expresses . . . the bloodshed of the battle that destroys the prince of this world, that breaks in us the guilty entail, and establishes the holy kingdom.'

[4] To be distinguished from the 'modernised theology' which he approves. This is concerned with a moralising of doctrine, and the criticism of intellectual categories which have ceased to be relevant, together with the abandonment of the old conception of Biblical inspiration and authority.

[5] *Positive Preaching*, p. 333.

by the enduring of any penal affliction, but by revealing, as the representative of mankind, or, more strongly, the inclusive Man, that spirit of grief for sin and acknowledgment of its guilt, that positive holiness and conquest over sin, which, when displayed in its perfection—a perfection possible only to One Himself sinless—was the one perfect atonement for sin.   We shall see that there are differences of treatment within this covering unity of outlook, and it is not difficult to pass from this position to the view that the Incarnation itself, the bringing together of God and man in the Person of Christ, is itself the Atonement—a view that finds itself to some extent in the works of Dr. Westcott, and is represented in varying degrees by such writers as Mr. Eck, Dr. Foley, and Dr. J. M. Wilson.[1]

Dr. M'Leod Campbell's treatise, *The Nature of the Atonement*, is dignified by that grave and lofty spirit which almost all the classical contributions to the subject display. His own divergence from the strict Calvinistic doctrine of Owen, with whom, not quite correctly as I must think, he couples President Edwards, never blinds him to the religious interests which that doctrine was intended to conserve.   He is by no means confident that certain modifications of this theology which, though his name is not mentioned, can be referred back to Grotius are an improvement.   The grounding of the sufferings of Christ in the demands of ' rectoral or public justice ' rather than in ' distributive or absolute justice ' does not satisfy him. ' Unless,' he says, ' there be a rightness in connecting sin with misery, and righteousness with blessedness, looking at individual cases simply in themselves, I cannot see that

[1] Mr. Eck, though he speaks of 'the redemption of human nature by its assumption into God,' goes on to describe the Atoning Death as ' the representative act of all mankind, the means whereby man acknowledges his sin, confesses the righteousness of God's sentence, and pays the penalty which else he could not pay.'   He also quotes, with obvious approval, some of Dr. Dale's strongest and most characteristic remarks (*The Incarnation*, pp. 205-220).   Dr. Foley exalts the Greek idea of deification, while Dr. Wilson combines the 'moral influences' theory with the notion that the identification of the human and divine in the Incarnation is the Atonement: 'there is no other.'

there is a rightness in connecting them as a rule of moral government.'[1] Similarly he sympathises with the idea of imputation, though not with its intellectual expression, as testifying to the sense of dependence on Christ.[2] Nor does he hesitate to conceive of a proportion between men's sins and Christ's sufferings, for these are 'essential to the living reality of a moral and spiritual atonement.'[3] Where he breaks completely away from the older view is in his denial that these sufferings were penal. 'While Christ suffered for our sins as an atoning sacrifice, what He suffered was not—because from its nature it could not be —a punishment.'[4] By an elaborate and unconvincing argument,[5] he rules out from the cry on the Cross not only the idea of penal suffering but any suggestion of 'a hiding of the Father's face.'[6] There was no 'interruption of the continuity of that life which was in the consciousness of the Father's favour.'

In putting forward his own view Dr. M'Leod Campbell, while at every point in his book he approaches the question through the Fatherhood of God, never gives any excuse for the attribution to him of a doctrine of a genial God, unmoved to wrath by sin. 'The wrath of God against sin is a reality . . . nor is the idea that satisfaction was due to divine justice a delusion. . . . And, if so, then Christ, in dealing with God on behalf of men, must be conceived of as dealing with the righteous wrath of God against sin, and *as according to it that which was due.*'[7] Christ deals with it by making a perfect confession of men's sins. The thought which entered Edwards' mind, but which he rejected without more ado as impossible, of 'an equivalent sorrow and repentance,' becomes central. That perfect confession which 'was only possible to perfect holiness'[8] was offered by Christ to the Father. 'That oneness of mind with the Father, which towards

---

[1] *Op. cit.*, p. 68 (sixth edition).   [2] P. 139.   [3] P. 248.   [4] P. 101.
[5] Dr. Moberly (*Atonement and Personality*, p. 409) says there is in it 'a painful sense of unauthorised and almost wilful minimising.'
[6] P. 241.   [7] P. 116.   [8] P. 260.

man took the form of condemnation of sin, would in the
Son's dealing with the Father in relation to our sins take
the form of a perfect confession of our sins. This confession,
as to its own nature, must have been *a perfect Amen in
humanity to the judgment of God on the sin of man.*' [1] Such
confession, commensurate with the evil of sin and God's
wrath against it, was rendered possible by the Incarnation
alone ; but the Incarnation made it more than possible,
it made it inevitable, and in it was the perfect expiation
of sin, and the earnest of that pardon which men need,
not simply from their Judge, but from their Father. We
must think too of Christ's intercession along with His
confession. This is a part of His sacrifice ; 'its power
as an *element of atonement* we must see, if we consider that
it was the voice of the divine love coming from humanity,
offering for man a pure intercession according to the will
of God.' [2] Christ's atoning work culminated in His death ;
to Him alone as perfectly holy could death have ' its perfect
meaning as the wages of sin,' as the withdrawal of God's
gift of life ; and so ' *death filled with that moral and spiritual
meaning in relation to God and His righteous law* which it
had as tasted by Christ, and *passed through in the spirit
of sonship, was the perfecting of the atonement.*' [3] Thus
Christ makes in humanity ' the due moral and spiritual
atonement for sin ' ; [4] He, on behalf of man, ' responds to
the divine wrath against sin, saying, " Thou art righteous,
O Lord, who judgest so " . . . and in that perfect response
He absorbs it.' [5]

Not the least important feature of Dr. M'Leod Campbell's
theory is the stress he lays and the use he makes of what
he calls the ' prospective aspect of the atonement.' The
atonement is conceived as directly related to the gift of
eternal life, which is manifested in the life of Sonship ;

---

[1] P. 116.   [2] P. 127.   [3] P. 261.   [4] P. 270.
[5] P. 117 ; cf. the very similar language of Dr. Forsyth (*The Work of
Christ*, p. 157), 'The whole of His work was not the bearing of punishment ;
it was not the acceptance of suffering. It was the recognition and justification of it, the " homologation " of God's judgment and God's holiness in it.'

thus deliverance from sin rather than from the punishment of sin becomes the direct and foremost blessing of Christ's work ; if we suffer the atonement ' to inform us by its own light why we needed it, and what its true value to us is, the punishment of sin will fall into its proper place as testifying to the existence of an evil greater than itself, even *sin* ; from which greater evil it is the *direct* object of the atonement to deliver us—deliverance from punishment being but a secondary result.' [1]

For the doctrine of vicarious punishment, however expressed, Dr. M'Leod Campbell substitutes a doctrine of vicarious repentance and confession. The possibility of such action on the part of Christ is due to His relationship on the one hand to God, on the other to men. Nevertheless, it is a true criticism of Dr. Moberly's that ' Dr. M'Leod Campbell appears to me to have discerned with more complete success the nature of the relation of Christ to God than that of the relation of men to Christ ' ; [2] all externalisation of the atonement has not been avoided in the avoidance of its most common form. Another weakness to which Dr. Moberly draws attention is the ignoring of Pentecost, a weakness which he also associates with the work of Dr. Dale : neither writer realises ' the impossibility of explaining atonement in its personal relation to ourselves, apart from the doctrine of the Holy Ghost.' [3] Whatever may be thought of Dr. Moberly's own formulation of the doctrine, to which we must now turn, it is certain that he has applied himself to the most thoroughgoing rectification of these weaknesses.

Dr. Moberly's conclusion is reached through two premisses, one of a moral, one of a theological, character, which themselves are not taken for granted, but are the outcome of a course of critical investigation of the relevant subject-matter in either case. The first is that since any sort of penitence must imply a degree of reidentification

---

[1] P. 164.   [2] *Atonement and Personality*, p. 402.
[3] Moberly, *op, cit.*, p. 409.

on the part of the penitent with righteousness, perfect
penitence would imply a completely reidentification.
But such penitence is impossible for one who has sinned,
since the power of sin is within the self, and ' the reality
of sin in the self blunts the self's power of utter antithesis
against sin.' [1] So follows the ' irresistible—if paradoxical
—truth : that a true penitence is as much the inherent
impossibility, as it is the inherent necessity, of every man
that has sinned.' [2] In other words ' penitence, in the
perfectness of its full meaning, is not even conceivably
possible, except it be to the personally sinless.' [3]

Something then is necessary to atonement—for ' perfect
penitence would be such a change of self as would by
contradiction make the past dead ' [4]—which is not within
the power of sinful man. How then is man to be saved ?
A second support is needed if any satisfactory conclusion
is to be reached. It is found in the Person of Christ and
the character of His Humanity. Christ who is ' identically
God ' is also ' inclusively man.' [5] Christ's Humanity includes and consummates the humanity of all other men.
So we have the means of transcending the differences
which separate Anselm and Abelard, and the upholders
of ' objective ' and ' subjective ' views. Christ does not
' deal with the Father in relation to men ' by way of
vicarious expiatory confession of sin, but ' Christ *was*
humanity perfectly penitent, humanity perfectly righteous,
humanity therefore in perfect accord with, and response
to, the very essential character of Deity.' [6] And this
perfect penitence involved death, not in any way as the
endurance of punishment—punishment is not primarily
retributive, and as retributive could not be brought into
any connexion with the perfect penitence of Christ—but
as its own consummation. ' In the bitter humiliation of
a self-adopted consciousness of what sin—and therefore
of what the damnation of sin—really is, He bowed His

[1] P. 42.   [2] P. 43.   [3] P. 117.
[4] P. xviii.   [5] P. 86.   [6] P. 404.

head to that which, as far as mortal experience can go, is so far, at least, the counterpart on earth of damnation, that it is the extreme possibility of contradiction and destruction of self.'[1] This is the atonement as an objective fact, 'external, objective, historical, consummated adequately and once for all,' but, in order to the salvation of persons, it must become subjective; it must pass into and transform personalities. This necessarily leads on to the doctrine of the Holy Spirit; 'it is Pentecost, it is the gift progressively transforming, it is the indwelling of the Spirit of Holiness, the Spirit of the Crucified, which is the transfiguring of human personality; a transfiguring in which at last, for the first time, self has become fully self, and the meaning of human personality is consummated and realised.'[2] Calvary, in fact, must lead on to Pentecost, and apart from Pentecost no intelligible link unites man with Calvary.

Dr. Moberly's book is much more than a treatise on the Atonement; it is an outline of systematic theology, and the parts hang so closely together that it is difficult to give a fair impression of the whole without going through the chapters one by one. The impression which it produced on publication was immense, for it appeared to be an exposition of its subject, absolutely loyal to the orthodoxy of the Creeds, careful not to give away the 'objective' side of the atonement,[3] free and modern in its treatment of such problems as punishment and personality. All this

[1] Pp. 133, 142. [2] P. 153.
[3] Unless I much misunderstand him Principal H. G. Grey, in his preface to Dimock's *Death of Christ*[2], regards Dr. Moberly as the expounder of a *merely* subjective view. This is quite certainly not the case. As I have referred to this preface I should like to draw attention to Dr. Grey's words, 'the free objective forgiveness purchased by the death of Christ.' What does this mean? Does it mean 'possibility of forgiveness'? If so, the actualising of this possibility must involve in the individual the presence of that 'forgivableness' on which Dr. Moberly lays stress, but without making it, as Dr. Grey seems to think, the 'real atonement.' On the other hand, if Dr. Grey rejects the gloss, 'possibility of forgiveness,' he is using the word in an impersonal and not very intelligible sense. Nor can I think it at all right to read into the idea of forgivableness the idea of merit, as Dr. J. G. Simpson does (*The Religion of the Atonement*, p. 37) when he says

tended to cover up the serious difficulties involved in the paradox: True penitence is a necessity for the sinner, it is possible only for the sinless. In addition to this the view taken of Christ's humanity needs very rigorous examination, as well as the conception of punishment and the use made of that conception in different parts of the book.[1] Moreover, it cannot be denied that though Dr. Moberly should not be classed with advocates of the 'moral influence' theory, it would be perfectly possible to drop his special view of Christ's penitence, which is the objective side of his doctrine, and so make the transition to that theory which finds support in much of his argument. That *Atonement and Personality* is, despite all criticisms, a great book, is, to me, unquestionable: but not less certain is it that the revision of Dr. M'Leod Campbell's theory which it contains lacks the true note of permanence.

The last writer who has to be considered is Dr. Du Bose. Perhaps he has suffered a little from being discovered as a prophet by Dr. Sanday [2]—the rôle is not an easy one to fill, still less to sustain—but the unrhetorical character of his theological audacity (without any fireworks he can take his reader's breath away), and the exceptional

---

that the wideness of the mercy of God's love 'depends on the fact that there is nothing "forgivable," in other words no merit, of which it takes account.' How the divine love is to function as forgiveness, apart from some re-orientation of the desires and the will of the individual sinner I cannot imagine, but that is not to introduce the idea of 'merit.'

[1] Every one who can should read Dr. Hasting Rashdall's review in the *Journal of Theological Studies*, iii. 178-211. It is an exceptionally fine and stimulating piece of criticism, and Dr. Rashdall's own standpoint—the elaboration of which in this year's Bampton Lectures on the Atonement will be eagerly awaited—whether acceptable or not to the reader, is hardly obtruded at all, and never to the dislocation of the matter in hand. He finds two great confusions running through the book: (1) 'The confusion between an effect produced upon the character of the sinner, and an obliteration of sin or guilt which takes place independently of any such effect'; (2) 'The confusion between the retributive view of punishment and the disciplinary.' I may also refer to the chapter on the Atonement in Mr. R. A. Knox's *Some Loose Stones*, which is directed at Mr. W. H. Moberly's article in *Foundations*. (Mr. W. H. Moberly's position is essentially that of his father.) So responsible a judge as Professor H. R. Mackintosh, writing in the *Review of Theology and Philosophy* (Feb. 1914), gives it as his opinion that Mr. Knox has fairly disposed of the theory of vicarious penitence.

[2] See *The Life of Christ in Recent Research*, p. 259.

thoroughness with which he pursues his leading thoughts
to the end, make him worthy to rank with Dr. M'Leod
Campbell and Dr. Moberly.   Above all, Christianity is
an extraordinarily living thing in his books.   His doctrine
of the Atonement is controlled by two ideas.   The first is
that what Christ did He did initially for Himself.   ' Jesus
Himself in His humanity needed the salvation which all
humanity needs.   Salvation for Him, as for us, demanded
that conflict with sin and conquest of sin which was pre-
eminently His experience and His achievement.' [1]   ' Jesus
Christ was no more saved by any accident or fact of nature
than we are ; He was saved only by the personal act of
His own holiness and life in the nature.' [2]   In this conception of Christ's life as moral action there is obvious affinity
with Dr. Forsyth's conclusions. [3]   The second controlling
idea we have met with in reviewing Dr. Moberly : it is the
inclusive character of Christ's humanity, and Dr. Du Bose
seems to me to go beyond even Dr. Moberly in the stress
that he lays upon this fact.   In countless ways and connexions he elaborates the notion that in Christ humanity
was redeemed and sin conquered, as alone it could be
conquered, by the victory of holiness.   This is the atonement, an atonement not by the union of the divine and
the human in the Person of Christ—Dr. Du Bose completely
subordinates the physical to the moral [4]—but by that
death of humanity to sin which is contained in the death
of Christ.   Such language as the following is typical :
' The Incarnation was in humanity, not only in a man.' [5]
' Sin was actually abolished in humanity in the person of
Jesus Christ, in whom in the most literal and actual sense

[1] *The Gospel according to Saint Paul*, p. 127.
[2] *High Priesthood and Sacrifice*, p. 78.
[3] Dr. Forsyth has worked out his thought in connexion with Christology
in the last chapters of his *Person and Place of Jesus Christ*, entitled ' The
Kenosis or Self-emptying of Christ,' and ' The Plerosis or the Self-Fulfilment
of Christ.'
[4] Cf. *The Gospel according to Saint Paul*, p. 222, ' Sin or holiness cannot
be in mere nature or condition ; they can be only in what *we* are or do in the
nature or the condition.'
[5] *High Priesthood and Sacrifice*, p. 217.

humanity died to itself and so to sin, and lived to God and
so to holiness and righteousness and eternal life.'¹ 'We
exactly express or explain any act of His, and so the
supreme and decisive act, when we say that humanity did
it in His person, and that it was just precisely what
humanity needed to do in order to its own redemption
and completion. In His person humanity righted itself
with God, redeemed itself from sin, raised itself from
death . . . by undergoing that spiritual, moral, and natural
change or transition, from the evil it needed to be saved
from to the good it needed to be saved to, which was in
itself necessary to constitute its salvation.'² Dr. Du Bose
is aware of the possible charge that he is reviving a realistic
philosophy with humanity as an universal apart from
particular men, and counters it with the argument which
Dr. Moberly had also used that Christ's humanity is the
humanity of Deity, and therefore capable of an universal
relation ; 'the universality of our Lord's humanity is
only explicable upon the fact that His personality is
a divine one. . . . The concrete universal of humanity
which may be found in Jesus Christ belongs to it not as
humanity but as God in humanity.'³

It would be a great mistake to suppose that Dr. Du
Bose is indifferent to the Cross. He makes much of death
in general—though his argument on this point seems very
free of the New Testament—and of Christ's death as His
supreme act. Death, because of all that it implies of
possibility of change and development, is man's great
opportunity ; 'it is,' if it be death with Christ, 'the
death of the nature in which we cannot but sin, and of
ourselves who cannot but sin in it.'⁴ Commenting on
the words περὶ ἁμαρτίας of Romans viii. 3 he writes, 'Jesus
Christ had come *for* or *about* sin, and as an offering or
sacrifice for sin. That which He offered up in sacrifice

---

¹ *The Gospel according to Saint Paul*, p. 93.
² *Op. cit.*, p. 126.   ³ *Op. cit.*, p. 297.
⁴ *High Priesthood and Sacrifice*, p. 22.

to God, that which He carried back with Him to God
from His divine mission to men, was humanity in His
person, dead in its old self in the flesh, and alive to God
in the spirit. . . . It was humanity in Christ that condemned and abolished sin. Our Lord took our flesh of
sin only that in it He might accomplish that death to sin
which is our own and only salvation from sin.' [1] In
another place his language more nearly resembles Dr.
Moberly's : ' Jesus Christ, or humanity in Him, accomplished salvation or holiness through a lifelong and death-
completed act of perfect repentance and perfect faith.' [2]
Of course this objective work, ' God's at-one-ing Himself
with man in and through the responsive act of man
at-one-ing himself with God,' [3] like the redemption of the
world in Dr. Forsyth's scheme, does not leave individuals
with nothing to do. The crucifixion and resurrection of
Christ must be reproduced in the individual's co-crucifixion
and co-resurrection with Christ. At this point Dr. Du
Bose expresses himself in what at first sight is a highly
individualistic and even Pelagian manner. ' Only the man
himself can make himself either sinful or holy,' ' Human
salvation is a definite act, and a definite act of our own,' [4]
—it is such sentences as these which make him no writer
for babes and for people quick to jump to conclusions.
Not more is implied than that if salvation is to come to
man through his will, that will must not be moved from
without as though it were an automaton.[5]

Dr. Du Bose is a theologian, who leaves himself open
to attack at many points, in Theology proper and Christology as well as Soteriology. We are immediately con-

[1] *The Gospel according to Saint Paul*, p. 230.
[2] *The Gospel in the Gospels*, p. 158. It must be remembered that for Dr.
Du Bose Christ's death was a necessity, because death is a necessary condition of human salvation. See his chapter, ' Human Destiny through
Death,' in *High Priesthood and Sacrifice*.
[3] *The Gospel according to Saint Paul*, p. 226.
[4] *High Priesthood and Sacrifice*, p. 14.
[5] Dr. Du Bose's language is defensible enough, but on the wider matter I
am not confident that a vital union has been made between humanity in
Christ and what it does, and individuals and what they do.

cerned with the last alone, though it is especially hard,
in his case, to break up his dogmatic into fragments.
And if I were to put briefly what presents itself as the
root-defect in his treatment of atonement and salvation,
a defect less marked in Dr. Moberly and hardly observable
at all in Dr. M'Leod Campbell, it would be that his ' intense
moral earnestness,' [1] truly indicated by Dr. Sanday, yet
lacks the tragic note.   Experience is curtailed of elements
whose loss weakens the total formulation in more than
incidental respects.   Such a phrase as ' the half grace
of forgiveness ' [2] is defensible when taken along with the
ethical demand for the extermination of sin—' the only
ultimate and complete thing to be done about sin is to
abolish it ' ; [3] nevertheless, Dr. Simpson rightly objects
to its use on Scriptural and experiential grounds.[4]   In
a complete moral synthesis forgiveness would be a means
to the end, perfect holiness, and not the end itself ; indeed,
the end reached, it is difficult to see how forgiveness, as
a present reality, could hold any place at all ; but such a
synthesis is quite out of the question under the conditions
of this world, and the experience which testifies to forgiveness as an end in itself is the only kind of experience which
answers to the necessarily fragmentary character of our
moral existence.

Had space permitted I should have liked to notice some
modern books which approach the subject from particular
angles, to show how this or that current of scientific or
philosophical thought throws light upon the idea of
atonement, and helps towards the construction of an
adequate Christian doctrine.   Professor Lofthouse's *Ethics
and Atonement*, with its argument that atonement in the
sense of reconciliation was the necessary expression of
God's nature face to face with sin ;   Mr. M'Dowall's
Evolution and the Need of Atonement, in which advance is

[1] Sanday, *op. cit.*, p. 298.
[2] *The Gospel according to Saint Paul*, p. 102.
[3] *High Priesthood and Sacrifice*, p. 143.
[4] *Religion of the Atonement*, p. 37.

made from the side of biology and evolution, and the teleological implications of the world-process find their vindication, and the opposing ' katabolic ' forces their defeat, in the work of Christ ; Dr. Douglas White's *Forgiveness and Suffering*, written to show the inseparability of the one from the other, and that God Himself must suffer if He is to forgive—these works and others would have repaid detailed attention.

But it is time to turn from particular writings, and, in a final chapter, to apply a wider criticism, in which, it is hoped, will be revealed the elements most necessary to the construction of a satisfactory positive doctrine.

CHAPTER VII

TOWARDS A DOCTRINE

WE have now tested the Biblical foundation on which, with more or less of faithful correspondence to the character of that basis, successive doctrines of the Atonement have been reared. We have also passed in review the most important of those doctrines, the historical environment and the metaphysical presuppositions often providing an explanation and a criticism of this or that conception. Debt—Honour—Public Justice—Representative Headship —we have seen what large parts such terms have played, and how theory has been not only regulated by but constituted in one of them. With a sense of bewilderment we observe that the doctrine which, of all others, most closely links together the counsels of God and the destiny of man, the doctrine that ' Christ died for our sins ' (those who make the Incarnation itself the atonement do not deny that the atoning Person passes through the atoning life to a climax in the atoning death), has been so variously interpreted that an Hegelian synthesis of all differences, a discovery of unity in diversity, is, at best, a mere strained-off residuum, which, in effect, is equivalent to a return of the problem to its starting-point through the elimination of everything that has given to the problem's answer a definitive meaning.

All this is true, but it is not the whole truth. The student all at sea with conflicting charts and unsteady compass must seek help from the preacher, the priest, and the minister. Let us beware of hard-and-fast divisions, of unreal distinctions of practice from thought. But with this caution we must admit the existence of different spheres of activity, suited for men of different powers, and looking, immediately at least, for different results. And of the minister of the Gospel the one constant theme is the Atonement. As Bengel says of the last months of our Lord's ministry *jam habitabat in passione sua*, so the ministry which presses upon man whether at the altar,[1] or in the pulpit, or at the penitent form τὰ περὶ Ἰησοῦ, dwells continuously upon that death and passion. Cardinal Wiseman loved the Yorkshire Methodists, because they from the pulpit as he from the altar pleaded the one great sacrifice.[2] There is not so much preaching about the Atonement as was once the case; this is, in part, a weakness, and from it we can judge how the student's perplexities react upon the preacher; but the fact of the Atonement conditions the life of the Church throughout, and in the simple statement of the fact there is demonstrable power. To this extent there is truth with those who contrast fact and theory; but if we were able more deeply to search the minds of those who hear and respond to the fact we should, I believe, find there some faintest suggestion of a theory hidden.

In such recollections even those of us who shrink from a facile, adaptable pragmatism may take heart. 'The elephant rests on the tortoise, but what does the tortoise rest on?' 'Never mind,' says the pragmatist, 'as long as the tortoise can do its job.' So he might ask, 'Why trouble about the theory of the Atonement? You will find it work if you preach it as a fact.' The statement is true, and the question may be relevant to many a troubled spirit. But we answer that the statement would not be true at all unless there were a theory, rather a doctrine,

---

[1] It is surely only by an oversight, an overmuch love of antithesis, that Dr. Simpson, in his *Religion of the Atonement*, welcomes 'Catholicism at the altar, but Evangelicalism in the pulpit.' Is not the altar 'evangelical' or nothing?

[2] I have not the exact quotation and reference.

of the Atonement, though it were known to God alone. We do not reach bed-rock in preaching facts : they may be mere phenomena, dependent for their existence on associations of a heterogeneous character, which have yet gathered round them. A true fact is rooted in that final reality which we call God, and is proclaimed as a revelation of His purposes and activities. Such a fact carries with it something, at least, of its own interpretation. And remembering that it is into a fact of this kind that the life of the Church is integrated, we may go forward with better heart to explore lines of thought, at the end of which, could we penetrate far enough, the goal of our search may lie.

He who should wish to make of the Atonement a luminous reality for himself and others must ever strive to do justice to three things—to the meaning of the Bible, to the meaning of the moral consciousness, and to the meaning of Christian religious experience. If he is at all successful, even if he is at all in earnest in his attempt, he will be secure against the lamentable failures which result when the Atonement is treated as an intellectual problem, the truth of which can be vindicated or the falseness shown by Euclidean methods. A doctrine which supplies at any rate the immediate, possibly, or even probably, the final cause why God was manifest in the flesh must be handled with an adequate appreciation of its supernatural [1] character. Now the Bible, the moral consciousness, and Christian religious experience, if what they profess to register is part of reality, or reality under a certain aspect, are essentially supernatural. Each one of the three rises above the level of natural life, thought, and inclination ; this is as true of the moral consciousness as of the other two. In other words we are in the presence of mysteries. Mystery is not a word invented by a theologian in a fix,

[1] I do not care for this word, and look on it as fraught with more philosophical difficulties than the word 'miraculous.' But the word 'miraculous' has gathered various associations which may mislead like πρόσωπον in the third and fourth centuries.

though he may make illegitimate use of it at times. Whether we will or no, *omnia abeunt in mysterium* ; the only question is as to the ultimate nature of the mystery. The Christian, not alone in this respect, affirms that the mystery is theological,[1] and not only theological but moral ; that is, not simply one which reaches back to God, but to a God of a particular kind, a God of whom the word character can be employed. Only the Christian goes further, and not just a little—or a great deal—further along the same road. He strikes off on a road of his own. For him the mystery includes as a realised fact the revelation of the mystery in the Person and Work of Jesus Christ. So the appearance of Jesus Christ in the world is a supernatural event. It is not something which leads to great, holy, even divine results. It is something in which the results are necessarily contained, *a priori*, not merely *a posteriori*. Thus the mystery of eternity is revealed in time, but the element of mystery is not thereby abrogated. When the Church confesses the doctrine of the Incarnation, of God manifest in the flesh, she does not claim a rationalistic triumph ; what she contends is that eternal mystery has come into special contact with men through temporal mystery, and that the knowledge of the truth has thereby been increased. Truth did come through Jesus Christ, not ultimately because He spoke true things, but because He was the Truth.

To this the supernatural Bible, and the supernatural Christian religious experience, bear direct witness. The supernatural moral consciousness does not bear direct witness. Nevertheless, it bears a witness, which, when taken along with the other two, may be found to have an entirely relevant place in reference to the mystery of the Incarnation. And apart from it the testimony of those two may appear as incomplete and therefore as less convincing.

[1] I do not say ' religious,' since some writers, *e.g.* Mr. Lowes Dickinson, use that word without introducing the idea of God.

O

In a very real sense, then, the Atonement must be a mystery ; we approach it by way of mysteries, and the religion of which it is either the central point, or at least an inexpugnable doctrine, is a mystery. With this necessary warning we may begin to advance upon its meaning, and gain insight into its character. Insight is generally recognised as a singularly precious gift, and it is worth noting that it is not needed for something which lies like a map spread out before the observer.

' Christ died for our sins.' That is, the relation between Christ and sins not His own was such that He died, with some purpose not defined in view. Christ comes and deals with a particular situation in a particular way. That is the principle of intervention. But the principle of intervention is seen more clearly in other passages as the principle of mediation. The situation always remains the same ; it is the situation which results from sin. The intervention also remains the same. But the situation does not concern man alone—it concerns God as well. The situation produced by sin lies, as it were, between God and man. Therefore the intervention of Christ is His mediation between God and man. Let that plain fact have, for the moment, its own force. Christ's relation to God and to man may affect the character of that mediation ; His intervention may be interpreted (not rightly, I think, but still possibly) as operative upon man alone, and not upon God ; nevertheless, the result of that intervention is that the situation as between God and man changes. It changes not through direct dealing of God and man with one another, but through the action of Christ. Christ is a third to God and man, though He be both God and man, for He is neither simply God nor simply man. It is impossible to cut out of the New Testament this principle of mediation, manifested in and carried into effect by a Person.

From the New Testament we pass to the moral consciousness. Has that any primary verdict to deliver in regard

to sin ? The ground we tread is rough through much
controversy, and slippery with the subtleties of analysis.
Yet there is a primary verdict, that sin deserves punishment. Contentious as this assertion is, which involves
one out of many possible attitudes towards the philosophy
of punishment, it is, I believe, justifiable on two grounds.
In the first place, the connexion between sin and punishment, of which we may fairly say that we have no knowledge
of a time when such connexion was not in existence, is
inexplicable on any grounds except that wrongdoing,
whatever is supposed to constitute wrongdoing, merits
punishment. Any other theory introduces elements of
analysis and of perspective quite beyond the powers of
humanity in the earliest times of which we have knowledge.
But secondly, and of equal though rather different importance, the verdict that sin deserves punishment, and, to
make the matter perfectly clear, in the person of the sinner,
is one that is endorsed by the sinner himself when penitence,
however fragmentary, touches the soul. To use the word
' invariable ' is to lay oneself open to very natural charges
of rashness, yet I believe that the penitent consciousness
does necessarily and invariably re-echo the simple confession of the penitent thief, ' We indeed justly ; for we
receive the due reward of our misdeeds.' Now it is
perfectly true that punishment accepted in this spirit
ceases to be mere retribution ; its quality changes, and
becomes healing and restorative. But Dr. Moberly's
chapter on Punishment, acute as it undoubtedly is, seems
to me to suffer very seriously from his omission, curious
in one with such insight into psychological conditions, to
do any justice to the particular state of consciousness and
the verdict which it pronounces, to which I have just
referred. The result is that he involves himself in real
difficulties as to the retributive aspect of punishment,
an aspect he does not deny but regards as arising when
punishment fails to accomplish its proper, restorative
task. All the criticisms which Dr. Rashdall makes of his

inconsistencies at this point are unanswerable. Unless there is some primary and necessary connexion between sin and punishment as retribution it is impossible to justify any kind of retributive punishment. To the question, If punishment does not restore, why should it continue ? there is no possible answer except that whether it restore or not it is the due reward of sin. But if it is the due reward of sin at the end of the process, how is it possible to say that it was not so at the beginning of the process ? Dr. Moberly's order is wrong. Rightly considered, punishment begins as the due reward of sin, that is, as retributive ; penitence changes its character from retributive to restorative ; but penitence involves the acknowledgment of the righteousness of retribution. Similarly, the exactor of punishment has as his first object the infliction of the due penalties of wrongdoing. But this by no means implies that the purpose of restoration is not always potentially present, and may not, in correspondence with the penitent confession of the punished, oust the retributive and vindicative aspects of the act of punishment. If authority be sought for such a conception it may be found in the words of Kant, ' Though he who punishes may at the same time have the gracious purpose of directing the punishment to this end also ' (*i.e.* the true felicity of the sufferer), ' yet the infliction must first be justified by itself as punishment—*i.e.* as pure evil. In every punishment as such there must first be *justice, and this constitutes what is essential to the notion*.' [1]

Next we must ask, ' What is the verdict of Christian religious experience in this matter ? ' A sharp separation of this experience from the general moral consciousness is neither possible nor desirable. But a new factor is introduced. Forgiveness may be implied in punishment which passes from the retributive to the restorative stage ; yet forgiveness has a peculiar quality which is not clearly seen till wrongdoing is viewed as sin, that is, as an offence

[1] See Ritschl, i. 396 (E.T.).

which creates a situation between man and God. Now
the moment we set foot on this theological ground we see
that the penitence which brings with it a change in the
character of punishment is not simply the acknowledgment
of the justice of punishment, but the conscious valuation
of wrongdoing as sin against God, and the earnest desire
that the primary effect of sin, estrangement from God,
may be abolished. That desire does not include the wish
that the punishment, now acknowledged as just, shall
forthwith stop. God's response to this penitence is
forgiveness. It is quite truly urged that forgiveness
cannot be equated with cancelling of punishment; but
it does cancel a situation which, so long as it lasts, leaves
punishment in its primary character of retribution, and
prevents the actualisation of its latent, potential quality
of restoration.

We need to guard against a certain sophistication
as regards punishment, penitence, and forgiveness. Dr.
Moberly has not escaped this danger. As to punishment
I must needs think his order of ideas simply wrong : as
to penitence and forgiveness he is over-occupied with ideal
ends, which are not attainable in this world. Penitence
may be spoken of as reidentification of the self with
righteousness, but it is such as aspiration rather than as
fact. The moral results of penitence are latent in penitence;
penitence is an ethical act, nor is it anything but true to
connect that act with the presence of the Holy Spirit in
the heart of the now penitent sinner. But I distrust an
analysis which can find no place for a true penitence except
by reference to the perfect penitence of the personally
sinless, and its weakened echo in men's hearts through the
power of the Holy Spirit.

On the other hand, there is real need for a fuller explanation of some of the phrases used to indicate the nature of
the Atonement than is often given. The acceptance of
the retributive view of punishment as primary does not
in itself make clear the meaning of such expressions as

'Christ died our death,' or 'He bore the penal consequences of sin.' We still feel that the way does not lie open to an understanding of the content of Christ's death.[1] We must go on, with the help of Scripture, the moral conscious- ness, and Christian experience, towards a more satisfactory reply to the question, 'How does salvation depend upon the death of Christ ?' And we must remember that our answer must include answers to those objections, thrown in the form of questions, which are real and not artificial difficulties, as when men ask, 'If Christ had not died, would it have been impossible for God to forgive and save us ?' or, 'How can the death of Christ affect those who lived before His time, and those who have never heard of Him ?'

Now I take it that the strength of what we call the penal theory, elusive as the phrases may be in which that theory is defined, lies, apart from its supports in Scripture, in the sanctity with which it invests the conception of moral law. Hence the thought of reparation and satisfac- tion. An improved attitude on the part of men towards the law, a moral reidentification with it, is not sufficient, because the temporal future cannot meet the demands of the temporal past. The law's quality is not seen in successive demands, linked by the passing of time, but in its absolute eternal character of holiness. Nothing can make amends for the violation of this except some act of a quality equal to the law's own essential quality. The foundations of this conception are far too deeply engrained in the records of the human race to be rejected as mythological. The weakness of the penal theory appears whenever the reparative act fails to find any true link with the guilty persons and race who are the occasion of it, when it is presented as done 'over their heads.'

---

[1] Dr. White (*Forgiveness and Suffering*, p. 25) puts the difficulty very fairly, 'If physical death be the penalty of sin, then Christ's death does not in fact save us from this penalty. But did Christ then suffer *eternal* death, commonly called damnation, in order to save us from that penalty? Obviously not. So it is not clear, to say the least, in what sense Christ did in fact endure the penalty due to mankind'

For the object of the act is *ex hypothesi* not only to serve the demands of the law, but also to serve the needs of men. And there is an unreal disjunction of the two objects which the act has in view when a 'plan of salvation' is framed, of which it can be said that 'the scheme has, in itself, nothing to do with an actual salvation; it is a process which precedes the real work of saving men; it is wholly outside and independent of their moral life of experience.' [1] It was with this disjunction continually in view that Dr. Moberly wrote his book, and the stress he laid upon 'Personality' in connexion with 'Atonement' was the guiding principle in his effort to overcome it.

In opposition to the penal theory every other kind of doctrine finds its strength at just this point. The Atonement, whatever it be, must directly affect man in his moral life. Whatever else it may be it is only completed as it functions within man, as it is seen to be the at-one-ment of man with God. Now the fact that teaching such as this has found a welcome where the penal theory has met with complete coldness, or even indignation, ought not to be attributed to moral shallowness and belief in a good-natured God. Such defects may here and there enter in, but they are not the bed-rock upon which the whole conception rests. There are portions of Scripture, and real moral instincts on which the theory builds. Its weakness consists primarily in its impatience. The good is here very conspicuously the enemy of the best. Neither Scripture, nor the moral consciousness, nor Christian experience, is done justice to throughout, and presented as a whole. This is true even of such penetrating works as those of Dr. Moberly, Dr. Du Bose, and Dr. Stevens.

Any adequate doctrine of the Atonement must begin

---

[1] Stevens, *op. cit.*, p. 171. One sees the inattention to the element of personality in such an account as Dr. Shedd (*History of Doctrine*, ii. 256) gives of the Anselmic theory; 'the vicarious satisfaction of law in the Anselmic theory . . . denotes the substitution of an exact and literal equivalent—as when a debt of one hundred dollars in silver is paid with one hundred dollars in gold.'

with a realisation of the greatness of the thought—the Son of God died, Cyril's ' God suffered in the flesh.' Even if it involved no more than God's desire to bring Himself near to man by an entry into the actual conditions of human life, including the cessation of physical life itself, it would leave us increasedly in debt to Him who had sacrificed so much.   Add to this the knowledge that God had so acted because there was no other way to draw our hearts to Him, and, at the same time, to show that there was no act of love and sacrifice which man could do that had not been outdone by God, and the force of the appeal of the Cross would be intensified.   It would be quite unfair to depreciate such an act as an objectless display of love. Though no other purpose than this were found in the Incarnation it would remain a high moral act ; we could speak of it as good news.[1] But it is not easy for the Christian consciousness to halt at this point. A good example may be found in the work of Dr. Foley.   His sympathies are very much more with Abelard than with Anselm, but he sees that there is more to be said, and more of a different kind, than Abelard's theory allows.   So he writes ' the atonement is more than an at-one-ment, at least in the sense that an effective work was performed by the historic Christ, distinct from its consummation in our personal reconciliation. . . . We come to be one with God because what Christ was and did centuries ago mediated for us what we could not do for ourselves.' Such words are not to be pressed as implying anything of the nature of a penal theory, but they are indicative of a dissatisfaction with any representation of Christ's work which does not attach to it an independent value prior to our response to it.   The real question is as to the character and special reference of that work of independent value.

[1] Both Professor Denney and Dr. Forsyth seem to me to go wrong in their comparative depreciation of the Incarnation except as the necessary presupposition for a true expiatory atonement. Incarnation without this latter does not necessarily drop to the level of a misty doctrine of divine immanence, though I should admit that some of our Christian mysticism now so much in vogue has dangerous inclinations in this direction.

Dr. Moberly preserves the independent value of Christ's work by his notion of vicarious penitence, while his doctrine of Christ's inclusive humanity and his insistence on the mediating work of the Holy Spirit enable him to pass from the 'objective' to the 'subjective' aspect in a natural way. But the position taken as a whole is rather a halting-ground than suitable for permanent occupation. We have already seen some of the difficulties in which Dr. Moberly's theory is involved. Not the least of these is the very idea of Christ's inclusive humanity, which has as its object the removal of the objections raised when Christ is thought of as essentially 'other' than the rest of mankind. But this idea, though attractive and appealing in itself, gives rise to very great perplexities the moment the attempt is made to treat it as in any way a truth for scientific know-ledge. For humanity, apart from the individuals who compose it, is an abstraction ; and yet it would appear as though for Dr. Moberly it were much more than this. He pushes the Irenæan *recapitulatio* to a point where a crude realism seems the inevitable result, for since, as Dr. Rashdall puts it, 'the question is whether we can say that all men suffered because Christ suffered,' [1] and the answer which Dr. Moberly's treatment of the subject presupposes is an affirmative one, humanity must logically be regarded as a concrete and inclusive term. That Dr. Moberly would have refused to admit this to be the outcome of his theory, or as a true representation of it, is exceedingly probable ; but how he could legitimately repel this attack, while at the same time retaining all the force of his assertion, 'Christ is Man, not generically but inclusively,' is a riddle unsolvable by any save himself, and he has not left us the solution.

Let us get back to firmer and less disputable ground. However it be with vicarious penitence, vicarious suffering —suffering for the good of others and in their place so that they may not have to suffer—is a fact of life which,

[1] *J.T.S.*, iii. 202.

whenever found, excites the deepest admiration as the fact
above all others which reveals man in his noblest because
least self-centred light. It may be said that the lower
animals also are capable of this altruism. This is true, but
two relevant considerations manifest the wide difference
between such an act on the part of a man and on the part
of an animal. Firstly, the man acts with conscious
intelligence, gauging all that the act may involve for
him up to the loss of life ; he triumphs over counter-
considerations which, in any individual case, may appear
of almost overwhelming force. The animal, on the other
hand, acts instinctively ; it may be impossible to say
that the consequences of the act are entirely concealed
from it ; at least they are not patent. Secondly, man
may exhibit this willingness to go to meet suffering in the
interests of one to whom he is bound by no urgent ties of
kinship or affection ; the animal acts impulsively in defence
of its mate or offspring. Both are acts of love, but the
character and moral quality of the love differ profoundly.

The act which consents to vicarious suffering is supremely
moral. But what of suffering itself ? In itself, in isolation,
if we can for a moment disregard every single circumstance
attending it, it is simply an evil. A physical evil, it may
be said. But at this point Professor Denney's warning
against false abstractions is true and valuable. On the
scale of human life physical evil is so closely linked up
with moral evil that there is everything to be said in favour
of the supposition that some inner relationship exists
between the two. The problem of sin and suffering is
not a double but a single problem. Of course one cannot
write the matter off in easy fashion by saying that suffering
is always and everywhere the penalty of sin. That leaves
the problem of the suffering of the animals untouched,
and the Book of Job was written to show how precarious
such an argument is as to any particular man. Nevertheless, it is obvious in how many cases suffering is the scourge
on sin, and how firmly fixed in our moral sense as well

as in our legal institutions is the principle δράσαντα παθεῖν. Suffering has so constantly the force of penalty, of judgment upon sin, that though suffering may be undergone in the noblest cause, though in stepping into the place of another, where that is possible, and suffering for him, man rises to the grandest potentialities of his moral personality, yet he embraces something which is not mere physical evil, but physical evil with a further moral reference.

Of all that falls within the bounds of physical evil, death is the culmination. In itself it is the last enemy and the worst of evils; as the quality of suffering may be transmuted by the spirit of the sufferer, so with death. But that which is good and noble does not subsist in death any more than in suffering, but in the spirit of him who finds himself face to face with it.

Christ suffered and died. He entered into and penetrated the region of evil. He submitted to the final curse upon the race, the curse of death. Was this of purely physical relevance for Him? The Cry of Desolation from the Cross, hard as it is to find a way to its positive content, at least answers this in the negative. The suffering of the Cross meant for Him at some moment, for some length of time while He hung there, the obscuring of His Father's presence. Christ, the old commentators used to say, was bowed under the burden of the sins of the world. The language must be metaphorical if it is not strictly arithmetical—so much suffering exactly, and morally, equivalent in value to so much sin. But the language is true metaphor, not false. The moral connexion between human death and sin was not broken when Christ died, who knew no sin. For Himself the connexion was irrelevant, but this heightens and does not lighten the mystery of the Cross. We only know of the death of sinners. We do not know, and it is useless to inquire, what kind of a thing death would have been in a world of sinless personalities. But Christ's was the death of a sinless Personality in a sinful world. He did not evade that fate which for all His brethren makes up, as the culmination of suffering and along with, not in detachment from, sin, the moral problem of human life. If we use such an expression as He died our death it is this meaning that we intend to convey.

Christ suffered and died. Did His sufferings and death leave the facts of suffering and death exactly as they were before He passed through them ? Without any hesitation we answer ' No.' The fact that He suffered and died does not turn suffering and death, considered in themselves, from evil to good ; nor does it quit them of their reference to sin. But it does alter the nature of that reference. The element of judgment, universal in death, spends itself in the Cross ; it is not destroyed ; we can still speak of a death being a judgment. But this force is potential only ; it concerns this or that particular death. For humanity death has become other than it was since Christ died, for the race that is, regarded as a unity. What is involved is not primarily a subjective change, humanity's reorientation of itself in the fact of death. It is this only because death as a fact is not what it was before Christ died.

But, it may be asked, is not this due to the Resurrection ? We remember what Harnack says of the grave being the birthplace of indestructible belief in immortality, eternal life.[1] This is true. The Cross can be interpreted in the light of the resurrection alone. Christ could not have changed death if He had not risen. But that does not mean that Christ could so have changed death had He not died, had He, as was told of Mithras, ascended into heaven without passing through death. Death is transmuted for sinners because the Son of God died. If He had left life's tragic end untouched no difference that we can see would have been made to death in its relation to men.

I do not therefore think that we need shrink from saying that Christ bore penal suffering for us and in our

[1] *What is Christianity ?* p. 165.

stead. But still the question presses—how does such
endurance redound to our advantage ? How does it
enable God to forgive us ? Nothing yet has been said to
justify the language of the hymn, which may be taken as
typical in this matter.

> Had Jesus never bled and died
> Then what could thee and all betide
> But uttermost damnation ?

The first thing I would say in answer to such questions
is that though the idea of Christ's humanity as an
' inclusive ' humanity passes beyond the range of scientific
knowledge and entangles itself in great difficulties and
even contradictions, it is not untrue to say that Christ's
acts, working up to their climax in the greatest of His
acts—His deliberate surrender of His life in death—stand
in a quite unique relation to the life, that is, the action,
of the race. His whole career revealed the right way of
life. His death, inasmuch as it was a voluntary act,
showed His willingness to undergo that which, as we know
it, has in it God's judgment upon sin. Now Christ's
action was not the action of humanity in Him ; it is
impossible to treat such a conception at once seriously
and lucidly ; nor is it the meaning of St. Paul's ' one died
for all : therefore all died.' Our modern feeling of the
solidarity of mankind does not presuppose anything in
the least similar to this type of mystical doctrine ; what
it does presuppose is the almost limitless reaction of
individuals and their acts upon other personalities. This
is the true analogue to the work of Christ. But His work
has a far fuller scope. As Man He obeys the law, and
suffers the final earthly judgment upon the law's violation.
He unifies through His life and death the two moral
necessities—the keeping of the law, and the willingness
to suffer when the law is broken. As Man He does all
that man needs to do. Now if from this there followed
any kind of mechanical salvation for men, as has been

said to be the logical consequence of the older penal theory—that a superabundant penalty for all men or for the elect having been paid, neither could faith be justly required nor sin regarded as an impediment to salvation —then it might fairly be argued that human salvation had been brought into no inner relationship with that which Christ had done. But this is not the case. The necessity for faith implies that the individual man must identify himself by way of aspiration with the work of Christ. It is not his work, it is Christ's work ; but it is also not the work of a divine non-human redeemer, but of Christ as Man fulfilling human obligations. Is there anything immoral if God looks at men's inchoate moral achievements and forgives their moral shortcomings, that is, their sins, in the light of the moral completeness of Christ's life ? If He reckons faith as righteousness, when in the act of faith man recognises the moral obligations that press upon him for fulfilment, confesses his own failures, admits the justice of punishment as that which he has deserved, and at the same time points to the complete fulfilment of the law, the complete confession of God's holiness, and the voluntary endurance of penal suffering and death by Christ from within humanity ? We go beyond what we have a right to assert if we say with Anselm that God was bound by the satisfaction which Christ provided and the merit which He won to treat man after a particular manner ; but we have a right to say that it is neither unreasonable nor immoral that He should do so.

And this brings me to the second point in the reply to the question : If Christ had not died, were men debarred from all hope of forgiveness and salvation ? Our present unfamiliarity with the thought of predestination in any form often causes us to forget the truth of God's eternal counsels and purposes. But it is essential, especially in connexion with such a doctrine as the Atonement, that we should remember them. The only thing that God does not purpose, and has not eternally purposed, is sin. The

Atonement as the counter-stroke to sin is of God's eternal purposes ; it is not an afterthought. The expression 'Eternal Atonement' is not, I think, a happy one. It detrimentally affects our understanding of the only plane upon which atonement for human sin can be wrought, the plane of human life and moral action. But if by the phrase no more is meant than that God eternally purposed an atonement made in one and only one way, then it must be welcomed and urged. And if this be so the question what would have happened to men had Christ not died becomes totally unmeaning. It is like asking what would be the result if the law of thought that a thing cannot at once both be and not be were untrue. The attempt to conceive of something as not a fact which God has always conceived of as a fact is doomed to like fruitlessness. Human salvation is from all eternity hinged upon Christ ; what measure of subjective appreciation of this is necessary, under what conditions conscious faith is dispensed with as a necessary means, what ethical actions and states are reckoned as filling the place of the concentrated ethical act which we call faith—to such inquiries we may give various answers without in the slightest degree invalidating the apostolic statement that there is no other name given under Heaven whereby we must be saved. That is the last word on the efficient cause of man's salvation, because that cause returns for its own sanction to God's eternal purposes.

Much of the objection felt towards any doctrine of the Atonement which refuses to dispense with substitutionary and penal conceptions centres round the supposition that these connote either that God the Father was Himself anxious only to punish, while God the Son satiated that desire for vengeance by taking the punishment upon Himself, or that other ways to atonement being open God chose a way which entailed the infliction of suffering upon His innocent Son. On moral and theological grounds, by the refusal to elevate punitive justice above love and to revive Marcion's ditheism in a new form, whatever appears to induce such conceptions is rejected. But if it is once made clear that God's eternal counsels are the eternal movements of His love, and that the Incarnation, a doctrine inexpressibly dear to all who believe in it as being the temporal actualisation of those counsels and the record of that love, necessitates in a sinful world the endurance of a suffering and a death in which the penal element is inevitably included, then the objections lose their force.

I conclude that we cannot dispense with that point of view which finds notable expression in the works of Dr. Dale, Professor Denney, and Dr. Forsyth, and is assumed in the soteriological teaching of the Roman Catholic Church. On this last point I should like to lay some stress. Those who derive their knowledge of the history of the doctrine from the pages of Dr. Moberly, or still more, of Mr. Oxenham, might be led to think that the notions so forcibly presented in Reformation and post-Reformation theologians were mere provincialisms in Christian thought, to be contrasted with a Catholic doctrine of the Atonement rotating on quite a different centre. Ignorance of authoritative Roman Catholic work tends to foster this delusion, and to deprive the notions indicated of that background in history and support in contemporary non-Protestant theology to which they are justly entitled.

That more sympathy is not gained for these ideas is partly due to the appearance of hardness which now and then accompanies those works in which they are set forth. Theological ability triumphs over the note of appeal. In preaching a reaction from every sort of sentimentalism not enough allowance is always made for weaker brethren. The welcome which greeted *Atonement and Personality* was, I believe, due as much to the spirit which informed it as to the freshness and comparative novelty of its arguments. Its appeal was in part æsthetic; in the hands of the master Christianity stood revealed as a thing of beauty, to be desired because it was altogether lovely. And it is important to realise that Christian doctrine has its æsthetic side ; it is a true and noble and necessary side, and as long as it does not obliterate other even more important aspects, it may rightly be pressed in the interests of apologetic, to which it would add a most desirable element, far too much neglected at present. But even in Dr. Forsyth, who knows well the power of the æsthetic appeal,[1] I miss, sometimes when it would be most in place, that willingness to commend theology and the doctrine of the Atonement along these lines, so that upon the reader's soul may descend a sense of heavenly beauty.

For the Atonement, as fact and doctrine, should evoke feelings not only of respect and self-surrender but of worship. The Lex Credendi should be also the Lex Adorandi. That Eucharistic worship which is to many the highest possible expression of their adoration of God is the worship of the Crucified even more than of the Incarnate Christ. We must not speak of the sacraments as the extension of the Atonement, but to call them the extension of the Incarnation hinders insight into their dependence upon the Cross. Yet in the New Testament it is the Cross which determines their content. They are Sacraments of the Gospel, and if the Cross is not the whole Gospel it is the Gospel's centre and enlivening power.

With Christians of old time we worship Christ as God. And when we worship Him we turn away from ourselves, even from what He is to make of ourselves. In another way is the Lex Adorandi the Lex Credendi. We worship Him for what He is, and in that which He is lies that which He has done. And that which He has done He did first unto God by victory over sin through the gateway of seeming defeat, by breaking that chain of guilt which

---

[1] See his books *Religion in recent Art* and *Christ on Parnassus*. It is true that he is always on the lookout for the ethical note in æsthetics, but no reader of these books can doubt his feeling for the beautiful in itself.

P

bound down the noblest and most God-like part of God's creation, by the establishment of the new Kingdom grounded in holiness and sacrificial love. This is the fruit of His death, and this the secret of the Adoration of the **Lamb.**

SELECT BIBLIOGRAPHY

FROM the foregoing pages the student will already have become familiar with many of the works most serviceable for a thorough study of the doctrine. In the following list an attempt is made to bring together the writings most relevant to each special portion of the subject.

CHAPTER I

§ 1. ARTICLES IN DICTIONARIES : *Hastings' Dictionary of the Bible, Encyclopedia Biblica, Encyclopedia of Religion and Ethics, New Schaff-Herzog Encyclopedia of Religious Knowledge,* etc. Especially S. R. DRIVER, *Expiation and Atonement* (Hebrew) in *E.R.E.* ; S. R. DRIVER, *Propitiation* in *H.D.B.* ; G. F. MOORE, *Sacrifice* in *E.B.* ; W. P. PATERSON, *Sacrifice* in *H.D.B.*

§ 2. OLD TESTAMENT THEOLOGIES :

W. L. ALEXANDER. *System of Biblical Theology.* 2 vols. 1888.
BERTHOLET. *Biblische Theologie des Alten Testaments* (a continuation of STADE'S work). 1911.
C. F. BURNEY. *Outlines of Old Testament Theology.* (3rd ed. 1910.)
A. B. DAVIDSON. *The Theology of the Old Testament.* 1904.
A. DILLMANN. *Handbuch der Alttestamentlichen Theologie.* (Posthumous, 1895).
G. F. OEHLER. *Theology of the Old Testament.* (E.T. 2 vols. 1874-5.)
C. PIEPENBRING. *Théologie de l'Ancien Testament.* 1886. (E.T. 1893.)
E. RIEHM. *Alttestamentliche Theologie.* 1889.
H. SCHULTZ. *Old Testament Theology.* (E.T. 2 vols. 1892.)
R. SMEND. *Lehrbuch der alttestamentlichen Religiongeschichte.*
B. STADE. *Biblische Theologie des Alten Testaments.* 1905.

§ 3. SPECIAL WORKS RELEVANT TO THE SUBJECT :

W. E. ADDIS. *Hebrew Religion.* 1906.
W. BOUSSET. *What is Religion ?* (E.T. 1907.)

A. CAVE.   *The Scriptural Doctrine of Sacrifice.*   (2nd ed. 1890.)
P. FAIRBAIRN.   *The Typology of Scripture.*   (2 vols. 5th ed. 1870.)
M. G. GLAZEBROOK.   *The End of the Law.*   1911.
T. HERRMANN.   *Die Idee der Sühne im Alten Testament.*   1905.
A. KUENEN.   *The Religion of Israel.*   (Vol. ii.   E.T.   1874.)
A. LOISY.   *The Religion of Israel.*   (E.T.   1910.)
M. LAGRANGE.   *Études sur les Religions Sémitiques.*   (2nd ed. 1905.)
K. MARTI.   *Geschichte der Israelitischen Religion.*   (4th ed. 1903.)
K. MARTI.   *The Religion of the Old Testament.*   (E.T.   1907.)
F. D. MAURICE.   *The Doctrine of Sacrifice deduced from the Scriptures.*
      1854.
C. G. MONTEFIORE.   *Lectures on the Origin and Growth of Religion.*
      (Hibbert Lectures, 1892.)
A. NAIRNE.   *The Faith of the Old Testament.*   1913.
R. L. OTTLEY.   *Aspects of the Old Testament.*   (Bampton Lectures,
      1897.)
R. L. OTTLEY.   *The Religion of Israel.*   1905.
A. S. PEAKE.   *The Religion of Israel.*   1908.
A. RITSCHL.   *Rechtfertigung und Versöhnung.*   Vol. ii.   (2nd ed.
      1882.)
J. ROBERTSON.   *The Early Religion of Israel.*   (Baird Lectures.
      2nd ed. 1892.)
H. W. ROBINSON.   *The Religious Ideas of the Old Testament.*   1913.
W. SANDAY (Ed.).   *Priesthood and Sacrifice.*   1900.
W. ROBERTSON SMITH.   *The Religion of the Semites.*   (Revised ed.
      1907.)
G. B. STEVENS.   *The Christian Doctrine of Salvation.*   Pt. i.,
      ch. i., ii., 1905.
A. C. WELCH.   *The Religion of Israel under the Kingdom.*   1912.

§ 4. COMMENTARIES:

T. K. CHEYNE.   *The Prophecies of Isaiah.*   (5th ed. 1889.)
FR. DELITZSCH.   *Commentary on Isaiah.*   (E.T.   1892 from 4th
      German ed. 1889.)
A. DILLMANN.   *Die Bücher Exodus und Leviticus.*   (3rd ed. 1897.)
K. MARTI.   *Isaiah* (kurzer Hand-Commentar, 1900).

      And volumes in the following series of commentaries:
            The Cambridge Bible (ed. A. F. Kirkpatrick).
            The Century Bible (ed. W. F. Adeney).
            The International Critical Commentary (ed. S. R. Driver
               and C. Briggs).
            Westminster Commentaries (ed. W. Lock).
            The Polychrome Bible.

CHAPTERS II AND III

§ 1. ARTICLES IN DICTIONARIES :

Add to those already mentioned the following : A. ADAMSON, *Reconciliation* in *H.D.B.* ; W. ADAMS BROWN, *Expiation and Atonement (Christian)* in *E.R.E.*, and *Ransom, Redemption, Salvation, Saviour* in *H.D.B.* ; J. O. F. MURRAY, *Atonement* in *H.D.B.*

Articles on N.T. persons and writings generally have a section in which the doctrine of Atonement *inter alia* is discussed ; *e.g.* G. G. FINDLAY, *Paul the Apostle* in *H.D.B.*

§ 2. NEW TESTAMENT THEOLOGIES :

W. BEYSCHLAG. *New Testament Theology.* (E.T. 2nd ed. 1899.)
W. P. DU BOSE. *The Soteriology of the New Testament.* 1892.
P. FEINE. *Die Theologie des Neuen Testaments.* (2nd ed. 1911.)
H. J. HOLTZMANN. *Lehrbuch der Neutestamentlichen Theologie.* (1st ed. 1897 ; 2nd ed. posthumous, 1911.)
A. SCHLATTER. *Die Theologie des Neuen Testaments.* 1909. 2 vols.
G. B. STEVENS. *The Theology of the New Testament.* 1899.
H. WEINEL. *Biblische Theologie des Neuen Testaments.* 1911.
B. WEISS. *Biblical Theology of the New Testament.* (E.T. In 1888-9, from 4th ed. 1884.)

§ 3. SPECIAL WORKS RELEVANT TO THE SUBJECT :

(*a*) For the Gospels :

(i.) Special chapters in treatises on the Atonement, particularly in R. W. DALE, *The Atonement* ; J. DENNEY, *The Death of Christ* ; M. KÄHLER, *Zur Lehre von der Versöhnung* ; G. B. STEVENS, *The Christian Doctrine of Salvation.*
(ii.) For incidental treatment of the subject. Lives of Christ, especially O. HOLTZMANN, *Life of Jesus* (E.T. 1904) ; T. KEIM, *Jesus of Nazara* (E.T. 6 vols. 1873-83) ; B. WEISS, *The Life of Christ* (E.T. 3 vols. 1883-4).

W. P. DU BOSE. *The Gospel in the Gospels.* 1906.
C. VAN CROMBRUGGHE. *De Soteriologiae Christianae primis Fontibus.* 1905.
A. E. GARVIE. *Studies in the Inner Life of Jesus.* 1907.
A. HARNACK. *What is Christianity ?* (E.T. 1901.)
O. PFLEIDERER. *Primitive Christianity.* (E.T. 4 vols. 1906-11.)
A. SCHWEITZER. *The Quest of the Historic Jesus.* (E.T. 1910.)
A. TITIUS. *Neutestamentliche Lehre von der Seligkeit.* 4 parts. 1895-1900.
H. WENDT. *The Teaching of Jesus.* (E.T. 2 vols. 1892.)

P. WERNLE.   *The Beginnings of Christianity.*   (E.T.   Vol. i.   **1913.**)
W. WREDE.   *Das Messiasgeheimnis in den Evangelien.*   1901.

(*b*) For the rest of the N.T. :

(i.) Special chapters in treatises see (*a* i.).
(ii.) On the soteriology of St. Paul.

F. C. BAUR.   *Paul the Apostle of Jesus Christ.*   (E.T.   2 vols.   1873.)
W. P. DU BOSE.   *The Gospel according to Saint Paul.*   1907.
A. B. BRUCE.   *St. Paul's Conception of Christianity.*   1894.
P. GARDNER.   *The Religious Experience of St. Paul.*   1911.
A. E. GARVIE.   *Studies of Paul and his Gospel.*   1911.
O. PFLEIDERER.   *Paulinism.*   (E.T.   2 vols.   1883.)   Also his
    Primitive Christianity.   (E.T.   4 vols.   1906-11.)
W. M. RAMSAY.   *The Teaching of Paul in Terms of the Present Day.*
    1913.
G. B. STEVENS.   *The Pauline Theology.*   1898.
W. WREDE.   *Paul.*   (E.T.   1907.)

The literature which compares or contrasts Jesus Christ and Paul
is worth consulting in this connexion.   See the works under this
or a similar title by Feine, Jülicher, Kaftan, A. Meyer, and J. Weiss
(English Translations of the last two).

(iii.) On the rest of the New Testament :

W. P. DU BOSE.   *High Priesthood and Sacrifice* (on the Epistle to
    the Hebrews).   1908.
G. B. STEVENS.   *The Johannine Theology.*   1894.

§ 4. COMMENTARIES :

Of older English commentaries, H. ALFORD.   Of modern commentaries on St. Matthew, A. PLUMMER; on St. Mark, A. MENZIES,
The Earliest Gospel ; and H. B. SWETE.   On St. Luke, A. PLUMMER
(in *I.C.C.*).   For the soteriology of the Epistles SANDAY and
HEADLAM on Romans (in *I.C.C.*) is indispensable for that epistle.
See also Lightfoot's commentaries on Galatians and Philippians
and Colossians ;   C. BIGG on 1 Peter (in *I.C.C.*); and A. NAIRNE,
The Epistle of Priesthood (on Hebrews) ; B. F. WESTCOTT on Hebrews
and the Epistles of St. John.   Of foreign commentaries may be
mentioned H. J. HOLTZMANN on the Gospels in the *Handcommentar* ;
PÈRE LAGRANGE on St. Mark ; A. LOISY, *Les Évangiles Synoptiques*
(volume on St. Mark now to be had separately) ; SCHANZ (R. C.)
on the Gospels; J. WEISS, *Die Schriften des N.T.*; J. WELL-
HAUSEN (four separate volumes on the Gospels); and, for a German
conservative view, the series edited by T. ZAHN, to which he has
contributed on the first, second, third, and fourth Gospels and
Galatians.

CHAPTERS IV AND V

§ 1. In the standard histories of Dogma either special sections are assigned to the doctrine of the Atonement, or soteriology is discussed in connexion with each leading theologian. See:

J. F. BETHUNE-BAKER. *An Introduction to the Early History of Christian Doctrine.* 1903.

G. P. FISHER. *History of Christian Doctrine.* 1896.

K. HAGENBACH. *History of Doctrines.* (3 vols. E.T. 1880-81. From 8th German ed.)

A. HARNACK. *History of Dogma.* (7 vols. E.T. 1893-99. From the 3rd German ed. 1893.)

F. LOOFS. *Leitfaden zum Studium der Dogmengeschichte.* (4th ed. 1906.)

W. G. SHEDD. *A History of Christian Doctrine.* (2 vols. 1865.)

G. THOMASIUS. *Die Christliche Dogmengeschichte.* (2nd ed., post-humous. 2 vols. 1886-89.)

J. TIXERONT. *Histoire des Dogmes.* (3 vols. 1909-12. 6th, 4th, and 3rd edd.)

§ 2. Works in which the soteriologies of particular individuals or schools may be studied:

F. C. BAUR. *Die Christliche Lehre von der Versöhnung.* 1838.

C. BIGG. *The Christian Platonists of Alexandria.* (2nd ed., post-humous, 1913.)

G. C. FOLEY. *Anselm's Theory of the Atonement.* 1909.

F. R. M. HITCHCOCK. *Irenæus of Lugdunum.* 1914.

J. RIVIÈRE. *Le Dogme de la Rédemption* (the completest history to the close of the Schoolmen). (E.T. 2 vols. 1909.)

H. N. OXENHAM. *The Catholic Doctrine of the Atonement.* (2nd ed. 1869.)

A. RITSCHL. *Justification and Reconciliation.* Vol. i. (E.T. 1872.)

M. SCOTT. *Athanasius on the Atonement.* 1914.

Moberly's chapter, *The Atonement in History,* is of much interest but restricted in range; perhaps most valuable on Athanasius and Abelard. There is a good historical sketch at the end of Dr. Scott Lidgett's *The Spiritual Principle of the Atonement.*

In these books the student will find references to exact passages in the original authorities. The Oxford *Library of the Fathers,* the *Ante-Nicene Fathers,* and the *Nicene and Post-Nicene Fathers* are the chief series of English Translations.

CHAPTER VI

§ 1. For the soteriology of the Reformers the Histories of Doctrine should be consulted. Calvin's position can be seen in the Institutes, vol. ii., of the English Translation. On Grotius Dr. Stevens recommends an edition with notes by Dr. Foster of Andover, U.S.A. The scholastic theologians of the seventeenth century are accessible only in the original Latin editions. President Edwards' treatise *Of Satisfaction for Sin* is in vol. viii. of his collected works (new ed. 1817-47). See also on the Edwardean School, E. A. PARK, *The Atonement, Discourses, and Treatises,* 1860.

§ 2. To catalogue modern dissertations on the Atonement would be an almost impossible task. In the following selection the attempt is made to bring together works of a similar tendency, and to note the most important.

(i.) Sections in the following systematic theologies :

C. HODGE.   *Systematic Theology.*   (3 vols.   1871.)

A. A. HODGE.   *Outlines of Theology.*   (New ed. 1879.)

W. G. T. SHEDD.   *Dogmatic Theology.*   (2 vols.   1889.)

A. H. STRONG.   *Systematic Theology.*   1886.   (The 1907 edition reveals the introduction of different elements, already indicated in the author's *Christ and Ethical Monism.*)

These works reproduce the old Calvinistic positions.   Cf. also :

E. A. LITTON.   *Introduction to Dogmatic Theology.*   (2nd ed. 1902.)

H. G. C. MOULE.   *Outlines of Christian Doctrine.*   1889.

For the Ritschlian standpoint :

A. RITSCHL.   *Rechtfertigung und Versöhnung.*   Vol. iii.   (E.T. 1900.)

J. KAFTAN.   *Dogmatik.*   (6th ed. 1909.)

For the modern 'positive' position.   (Haering has affinities with Dr. Moberly).

M. KÄHLER.   *Zur Lehre von der Versöhnung.*   1898.   (Being the second vol. of the first ed. of his *Dogmatische Zeitfragen.*)

R. SEEBERG.   *Die Grundwahrheiten der Christlichen Religion.*   (E.T.   1908.   *The Fundamental Truths of the Christian Religion.*)

T HAERING.   *Der Christliche Glaube.*   (E.T.   1913.   *The Christian Faith.*   2 vols.)

Un-Calvinistic :   'moral influence' theories.

W. ADAMS BROWN.   *Christian Theology in Outline.*   1907.

W. N. CLARKE. *An Outline of Christian Theology.* (6th ed. 1899;
    many later editions.)

For the Roman Catholic standpoint.

L. BILLOT. *De Verbo Incarnato.*
C. VAN CAMBRUGGHE. *Tractatus de Verbo Incarnato.* 1909.
L. LABAUCHE. *Leçons de Théologie dogmatique.* (Vol. i. 1911.)
J. LAMINNE. *La Rédemption.* 1911.
C. PESCH. *Compendium Theologiae Dogmaticae.* (Vol. iii. 1913.)
J. POHLE. *Soteriology,* being volume v. of his *Dogmatic Theology*
    (E.T. by A. Preuss).

For the modern 'High-Anglican' position. Reaction from
Calvinism, and sacramental interests prominent, but ideas of
satisfaction and expiation not abandoned. F. J. Hall's volume on
the Atonement in his *Dogmatic Theology* should be consulted when
it appears.

A. J. MASON. *The Faith of the Gospel.* (2nd ed. 1889.)
D. STONE. *Outlines of Christian Dogma.* 1900.
T. B. STRONG. *A Manual of Theology.* (2nd ed. 1903.)
        (ii.) Special treatises and works in which the doctrine is
        handled.

    (a) With ideas of expiation, and in some sense of penal suffering,
        prominent.

W. M. CLOW. *The Cross in Christian Experience.* 1908.
T. I. CRAWFORD. *The Doctrine of Holy Scripture respecting the
    Atonement.* 1871.
R. W. DALE. *The Atonement.* 1875. (9th ed. 1884.)
J. DENNEY. *Studies in Theology; The Death of Christ* (1903); *The
    Atonement and the Modern Mind.* 1903.
D. W. FORREST. *The Christ of History and of Experience.* (5th ed.
    1906.)
P. T. FORSYTH. *Positive Preaching and the Modern Mind* (1907);
    The Cruciality of the Cross (1909); *The Work of Christ* (1910);
    The Person and Place of Jesus Christ (1909).
H. C. MABIE. *How does the Death of Christ save us?* 1908.
G. CAMPBELL MORGAN. *The Bible and the Cross.* 1909.
J. ORR. *The Christian View of God and the World.* 1893.
J. G. SIMPSON. *The Religion of the Atonement* (1889); *What is the
    Gospel?* 1914.
D. W. SIMON. *The Redemption of Man* (1889); *Reconciliation by
    Incarnation.* 1898.
W. H. GRIFFITH THOMAS. *The Catholic Religion.*

(b) Works mediating between semi-penal and 'moral influence' theories :

   (i.) The conception of vicarious penitence.

J. M'LEOD CAMPBELL. *The Nature of the Atonement.* (6th ed. 1886.)
R. C. MOBERLY. *Atonement and Personality.* 1901.
W. H. MOBERLY. *The Atonement,* in *Foundations.* 1912.

   (ii.) Mediating Anglican writings : the 'representative' idea often prominent.

F. R. M. HITCHCOCK. *The Atonement and Modern Thought.* 1911.
A. T. LYTTLETON. *The Atonement,* in *Lux Mundi* (12th ed. 1891.)
J. O. F. MURRAY. *The Revelation of the Lamb.* 1913.
J. P. NORRIS. *Rudiments of Theology.* (2nd ed. 1878.)
L. PULLAN. *The Atonement.* 1906.
M. SCOTT. *The Atonement.* 1910.

   (iii.) Mediating works, classed by Dr. Stevens as 'ethical satisfaction' as opposed to 'penal satisfaction' views.

G. HARRIS. *Restatement of Orthodoxy.*
J. S. LIDGETT. *The Spiritual Principle of the Atonement.* 1897.
W. F. LOFTHOUSE. *Ethics and Atonement.* 1906.
W. L. WALKER. *The Cross and the Kingdom.* 1902; *The Gospel of Reconciliation or At-one-ment.* 1909.

   (c) Works setting forth, more or less completely, 'moral influence' or 'subjective' theories.

H. BUSHNELL. *The Vicarious Sacrifice.* 1866; *Forgiveness and Law.* 1874.
R. J. CAMPBELL. *The New Theology.* 1907.
C. A. DINSMORE. *Atonement in Literature and Life.* 1906.
W. M'DOWALL. *Evolution and Atonement.* 1912.
A. SABATIER. *The Atonement.* (E.T. 1904.)
G. B. STEVENS. *The Christian Doctrine of Salvation.* 1905.
T. V. TYMMS. *The Christian Idea of Atonement.* 1904.
D. WHITE. *Forgiveness and Suffering.* 1913.
J. M. WILSON. *The Gospel of the Atonement.* 1901.
J. YOUNG. *The Life and Light of Men.* 1866.

The two volumes of collected essays: *The Atonement, a Clerical Symposium* (1883), and *The Atonement in Modern Religious Thought, a Theological Symposium* (1900), may be compared as indicating general tendencies of thought at different times.

INDEX

231